STEVIE WONDER

STEVIE WONDER
Constanze Elsner

EVEREST BOOKS LTD
4 Valentine Place, London SE1 8QH

Published in Great Britain by Everest Books Ltd, 1977
ISBN 0905018 516
Copyright © Constanze Elsner, 1977

Printed in Great Britain by the Anchor Press Ltd
and bound by Wm Brendon & Son Ltd
both of Tiptree, Essex

To Monika,
who knows!

Contents

7

Preface

"It is hard not to love a man like him. Stevie's a powerhouse full of energy. A person like him is rare. And any kind of moments that you spend with him are precious moments."

Madelaine "Gypsy" Jones, singer

"I have never heard anyone say anything nasty about Steve. About Motown, his recording company, yes. But not about Stevie. That is two different pairs of shoes."

Elaine Jesmer, author of *Number One With A Bullet*.

"When Steve walks into a room, immediately electricity darts through it. He is just a magnet now."

Ronnie White, member of the Miracles.

"If you want to write a book about Stevie, you are in for a hard job. Because there are no scandals that you can dig out and everybody you are going to talk to will tell you the same thing: Stevie is 'beautiful people'. And that ain't no bullshit."

Lee Garrett, composer and singer.

It is indeed hard to write a book about Stevie Wonder. Not only does his story sound unbelievable but Stevie Wonder is also one of the kindest, warmest, most generous people you will ever meet in showbusiness – leave him alone his musical talent. I cannot think of anybody else who is either as famous or as rich as Stevie and yet so much loved by everyone – even by people he has sacked. At one point during the research on this book I was almost about to give up on him – who wants to read a book

about a saint, anyway? – but then I finally bumped into someone who assured me that even Stevie Wonder is "only human".
You cannot imagine the relief I felt when I heard that Steve
has a failing: his temper. And when he loses it, oh boy, you'd
better not be near.

Only: Even if you do catch Stevie in a mood like this, when
he goes wild and hits out – you cannot be angry with him for
long . . .

Constanze Elsner
Bochum, February 1977

Acknowledgements

This is to all the people who have helped me along with this book in one way or another.

Lee Garrett & Carole: thank you for making your house my home, for negotiating with Stevie and for all the happy days in "Hollyweird"! *Elaine Jesmer:* wish you could have been around longer – you are one of the most exceptional women I have ever met. And please – hurry up with your next book. Apart from myself I know hundreds of people who are dying to read it ... *Madelaine "Gypsie" Jones:* beautiful lady, thank you for making me feel good and for keeping my spirits up! *Pam Stine, Simon Wasserman & Kip Murray:* you took some heavy weight off my shoulders – thank you! *Elisabeth Merck-Wöhler:* Deine Stippvisite hat mein Leben – im wahrsten Sinne des Wortes – ganz *schön* verändert! Tausend Dank!

Monika Seeger: thank you for being. And thank you for being my friend – the best in the world! *Doug Kee:* sorry you missed the movie – here's a book instead. *Gene Kee:* you need not have worried. This is not a book about Motown but Stevie Wonder! *Clarence Paul:* thank you for your time and for the dreams you gave us ... *Ira Tucker, Sandray Tucker & Barbara:* thanks for being so honest! *Jim Gilstrap:* you're in the right groove – and that "nice lady" is not too far away either! *Ron White:* thank you for making Miracles and Wonders happen! *Anona Blackwell:* thanks for your moral support, the lovely LP and all your concern!

Chris de Burgh: God must love *you* a lot, too! *Brian Holland:* thanks for taking me back into "them good ol' days!" *Corinne:* thanks! An experience you could have done without was very useful to me! *Estelle Ullman:* you make Great Expectations and dreams come true, please carry on with it! *Lee Armstrong:* I'm glad I don't look too old for you to try and make me join the silly games . . . *Ken East:* it's not Stevie, it's the people around him! *Eve Helms:* thank you for the rainbows. I told you I would not forget!

Richard Gillinson: okay, this is number one. What are we gonna do next? *Joe Cocker:* it's about time you came 'round again! *Johanen Vigoda:* as you don't seem to find much time to read anything, I hope that someone tells you that I give you a thankyou! *Bob Fisher:* looks like there is no such thing as a deadline with anything in regard to Steve. Thanks for helping me with the "final mix"! *Ken Evans:* you encouraged me a lot – did you know that? Thank you! *Lee Wilder:* thank you for being a friend. I needed one. *Chris Eldridge:* thanks for introducing me to Lee! *Klaus Martens:* danke für die schöne Reise . . .

Billy Griffin: you helped a lot – do you believe it now? *Elli Smith:* you are terrific! Thanks for organizing things so fast! *Priscilla Presley:* thanks for wishing me good luck. I could not have done without it! *Gabi Schulze:* thank you for the hot line to New York! *Barbara Müller:* if there's anything I can do for you . . . Thank you very much! *Marsha:* thanks for making the impossible possible! *Pete Moore:* thank you for talking about everything so openly! *Lloyd Chiate:* thank you for lending me your ear . . . *CoCo:* now I understand what chanting is all about. *Debbie Torres:* hope you'll make it soon! *Suzanne Thomas:* thank you for preparing the ground in L.A.!

Peter Allen: thank you for your music and: why is it so hard to interview people you adore? *Mickey Stevenson:* stop working so hard! *Bobby Rogers:* gee, how could I say that? Of course I meant *Tracks Of My Tears* . . . *Dr. Larry Scott:* why do women have to have babies when we have a dinner date? *Joe Ramerez & Lillette:* hope I see you again soon. I miss you! *Frank Lutz:* thank you for taking me on that plane. That's my favourite high and you can't imagine how much I needed it! *Peter & Michael Boulton:* I did not forget you. How could you come to think that? *Rose Ann Nemes:* it's good you got away from it all!

Clive "Robin" Sarstedt: you were involved in all this more than you know. Thank you! *Peter Sarstedt & the lovely Joanna:* welcome back and how about a new album and I love you both. *Jochen Kraus:* thanks for digging up Steve's long deleted albums! *Lou Wilson:* you should write a book about your fun place! *René Rott:* you sure have a great sound system! Thanks for the info and the drinks! *Michael Davidson:* thanks for the sound! *Rosemarie Johnson:* surprise, surprise: he really is the most beautiful man in this world! *Jerrold Johnson:* little man, people come in all shades and sizes. But what is inside their hearts is what matters! *Astrid Binder-von Richthofen:* Dein Wort in Gottes Ohr! *John Carlin:* thanks for trusting me. Hope I see you in a movie soon!

Janis Ian: did I tell you that I like you very much? *Julien Pearson:* thanks for putting up with me! *Jim de Santiago:* thank you for the soul food ... *Henryk M. Broder:* Danke, dass Du meinen Kopf ausgelüftet hast. Frische Luft und ein "alter" Freund do a whole lot of good! *Ken:* thank you, pink, and Holland! *Ute Elsner von Richthofen:* danke, danke, danke für alles! Angefangen von der ständig gefüllten Kaffeetasse bis zu der riesigen Portion Liebe, die Du mir gibst! Und: hab Dich schrecklich lieb! *Ingrid Elsner:* danke fur Deine Hilfe – ohne Dich sasse ich jetzt noch an der Discografie. Und: sorry, dass Du deshalb eine Verabredung verschwitzt hast! *Ingeborg Herzer & Dr. Edith Kohlhepp:* danke, dass Ihr an 'nem schwarzen Schaf so lange 'rumgeschrubbt habt, bis die versteckten weissen Flecken zum Vorschein kamen! *Eva-Maria Sauer:* danke, dass Du so viel Kleinkram fur mich erledigt hast, damit ich weiter vor mich hin tippen konnte! *Heinz Elsner:* danke, dass wir uns wiedergefunden haben! *Joyce Watson-Smith:* ain't it funny how you "stop" and still bump into people? Anyway: love and thanks for the index.

And most of all thank you to *Stevie Wonder,* without whom this book would not have been possible. . . .

CHAPTER ONE

I Call It Pretty Music – But The Old People Call It The Blues...

No one knows why the little boy Lula Hardaway gave birth to on 13 May 1950 in Saginaw, Michigan, was blind. Her first two sons, Milton and Calvin Hardaway, who were four and one years old at this time, had been born without any complications and were completely healthy, normal little children. There are two theories of the reason for Steveland's blindness. One version goes, that it stems from a dislocated nerve in his brain; the other says that Steve's blindness was caused by a poorly regulated flow of oxygen into an incubator after his month-premature birth.

Fact is, though, that Steveland, who later became Stevie Wonder, has never experienced what it is like to see. Friends of his – like CoCo, a lady he was very close to after his divorce from Syreeta Wright; Herbie Hancock; or Lee Garrett, a long-time friend of his who co-wrote *Signed, Sealed, Delivered I'm Yours* and *It's A Shame* with Stevie and who was also born blind – are heavily into Buddhism and believe that whatever kind of handicap you have to live with is due to bad Kharma; that in this life you pay your dues for something you did in a former life of yours. But Stevie himself believes that his blindness is a gift from God:

"Being blind, you don't judge books by their covers; you go through things that are relatively insignificant, and you pick out things that are more important."

Lula Hardaway also took her third son's blindness as being God-given. Her strong religious belief – she was a Baptist – told

15

her not to question pain, and this made it easier for her to cope with it. But Stevie's father, whose name was Judkins, could not deal with this kind of burden. Stevie's family situation is quite a complicated one altogether:

His two elder step-brothers, Milton and Calvin, bear the name Hardaway. Stevie's birth certificate makes him Steveland Morris, although his full father's name is Judkins and Stevie's younger step-brothers Larry and Timothy as well as his little step-sister Renee have the name Hardaway again. So has his mother, Mrs. Paul Hardaway.

What exactly happened when Steve's father walked out on the family is not talked about officially. But Lee Garrett, who later lived with Steve's family in Detroit for a while, remembers one evening when they talked about the family situation.

"That night I thanked Lula for treating me like one of her own children and giving me a home. I told her that up to this point I had never experienced what it is like to have a family. I was one of thirty children – somewhere in between – and not only did my mother have little time for any of us, but also I was given less of her attention than anyone. 'The blind brat', as they used to call me, was pushed into a corner and forgotten about. Because he would never be able to do anything for them anyway. When I was telling Lula that story she shrugged her shoulders, saying that she knew the expression 'the blind brat' only too well herself. Judkins must have used it more than once. And if it were up to him Steve would have ended up in a corner like myself. He had told her not to worry too much about 'the blind brat' as she would never get anywhere with him."

It is not hard to understand why neither Stevie nor his family like to talk about this time of their lives too much. Luckily enough, though, Lula finally found another man. He was not only a beautiful and loving father to Lula's and his own children Larry, Timothy and Renee but also the most understanding and gentle step-father for the other three. He worked in a bagel bakery in Detroit and even when Stevie came to fame and money he refused to live off his step-son. After a hard working life he died in November 1976.

One of the very few times Stevie mentioned his full father was in an interview with Burr Snider for *Esquire*. He recalls two episodes: one trivial, one decidedly chilling.

"There's one thing I always laugh about when I think back to when we were little kids in Saginaw. My father used to tell us that Saginaw was only twelve miles from the North Pole, and me and my step-brother Calvin used to go around telling people that we were born twelve miles from the North Pole. I believed that for a long time."

The other thing Steve remembers in connection with Judkins is the time the young boy came to know what it means to be frightened. "It wasn't until I was about eight or nine that I really started to get out and roam around by myself, but I mostly had a sighted person with me so I was rarely put into situations where I was scared or would start to feel alone. I do remember one frightening thing, though. The, uh, father of me, this was after he and my mother had broken up – I must have been around seven or eight – he said to me, 'You want to go, Stevie, with me? We gonna go and get some candy and stuff, bubble gum and stuff . . . ride the bus and . . . c'mon!' And I say okay, you know, and I was jumping up and down and was excited about it, and we went over to his house and he had, uh, a piano over there and a saxophone . . . I never knew what one looked like . . . and I stayed there for a while, we stayed together . . . and then one day I remember him having to go off somewhere and he stayed away for a long time . . . and left me alone. That was the first time I got upset and I started to cry about that. But after a while I just said, hey, forget it, and I just went on to sleep. I was just afraid because the surroundings weren't familiar to me."

These early days in Saginaw, Michigan, were hard for all four of them. The space they lived in was very small, and apart from raising her three little boys Lula would work at night. She took on all kinds of jobs, but was badly paid and had to do all the dirty work. Being black she did not have many opportunities back in Saginaw – your only chance was to be healthy and strong enough to do whatever work you were given. Stevie's father was not around much and all the problems that came up in everyday life Lula had to face more or less on her own.

If one of the children got ill, she was the one who had to take care of them; there was no granny or grandad to take some of the weight off her shoulders. The ghetto-neighbours had enough problems of their own and did not need to acquire any more by watching other people's children. There was also no opportunity for Lula to send the little boys to kindergarten. That was an advantage that only white people had. Black children had to play in the streets.

Hoping that a larger city than Saginaw would offer Lula and the children a better life, they moved to Detroit. There the Hardaways lived in a street called Breckenridge. Today the house Stevie grew up in has been torn down. But then the slums in Breckenridge, on the East side of the town, were the worst: the people who lived there had the least well paid but at the same time tougher jobs (mainly with the Ford Motor Company, which Detroit, "Motortown" was known for). The children, black ghetto children, were rougher, too. But it was not until a few years later that Stevie mixed with other youngsters of his age. Instead of hanging out on the street little Stevie sat by the radio all day long and listened to the black radio station WCHB which had a program called *Sundown*. The first tune he remembers listening to – so goes the saga – was a Johnny Ace song called *Pledging My Love*. Here is what Steve told *Penthouse* interviewer Ken Kelley:

"One of the first tunes I ever heard in my life was a Johnny Ace song – he was a blues singer with a kind of country blues. the song was *Pledging My Love*. Johnny made a great impression on my life because I was such a little boy when I heard it. I was maybe two years old then or even younger."

But Stevie must have been at least four and a half, if not five, years old when he listened to that particular song. It was only in the late forties that Johnny Ace, who was born on 6 September 1929 in Memphis, Tennessee (as John Marshall Alexander jr.), went solo. Before that he had gotten some experience as a pianist in Adolph Duncan's Band and later the Beale Streeters (which then included B. B. King). The first time Johnny Ace –

who generally gave sensitive baritone performances of love ballads – hit the Rhythm & Blues charts was in 1952 with *My Song*. In 1954 Johnny Ace was voted the "Most Programmed R & B Artist Of The Year" but it was not until 1955 when *Pledging My Love* hit the charts. This song was a posthumous hit: Johnny Ace shot himself playing Russian roulette backstage at Houston's City Auditorium on Christmas Eve 1954. (Still Johnny Ace was not forgotten for a long time. Many other artists mention him as one of the influences on their music and in 1955 two bands recorded singles in his memory. The Ravens: *Salute To Johnny Ace* and Five Wings: *Johnny's Still Singing*.)

When talking about very early childhood days though, it seems difficult not only for Stevie – and other artists – but for everyone around them to remember exactly what happened when. There is also a tendency in everyone – most of the time probably not wilful – to mix reality with legend. Stevie tells of an early fascination with noise.

"I was always hitting things, like beating on tables with a spoon, or beating these little cardboard drums they used to give kids. I'd beat 'em to death. And I remember people dropping money on the table and saying: 'What's that, Steve?' That's a dime ... buh-duh-duh-duh-da, that's a quarter ... buh-duh-duh-duh-da, that's a nickel. I could almost always get it right except a penny and a nickel confused me."

At the same time Stevie's publicity refers to his very early musical outlet: "As a toddler, he sat on the kitchen floor banging a spoon against a pan in tempo with the music being played on the radio." Also there are various stories about members of the family or friends banging on cans and that Steve could tell whether they were empty, half full or whatever. The stories have surely been exaggerated over the years. But there is no doubt about Stevie having a very special ear and that he must have developed this sense of his at a very minor age. John Fischbach, Steve's recording engineer in Los Angeles, says that "Stevie can hit you with a roll of tape from across the room," just locating your position by sound. Ken Evans, Radio Luxemburg's ex-director in London, was amazed by Steve recognizing his voice – at a reception party, not at the radio station! – after not having seen him for two years. Miracles-member Billy Griffin told me: "One day I walked into the Chrystal Studio in L.A. where Stevie had just finished mixing and listened to a very loud, very funky tune. There were thousands of people in the studio and everybody was yelling 'Yeah, Steve, yeah, I love it, I love it,' and when I walked up to him and said 'Hey man, what's happening?' he said 'Hi, Bill.' Just like that. He memorizes voices – it's almost unbelievable. I can't imagine it's only the voice tone – maybe it's a pattern of the way you talk or something. But whatever it is – he picks out everybody's voice immediately."

Some of the stories told by the people around Steve have the air of myths. Clarence Paul, who spent the years from 1962 to 1967 with "Little Stevie Wonder" as his producer, friend, co-writer and even father-figure, tells: "I remember being with Stevie in a studio one day. He must have been in his early teens then. When the orchestra started playing, Steve didn't start singing but came to me and said 'One of the trumpets is flat. Can you tell them?' I wouldn't have dared, though. I said to Stevie that he'd better tell them himself . . ."

One thing is for certain, though: When anybody tells you any stories about Stevie's sensitivity of hearing, Steve is always on the winning side. You *never* hear the faintly malicious jokes like the story that in musicians' circles is told about Ray Charles, whose blindness was caused through glaucoma he suffered when he was six years old. The anecdote told about one of Ray Charles' studio sessions goes that the old master kept telling one of his studio musicians on the saxophone that he played flat. Ray is supposed to have stopped that particular tune for at least twenty times when the saxophone player is said to have finally lost his temper and shouted 'Can't you *hear* either . . . ?'

The time came when the little boy's interest in music and his wish to learn to play an instrument himself could not be overlooked any longer. Here again, the versions of which instrument little Stevie played first and who gave it to him, vary. In much of what has been written about Stevie he is said to have learned the piano at the age of four. "Encouraged by his mother," as Aaron Fuchs writes in *Fusion* and as numerous press releases published by various publicity agencies state. However, playing the piano at the age of four contradicts Burr Snider's quote on Stevie that the first time he ever knew what a piano looked like was at his full father's house when Steve was at the age of seven or eight. In a *Newsweek* article Maureen Orth says:

"When he was seven, a friendly neighbour left her piano for Stevie when she moved away from their housing project. (By this time Steve's family had moved to the West side of Detroit.) 'I kept asking, "When they gonna bring the piano over, Mamma?" I never realized how important that was going to be to me." '

Neither Miracles-member Ronnie White, who discovered Stevie at the age of ten, nor Brian Holland, who produced some of Stevie's first records on Tamla, remembers the child having played the piano by the time they met him. Ron: "He played the harmonica, but as far as I know he took up the piano later."

Steveland's first harmonica is also subject to different legends. In its article "Rock Giants from A to Z" the *Melody Maker* states that Stevie got this first instrument from his uncle Stevie. The latest biography on Stevie that Motown in L.A. hands out to journalists, leaves the generous uncle nameless, but in a 1973 biography Motown says the harmonica was given to Stevie by a friendly barber who is also mentioned in some articles. The reason for this confusion is that there were not one, but *two* harmonicas. Stevie's very first harmonica, a four-holed toy instrument that he used to wear with a chain round his neck, was indeed given to him by a barber whose nickname was Laud. The second one, Stevie's first Hohner harmonica, was a present from his uncle. This instrument was larger and Stevie says: "This chromatic thing was more expressive, it had more complexity and a different style, than the toy harmonica."

It probably will not come as a surprise to the reader to learn that the stories on Stevie's first drums vary, too. However, he must have been around four when he got his first toy drums which he – and this is about the only point on which the write-ups agree – usually got for Christmas but used to beat to death before Boxing Day dawned. "The first real set of drums," quoting *Newsweek* again, "Steve got from the Lions Club at a Christmas party for blind children." Stevie himself tells the story of the first real snare drum that he owned. "I started playing the drums on the wrong side. So they came over to me and said 'Hey, you don't do it like this, try it over on the other side' and I'd say oh no, I wanna hear the side with the snares." Stevie also tells about a picnic he was on when they sat him behind the kit and threw money at the kid with the great feel for rhythm: "But the most important to me was not the paper money at all – it was the pennies and quarters, because I could hear the sound they was makin' hitting the drums."

But whatever it was he *got* first, it is certain that the first instrument he *mastered* was the harmonica. He played it when Ronnie White auditioned him and also a day later when Ron, who was more than impressed by the tunes the child had played him, had Brian Holland meet Stevie for an audition for Motown. There is also no doubt that Stevie had gained quite a bit of harmonica experience by playing along with the music he heard on the *Sundown* program. Sitting at home and listening to the wireless was what Stevie liked doing best to pass the time. As he was an extremely introvert and shy child, it was hard for Stevie to make friends with the rough kids in the neighbourhood. His blindness also made him kind of an outsider, as neither his brothers not their friends were prepared to include Stevie in the games that they played. Not that Milton and Calvin did not love Stevie; but being young children themselves they wanted to join the crowd and run around instead of always having little brother to take care of. Stevie's mother was also happy that he did not make any trouble wanting to go out with Milton and Calvin and she even promoted Steve's love for the radio. She let him tune in to whatever station he liked to hear, and even when she was tired and exhausted from the long days and nights that she was busy, Lula did not ask her son to turn the radio off. The more Stevie listened to

Sundown, his favourite program of all, the more his harmonica playing progressed.

As his biggest influence in connection with harmonica playing Stevie names Little Walter (who was born as Marion Walter Jacobs on 1 May 1930 in Alexandria, Louisiana, and who is said also to have been the biggest musical influence on Sonny Boy Williamson I). Little Walter had developed a blues harmonica technique with a style steeped in jazz phrasing which was revolutionary at this time. Before Little Walter went solo in 1952 he accompanied Muddy Waters on recordings like *I'm Ready* and *Standing Around Crying* and backed Jimmy Rogers on *That's Alright* and *The World Is In A Tangle* to name but a few. In 1952 he topped the R & B charts with hits like *Juke*, then followed *Mean Old World, Blues With A Feeling* and *Last Night*. Until 1955 he was found constantly in the R & B Top Ten. He died on 15 February 1968. His death was caused by a fatal thrombosis brought on by injuries he had received in a fight.

Other major musical influences on Stevie were the Coasters, who had formed in 1955 and who then did things in their music that today are found in some of Stevie's songs. Their themes dealt with teenage and/or black ghetto life and there was an element of social criticism in their lyrics that was not found in other pop songs played in the fifties. Their biggest hits were *One Kiss Leads To Another* (1956), *Searchin'* (1957) and *Yackety Yack* (1958).

Nat "King" Cole left a big impression on Stevie. (Today he is good friends with Nat's daughter Nathalie.) In 1953 Nat "King" Cole was voted Top Male Vocalist by *Downbeat* and songs of his that Steve listened to at an early age were *Too Young* (1951), *When I Fall In Love* (1957), *Let There Be Love* and *Ramblin' Rose* (1962).

Stevie idolized Jimmy Reed, who was born in Mississippi on 6 September 1925 and who turned out to be one of the leading R & B guitarists. Jimmy Reed records were *You Don't Have To Go, Ain't That Loving You Baby* (1955), *Baby What You Want Me To Do* (1960), *Bright City Lights* (1961) and *Shame, Shame, Shame* (1964).

B. B. King, whose *Three o'clock Blues* in 1950 stayed at number one in the R & B charts for eight weeks straight and whose other hits like *Everyday I Have The Blues* (1955), *Sweet Little Angel* (1956) and *Sweet Sixteen* (1960) got a lot of needle time, later became a big admirer of Stevie's. In April 1973 Stevie took time out from his own recording sessions to join B. B. King at the Sigma Sound Studio in Philadelphia. There Stevie played clavinet on B. B. King's version of Steve's song *To Know You Is To Love You,* which he had written for Syretta Wright. They also recorded another Stevie tune *When Will The World Learn To Love* and added the lyrics in the studio.

Stevie still listens to the music of the Isley Brothers, formed in 1957, who had hits like *Twist And Shout* (1962), which would later be revived by the Beatles (at the end of 1963), and *This Old Heart Of Mine* (1966), that ten years later topped the charts again with Rod Stewart as the singer.

The black music scene of the fifties and sixties, which was such a big influence on Stevie's musical career, was a small world. Most of the musicians Steve admits to having idolized have also influenced each other and/or at one time played in the same groups. Clyde McPhatter, who was the Drifters' lead singer when they started out in 1953 (*Such A Night, Someday, White Christmas*) himself had been influenced by the blend of gospel phrasing and "bird group" harmony that the 5 Royales had developed. In 1956 he went solo and made the R & B charts with songs like *Treasure Of Love, Without Love* and *A Lover's Question.* McPhatter, who died in June 1972, again had a huge influence on Jackie Wilson, another of Steve's idols.

Jackie Wilson, for his part, not only showed Stevie a kind of musical direction but is also said to have been Elvis Presley's idol. Elvis is said to have learned his stage act from Jackie Wilson. *The Encyclopedia of Rock* says of Wilson: "If his influence has been limited, it is because the standard he set has proved too high." Jackie Wilson's high standard is partly responsible for the standards Stevie Wonder sets for himself today as he did in his childhood days. Wilson's million sellers – like *Lonely Teardrops* (1958), which Berry Gordy jr. co-wrote, *Night* and *Doggin' Around* – were part of Stevie's musical education.

Another big role in Stevie's upbringing was played by gospel music. Gospel music reached its Golden Age in 1945, and today does not play that big a part in the charts any more, but it became part of Steve when he was about eight years of age. At this time, Lula had already found a new father for her three sons and also given birth to Larry, who is four years younger than Steve. But before that, after Stevie's father had left the family, it had been solely up to her to raise the children.

The money Lula Hardaway got for their support was very little. "She tried to make a living for the four of them by scrubbing floors in the neighbourhood," Lee Garrett remembers. The love Lula had for her sons, she divided equally between Milton, Calvin and Steve. Although her youngest one was blind, Lula would not spoil or pamper him. Her theory was that *because* Stevie was blind he had to learn to be independent. Steveland himself was not aware of his blindness for the first few years of his life. He seems to have been about four when he realized that one of his senses was missing.

"I guess that I first became aware that I was blind – and I just vaguely remember this – when I'd be wallowing around in the back of the house on the grass, and I kept getting into the dog manure, and my mother would get on me about that. She explained that I couldn't move about so much, that I'd have to try and stay in one place. I never really wondered much about my blindness or asked questions about it, because to me, really, being blind was normal; since I had never seen it wasn't abnormal for me."

Some of Stevie's stories seem unlikely. "Oh, I remember a funny thing. Once when I was just a little baby I remember my brothers Milton and Calvin were messing around with a lot of stuff in the house, had stuff all over everywhere, jam and bubble gum and stuff . . . and they had a garbage can and some matches in the house, and they were saying, God, you know Stevie needs some more light. Wonder what we can do to get him some light? Maybe we can set this thing . . . like start a fire in here and he'll have some more light. So they went and started a fire and almost blew the house down."

25

His mother not only prayed for Stevie to see the light one day, but took the young boy to faith-healers. The preachers, who were empowered by God, would chant over him, pray over him, cajole him and then, instilling in him the confidence to see, seize his shoulders or touch his eyes so that the power of the Lord could flow through their hands to him. Congenital blindness, after all, was a disease, an affliction which could not be merely adjusted to, or accepted, but must be eliminated, once and for all. Stevie says that as a blind child the only hurdle he had to overcome was to help his mother and family deal with his lack of sight. Though they visited many doctors, medical science simply has not been refined sufficiently to perform delicate operations on the brain.

"They talked that stuff but they are crazy. They can't wake up the dead. There are things that they said they could do, but I went to more doctors that said if there was any way that they could do it they would definitely try.

"Sometimes I think I would love to see. Just to see the beauty of flowers and the trees and the birds and the earth and grass, but being as I've never seen I don't know what it's like to see. So in a sense I'm complete. Maybe I'd be incomplete if I did see. Maybe I'd see some things I don't want to see, I guess that to see is to compare – to compare the beauty of the earth with the destruction of man. It seems to me that when man takes one giant step forwards he takes two giant steps backwards.

"You see, it's one thing when you are blind from birth, you don't know what it's like to see anyway, so it is just like seeing. You have things you are familiar with. The sensation of seeing is not one that I have and not one that I worry about."

This last quote on Stevie never having missed the sense of seeing seems to be the one that comes nearest the truth. For his family, his friends, and all other people that *can* see, the thought of someone not being able to see is probably much worse than for a man who has never experienced what it is like to *look* at all the beautiful things that there are. With Ray Charles, who lost his eyesight when he was six years of age, the situation is different: he *knows* what he is missing. So if he got bitter about his fate, it is understandable. But Stevie – as cruel as it may sound – is *happy* not to see. This is what he has been saying in all his latest interviews, and also something that all his longtime friends I spoke to agreed on. Stevie does not even want to *try* what "seeing" is like. Elaine Jesmer, for example, who worked with Stevie when he was around 16 years of age, remembers that even then he refused to give it a chance:

"There was this guy who came up to Stevie and wanted to hook him on to one of those machines that they had developed that would bypass the eye. They said it could actually make him see by touching a certain part of his brain. They wanted to try it on him but Stevie said no way. No way would he try it. Maybe he was afraid that it would spoil something in him and also – it would probably scare the shit out of him. . ."

Madelaine "Gypsie" Jones, a very special lady who has known Steve since 1970 and has been singing with him on and off, says: "I think for him being blind doesn't matter. I can't say that he does not mind but I don't think that it hinders him so very much, not being able to see *visually*. He even kids about it a lot of times and people are always calling him 'blind boy' and 'hey, can't you *see*, stop running into me' and all that. He jokes about the way he handles cash when he has some on him like 'Only a blind man folds money and puts it in his coat like that. Hey, don't *you* know the difference between a five and a fifty dollar bill?' And there have been times at his hotel room, when Steve puts on a real show. Just knocking things over, sweeping stuff off tables and things and then he goes 'Oh, pardon me, you know I'm blind and I can't see what I'm doing.' He's so funny. He'd put wet toilet paper in your bed when you're not there or play other tricks on you. He's such a comedian. No, Steve is certainly not bitter or concerned about his physical blindness."

But there are certain things that Stevie would like to do. "Like I can't drive a car. But then a lot of people don't have cars and they ride with their buddies." There are also things that Stevie *has* done despite his blindness: "I've flown a plane,

27

a Cessna, or something, from Chicago to New York. The pilot was there and he let me handle this one thing and I say 'What's this?' and we went *whish, whoop*, and I scared the hell out of everybody."

When Stevie reached the age where he had to go to school, Lula Hardaway had him attend special classes for blind children in the Detroit public-school system. That was the time when Stevie found out that he was not only different because he could not see, but that there was also something else that made him belong to a minority. That there was such a thing as colour-difference. And that it was not just black and white but that it mattered. Being black was considered more of a burden than being blind.

"I remember a teacher telling me that I should go on and make sure I studied very hard, because the only thing that I could probably do was tune pianos – no, I'm serious! – or make baskets or potholders or rugs. And this lady was being sincere! She didn't mean no harm by what she was sayin'. Basically, she was brought up thinking that that was where it was all supposed to go. Being black and blind, that was all that was supposed to happen. That was it. That's what's left for you to do, unfortunately. She said, 'I'm sorry,' but at the same time made it very clear that there was no way out."

Steve gets upset about any kind of prejudice: "It's racial. The poor white man is told, basically, that because you're white, you're better, and you can do it all. The black man is told, you're black, and *because* you're black, you might as well forget it."

There are no stories about Steve to indicate that he, the black kid, was mistreated by his white schoolmates. It is quite unlikely, though, that Steve should have been the only black child not having to suffer from the prejudices of white children. Lee Garrett:

"In his early schooldays Steve went through exactly the same unkind experiences as we all did. Maybe he thinks that if he talks about it people will think of him as being resentful. But children are cruel. I would not say that being black was worse. I can assure you that being black *and* blind was the worst. The other kids grabbed the nigger kids first. And you did not know what it was all about. After a while you could tell white from black by the way they talked. I remember thinking, so what, white. What is white? It makes no difference. But they showed you that it did. And later on I used to think, I don't wanna be one of them niggers. Until one time you start thinking of your own colour as number one."

Becoming colour-conscious or race-conscious is a process that every member of a minority has to go through. And it is not necessarily right that Stevie's or Lee's blindness made it more difficult to understand what white and black is supposed to be all about. It seems that sighted children do not become aware of colour-difference until they reach the age of about eight.

An illustration of that was given to me by John Carlin, a white, 33-year-old ex-convict who, at the end of 1976 when I met him in Los Angeles, was working with Dustin Hoffman. John was teaching the actor how to think like a bankrobber, for the part Dustin is playing in the movie of the book *No Beast So Fierce*. John: "I grew up in a whorehouse in Texas, that my grandmother had started and that then was run by my mother. Naturally none of the white parents would let their children play with me. Consequently all my friends were black. All my friends. Until they got to the age of about eight or nine. Then I didn't have any friends, because all of a sudden they had a prejudice-thing, too. This time *they* rejected me, because they had realized that I was white."

Later on I discussed what John had told me with a number of black friends. They all agreed with what John had said, remembering either their own experience of becoming colour-conscious or watching their children go through that phase. "You don't grow into it," they said. "You suddenly become aware."

When Stevie went to school he learned that there was more to life than just sitting at home and listening to the radio. As much as Steve liked music, he discovered that quite a few other things could be a lot of fun. Even though he was already a musical genius, he was a very young – and lively – genius, after all. Having to rely on his other senses more than sighted people, he had by now developed them much more in order to make up for not being able to see. But he liked to explore and experiment like every little boy does. Roaming around the streets, he could not look out for a car coming nearer, but his ears would pick up the noise and he would know where it came from. He had also been taught not to run along the street but stay on the sidewalk; and instead of just walking off he became aware of the fact that he had better stay in familiar surroundings. Still – even if he got lost by accident he could always ask somebody to tell him the way back home. Steve: "Some people seem to think that being blind automatically includes being dumb and deaf as well. There is always someone you can *ask* for the direction and it still drives me crazy when people raise their voice when talking to me."

Unfortunately, most of the friends that Stevie had in his childhood, are not around any more. He lost contact with many of them when he moved away from Detroit at the age of 21. But some of them broke with him earlier, when Stevie had his first hit record *Fingertips*. Then he was touring a lot and whenever he was at home Stevie was either busy learning at school or in the studio recording. His friends did not understand that Steve just did not have the time that he had had for them before and considered him to have become arrogant. Others envied him and through Stevie tried to get into Motown themselves – but he could not help them so they said he had become selfish. Some of the children Stevie used to play with and who were his friends do not even admit to it any more: What kind of friendship is that, they say, when you cannot pick up the telephone and dial his number? Those times you want to talk about are long gone.

But in the days when he had never heard of Motown he had plenty of friends, and it is quite clear that little Stevie did not stay at home all the time. But again the stories about the games he used to play with them do sound like they have a dash of fantasy in them. He has told several interviewers that at the age of six he would give his mother fits by jumping from one roof to another. Here is one version.

"I used to hop barns with all the other dudes. You know those small sheds they used to have in the back of houses? In the ghetto where I lived, we'd hop atop them from one to the other. I remember one time my aunt came in and said, 'OK, Steve, Mama said don't be doin' that,' and I said, 'Aw, fuck you,' and there're some neighbours out and they said, 'Aw, child, you oughta be ashamed of yourself, I thought you was a child of the Lawd, you out there cussin' 'n' everything.' That was like back of our house in the alley, you know, so I just kept on, just hopping the barns, jumping around and everything, 'til all at once I jumped and fell right into my mother's arms. The ironing cord, the whipping. The Magic Ironing Cord Whipping."

Somehow this whole statement seems unlikely. First of all, at this age little Stevie would not have dared to say "Fuck you" to anyone. He was a comedian and his head was always full of funny jokes to play on people, but he would not have sworn like that. Even if Stevie did not know the exact meaning of this expression, he sure would have sensed how strong a four-letter-word it is to say – especially to an aunt! Secondly, Stevie was one of the shyest kids around – unless he wanted someone to hear his music, then he knew how to insist. Even at the age of sixteen he would not open his mouth. Elaine Jesmer: "Stevie was so shy, when I worked with him, he hardly ever said a word. It's funny to see him now and remember him as being so shy then. He is modest but he is a little dirty old boy. I mean today this little 16 year old boy is pinching my ass. I mean I just can't make him into an adult. I'm always gonna think of him as 16 years old . . ." Ron White: "The amazing thing about Stevie was that apart from his talent which even at his young age came through and made you enjoy being with this kid, Stevie was very well behaved. He had good manners."

But according to him, he did not only climb apple trees to steal apples, and in total defiance of his affliction jump from the roof of one woodshed to another, but he also stole coal: ". . . like when I was younger my mother, my brothers and I had to go on this drydock where there was coal and steal some to keep warm. To a poor person that's not stealing, that is not crime; it's a necessity."

After the coal-stealing story was published in *Newsweek*, Stevie told *Penthouse*: "My mother wasn't very happy with the reference to the fact that I stole coal when I was young. I'm not ashamed to talk about it, but my mother felt very bad. I tried to explain to her that I told the story only because it's *sad* that in a country that is as wealthy as the United States stealing for survival is a *necessity* as well as a *crime*: You know, the *Newsweek* article didn't get into the politics of this country – they were much more interested in the politics of the record business, making me the centre of some bullshit that I don't even care about."

Apart from the fact that the *Newsweek* article said that they *all* had stolen coal, whereas in *Penthouse* Stevie only referred to himself as the thief, Lula Hardaway still does not like the whole thing. "Politics or not," she said, "we never were *that* badly off. I don't know why Steve says things like this, but on the other hand, he couldn't care less what's in the papers."

Johanen Vigoda, Stevie's lawyer since 1971 (who also used to work for Jimi Hendrix and Ritchie Havens) also told me that Steve has given up worrying about what people write about him: "Steve has been misquoted so often, or found things that he said quoted completely out of context, that the only way to deal with articles is not to take them seriously. It is his music that counts after all, isn't it?"

It is quite possible that Stevie does not bother too much about answering with a certain laxity questions that he might not think "helpful" to anybody. At the same time though Stevie *is* aware of being in *showbusiness*. If he disliked all the articles written about him that much, he would have stopped giving interviews a long time ago. Instead he is friendly, helps journalists make their living and if they ask for it, he gives them a good story. Like the story he tells of how he discovered the difference between boys and girls.

"We tried to sneak and do it to little girls. I used to get into a lot of shit. I got caught trying to mess with this girl. I was about eight years old. It was the play house trip. And I really was like taking the girl's clothes off and everything, I don't understand how I did that stuff, you know, I mean, I was *in* it! I had her in my room with my clothes off. And she gave it away 'cause she started laughin' and gigglin' 'cause I was touching her."

There are also many stories about Stevie's childhood dreams of what he wanted to become as a grown-up. Most journalists repeat the quote from the Motown press releases according to which Stevie is supposed to have said: "Once I had plans of becoming a minister, but then I decided to be a sinner instead." Steve also recalls: "I had visions of becoming a minister and I had also visions of being a doctor and an electrician." But he told *Penthouse*: "All I ever wanted to be was a disc jockey. Even now I fantasize about that – 'WBMB, Blind Man's Bluff Radio'." Still – in most articles you find written about Stevie's dreams the Whitestone Baptist Church in Detroit plays a big part. There, they say, Stevie was a junior deacon and in one story Stevie even tells how he left church:

"We [Stevie and his friends] used to get pretty big crowds of people playing [music] on the porches in front of the houses on Horton Street. I remember this one time, ha, this lady who was a member of our church, she was Sanctified Holiness, but she was still a member of our church, the Whitestone Baptist Church, and she came along and she said, 'Oh, Stevie, I'm ashamed of you for playing that worldly music out here. I'm so ashamed of you.' Ha, I really blew it, boy. I'd been a junior deacon in the church and I used to sing solo at the services. But she went and told them what I was doing and they told me to leave."

Again, it seems unlikely that Stevie would have had to leave the church just because he was playing "worldly music" on porches. After all he was just a child and nobody would expect a young boy to sing and play sacred music *all* the time. On another occasion Stevie stated: "When I left the church and started singing that rock'n roll, they said that I was backsliding."

Strangely enough though, ex-Motown producer Hank

Cosby, who in 1967 took over working with Stevie from Clarence Paul, said: "He'd never been to a Baptist church. So when we did the song *I Was Made To Love Her* I wanted Stevie to use the shouting and screaming element that black Baptist preachers use in their singing. But you can't explain this sort of thing, you have to *listen* to it. So I took him to a Baptist church for the first time in his life." Regarding all other stories about Stevie's strictly religious upbringing, this statement that Hank Cosby made is quite astonishing. But not so for Motown employees. More than one of them told me: "Churches are always good for publicity and there was a lot of hype going on about Stevie in the early days." As the reason why Stevie still sticks to those deacon stories they say: "Stevie has always been very loyal to Motown. He would never do anything to make them look stupid. After all, it doesn't hurt anybody to believe whatever Steve's early publicity said. . ."

Nevertheless, whether Stevie did go to church or not, and even though he sang "that rock'n roll", gospel music has had a great influence over his musical development. He used to listen to the Staple Singers, a family gospel quartet that in the mid-fifties had original hits like *Uncloudy Day, Help Me Jesus* and also topped the charts with traditionals like *Will The Circle Be Broken* and *Swing Low*. In later years they hit the R & B charts with *Why (Am I Treated So Bad)* and *For What It's Worth*. Mavis Staple is supposed to have been a secret love of Stevie's for a long time. "She's a Cancer, you know, and Cancer women are very, very warm. It's like a hypnotic effect they have on you. I met her later on and her eyes are just like that. I mean from what I understand. I could never see them of course, but I felt the pressure. You can feel them shining on you."

Stevie also listened to the Dixie Hummingbirds, a gospel group that was founded in Greenville, South Carolina, in 1928. With them Stevie later had a very strong relationship. Not only did they support him on a number of concerts but the children of lead singer Ira Tucker would work with Stevie and his band: Linda and Sundray Tucker were one time backing vocalists in Wonderlove and Ira Tucker jr. became Steve's publicist in 1972.

Stevie also listened to Mary Wells, who was born in Detroit, Michigan, on 13 May, the same birthday as Stevie's only she is seven years older than him. Mary, who had started singing in local churches at the age of ten, was later also discovered by Motown and in 1961 had hits like *Bye Bye Baby* and *You Beat Me To The Punch*. Her biggest hit was *My Guy* in 1964, just the time when Mary left the label.

Sam Cooke, another idol of Stevie's, had also started out singing in his local Baptist church (together with three other children as the Singing Children) at the age of nine. Sam Cooke, who managed to retain a vital relationship with the black audience and at the same time delivered to the pop market, is said to have been a great influence not only on Steve but Al Green, Otis Redding, Smokey Robinson and Marvin Gaye; and British performer Rod Stewart is supposed to have modelled his style after him. Cooke, who was born in Chicago on 1 January 1931 had hits like *I'll Come Running Back To You* (1957), *Only 16, Wonderful World* (1959), *Cupid* (1961), *Twisting The Night Away* (1962), *Little Red Rooster* (1963 with Ray Charles on piano and Billy Preston on organ), *Ain't That Good News, Tennessee Waltz* and *Shake* (1964). Cooke was murdered like Little Walter and the great rock saxophone player King Curtis (*Ode to Billie Joe*, 1962) who got stabbed to death in Harlem on 13 August 1971. Sam Cooke was shot at a Los Angeles motel on 10 December 1964.

Other great artists that left a big impression on Stevie lived like him in Detroit, and now it was only a matter of a few years until he would meet them personally. Like David Ruffin, son of a Baptist preacher and born on 18 January 1941 who was signed to Anna Records (a label owned by Berry Gordy's sister Gwen) as a solo artist but soon joined the Temptations. The Temptations were another group Stevie liked listening to, and although they did not have any hit records until 1962 were well known in and around Detroit. (Temptation hits in the mid-sixties were *My Girl* and *Ain't Too Proud To Beg* to name but two.)

35

John Lee Hooker (born in Clarksdale, Mississippi, on 22 August 1927), who had started playing in Memphis and in 1943 moved to Detroit, mixed the Afro-American rhythm with the blues and made it his trademark. Hooker hits were *Boogie Chillen*, *Hobo Blues* and *I'm In The Mood*.

All those musicians and the ones mentioned earlier had had a great impact on Stevie's musical direction, as well as they had had on Elvis Presley. Even though in the fifties and sixties it was white rock stars like Elvis and Janis Joplin who dominated the rock scene, who made the big money and caught the mass white audiences, they too had learned what they were doing from black artists. Elvis' first musical experiences had been those of gospel singing and later the white singer with the black voice had cut quite a few tracks that were songs from Little Walter, the Coasters, the Drifters etc. Janis Joplin, the white lady who sang the blues, had found her musical direction from listening to recordings of the black folk musician Leadbelly and Bessie Smith – whom Billie Holiday and other famous singers named as "the greatest woman ever to sing the blues".

Still, in those days when Stevie grew up it was white stars who dominated the music scene and few white people – other than those in the music business – would listen to black music. Steve remembers: "When I was little I used to listen to this black radio station in Detroit on my way to school. Like I was the only black kid on the bus, and I would always turn the radio down, because I felt ashamed to let them hear me listening to B. B. King. But I *loved* B. B. King. Yet I felt ashamed because – because I was *different* enough to want to hear him and because I had never heard him anywhere else."

And then Stevie talks about the respect that you have to demand as a black man and a black entertainer: "Let me say this: I would never go around saying, 'Hey, I *am*.' But so many of us have to demand respect. Do you know how much noise Muhammad Ali had to make before he was respected? It's ridiculous, it's absurd. At his age – and he is old in the fighting world – he had to prove himself. Those are the things which hurt – me, you. And that is where freedom begins.

In the simplest things, even in such things as feeling free enough to turn on a radio to a particular station. You have to seize that for yourself and then demand that kind of freedom from others."

The freedom, to tune the radio to the black station, Stevie had taken. But what freedom and being black meant to black artists and to black recording companies, Stevie had yet to find out.

Elsewhere in Detroit another talented black man was fighting for another kind of freedom. His name was Berry Gordy jr., and he had set out to start the biggest independent recording company in the world – Motown.

CHAPTER TWO

Hitsville

Detroit, Michigan, today the fifth-biggest city in North America, was founded by the French in 1701. Its convenient position next to the Canadian border made Detroit into an industrial city and an important base for furriers.

In 1805 Detroit burnt down to only one house and was rebuilt. Almost one hundred years later Detroit became known as "Motortown": Henry Ford I (born in Dearborn, Michigan, on 30 July 1863), had built the first car to drive through Detroit's streets in 1896. (Ten years before the Germans Gottlieb Daimler and Karl Friedrich Benz had built a three wheel-car with a four-cycle combustion-engine and introduced the novelty in Mannheim, West Germany.) In 1903 he founded the Ford Motor Company which was run by Ford himself and his son Edsel, until they both died (Edsel died on 25 May 1943 at the age of 39 and Henry Ford I on 7 April 1947). Then the company was taken over by Edsel's son Henry Ford II.

The main reason for the success of Ford's motor company was that he had developed radical new business and technical methods: extreme rationalization, flow-production and the employment of mainly untrained workers.

It's not much fun to work the assembly line at Ford's and Berry Gordy jr., who in the early fifties was one of the motor company's flow-production workers, had bigger ambitions than to spend all his life at the assembly line. Berry Gordy, who had grown up in a Detroit black ghetto, was now in his twenties and had already tried a few other jobs that he did not like. He certainly did not want to work in his father's little shop and prize-fighting, which he also tried, was not his dream come true. The only thing that Berry really dug was music. So one day he just skipped the job at Ford's and got involved with a record shop. It went bust. Still, Berry Gordy was not one of those who gave up easily. He started writing songs and he got two of them to Jackie Wilson. *Reet Petite* (1957) sold quite well and *Lonely Teardrops* was for Wilson, as for Gordy, the first million-seller. This was in October 1959. The teardrops that had turned into dollars now enabled Gordy to set up as a producer; making tapes and leasing them to various recording companies who would press and distribute them. He was also getting royalties on the songs he wrote.

At the end of 1959 Gordy had another big hit, this time as a producer – with the Detroit singer Marv Johnson and *You've Got What It Takes*. Shortly after that Gordy was lucky again: he bumped into the Miracles. Or they bumped into him – as usual, there are two versions.

The Miracles, then consisting of Smokey Robinson (christened William Robinson and born in Detroit on 19 February 1940), Claudette Rogers, Bobby Rogers, Ronnie White, Warren "Pete" Moore and Marv Tarplin, had formed as a high-school-band in 1955. Gordy recorded two singles with the group – both penned by Smokey Robinson – and leased *Got A Job* (an answer to the Silhouettes' smash hit *Get A Job*) to End Records and *Bad Girl* to Chess – the company that then distributed Anna Records, the label founded by Berry's sister Gwen.

Both singles were successful but did not make the kind of money that Gordy and Robinson had hoped for, as the biggest slice of the cake went to the publishers and not to the writer and producer. Berry Gordy and Smokey Robinson did some heavy thinking and came up with the decision that Gordy should form his own recording company. He did – using 800 dollars he had borrowed from his family – and called the new born baby Tammie Records. Both his wife and sister were called Tammy, and Debbie Reynolds had had a hit with a song of that name in 1957. Tammie Records did not last very long though, for copyright reasons. There either was a Tammie

Records already or Debbie Reynolds' recording company did not want Gordy to use the name – according to which version you want to believe. Gordy changed Tammie into Tamla. He then took over Anna Records' distribution ("Anna" named after another Gordy sister) and at the same time set up his own publishing company, Jobete, making his brother Robert head of it. Smokey Robinson became vice-president of Tamla and by 1960 Gordy not only had a distribution deal for Anna Records but for two more labels: Harvey and Tri-Phi, which belonged to Harvey Fuqua and had also been distributed by Chess.

There Fuqua had met Gwen Gordy, fallen in love with her, married her and decided that his labels might as well be worked on by his brother-in-law Berry Gordy. Apart from his labels Fuqua had brought a few acts with him like Junior Walker And The All Stars and Johnny Bristol who was later to write chart toppers like *Someday We'll Be Together* (for the Supremes), *Ain't No Mountain High Enough* (for Marvin Gaye and Tammi Terrell) and *Yester-Me, Yester-You, Yesterday* for Stevie Wonder. But the most important artist that Fuqua brought with him was a guy he had discovered who had played drums and sung with the Moonglows. His name was Marvin Gaye (born in Washington D.C. on 2 April 1939). Gaye was not only an artist of Fuqua's but also a close friend. To cut a long story short, Marvin married the other Gordy sister Anna and got signed to Tamla.

While Anna Records was doing quite well – besides making the Hot Hundred they also got into the Top Thirty with *Money* (sung by Barrett Strong and written by Berry Gordy) – Tamla was nowhere near the charts. Gordy was not particularly happy about his sister's label being more successful than his. The Miracles' first recording on Tamla had only been a hit locally. But instead of pushing things he was busy trying to set up the right staff for his company.

By 1961 Tamla began to get into shape. Gordy signed a handful of promising black writer/producers who – on the creative side – took some weight off his, Smokey's and Fuqua's shoulders. Gordy now had working for him Mickey Stevenson,

Norman Whitfield, Clarence Paul, Eddie and Brian Holland and Lamont Dozier – the latter three to become one of the hottest writer/producer teams of the sixties: Holland-Dozier-Holland.

Now that Berry Gordy's companies – and his expenses for all the newly hired staff – were getting bigger, he had a serious shortage of acts. He did have writers and producers, but what he needed now was performers. While Gordy was preparing the ground for what within the next five years would become one of the handful of black recording companies to survive and would turn out to be one of the most successful independent recording companies in general, neither he nor eleven-year-old Steveland Morris had the slightest idea of how soon they should meet.

Coming up to Stevie's discovery it is, of course, inevitable that since 1961 more than just one version of this event has cropped up. *Penthouse* accepted the touching story: the little boy taking care of his discovery himself:

"In 1959 a nine-year-old kid began hanging around a fledgling Detroit music company called Hitsville Studios. His name was Steveland Morris. He was black and he was also blind. The kid could play bongos, drums and the harmonica, and he was becoming expert at the piano. But he was a damned nuisance. He was always underfoot and he even started to butt into recording sessions. Still, he had an infectious way about him and the Hitsville people let him record a few songs, the first being *You Made A Vow*."

It is a good story, but it does not even come near reality. The version that Motown's London press office released in 1972 gets a little closer to the truth: "When he was twelve he was heard playing harmonica by Ronnie White, one of the Miracles. White was so overwhelmed by Stevie's unique harmonica style that he took young Stevie over to Motown to play for Motown's President Berry Gordy. 'I remember Berry was eating a steak when we went into his office. He told me to play and carried on eating. Then he stopped and began to listen.'"

Ronnie White was indeed the one who opened Motown's

doors for Steve. But when he himself tells what happened back in 1960 or 1961 ("I'm bad at dates"), it does not sound quite as exciting as Motown made it: "Actually, my brother Gerald was responsible for the audition. I was just a victim of my family. Like most people who are entertainers or who are artists, writers, or radio- or TV-personalities, I was asked by my family or friends to listen and audition other artists. Gerald did that to me. He asked me to come and listen to a friend of his that he thought was very good. He asked me several times and I kept putting it off. For some reason I never found the time to go over there. Until one day I had nothing much to do and remembered the favour I had promised my brother to do for a long time. When I went over to this house Steve was there with a guy who played guitar. Stevie was playing bongos and singing. I was very impressed by what I had heard and the next day, when I was at Motown I spoke to Eddie and Brian [Holland] about Stevie. They then had him over for an audition. I myself couldn't do anything else for Stevie, because the Miracles went on the road and I wouldn't have had the time to groom him."

Ron is proud, he says, "to have played a little part in Stevie's career", but at the same time he points out that *anyone* who had some understanding of music would have done the same thing: "You just knew that the potential was there. At this stage, of course, no one could *know* that Stevie would become the superstar that he is now. But even though he was very young when I met him I knew that he had a tremendous amount of talent. That he could become big if he were to realize his potential. He was good then and I knew that if he were to grow in the next ten or fifteen years and build upon what he already had the expectations were tremendous."

Stevie and the Miracles are still good friends today and Steve also acknowledges Ron as the man who discovered him. Miracle Pete Moore tells the following episode: "You know what happened earlier this year? The *Hollywood Reporter*, the magazine, paid a tribute to the Miracles. We are the only black act, and apart from the Beatles the only group, to have gotten this honour so far [up to 1976]. You know what Stevie did?

42

He put a full page ad in the *Hollywood Reporter* and the words were: 'A Miracle Discovered A Wonder! Thanks guys, Stevie.' That is what he was saying, and believe me: this page we cut out and framed. Stevie is really beautiful people. He doesn't think of himself as the superstar that he is but as a normal person. And I tell you something else: Stevie was the only artist at Motown and the only artist that we know as friends who actually gave a tribute to us."

It may seem strange, that neither Motown as a company nor any of Motown's other artists, who more or less grew up with the Miracles, paid a tribute to the group. After all, the Miracles had been friends with Smokey Robinson since their schooldays and they had been with Gordy's company right from the start. When Smokey Robinson left the group in 1972 – he wanted to pursue his solo career – the rest of the Miracles stayed at Motown for another few years but in 1976 changed labels and went to Columbia. It does seem quite a common practice at Motown, though: once you leave the company all other bonds are broken at the same time.

Apart from Ronnie White, Steve also feels that he owes thanks to Ruth Glover, a lady from his Detroit neighbourhood when he was a child. Steve dedicated a special thankyou to her in the booklet that goes with his 1976 album, *Songs In The Key Of Life*: "To Mrs. Ruth Glover to whom without, second to my mother, Stevie Wonder, the artist, would have never been. For you were the one who told all of the West 25th Street, 23rd Street, Buchanan, Breckenridge and Tillman Streets, the community and Motown about the 'little nappy headed boy'."

Once the people at Motown had heard about Stevie's existence, it all came together nicely. Although in most articles written about Stevie's first Motown audition it was nobody else but the big Mr. Gordy himself who was dazzled by the little boy's appearance, Stevie's introduction to the company was not all that glamorous. (Although Berry Gordy for a while was in the habit of holding regular Friday-open-house auditions for a few hours and listening to whoever wanted Gordy to hear him, Steve never attended one of those open auditions. It was Mary Wells who was discovered on one of those occasions.)

Motown writer/producer Brian Holland was the first of the company to listen to Stevie. This is how he remembers it: "First of all let me tell you one thing: all the stuff that you hear about it is crazy. You know, like Stevie coming into Motown and everybody running for him and offering him milkshakes on golden trays. It was nothing like that. He did not even come into the studio, because we had some kind of session going and so I met him outside. We sat on a kerb on the sidewalk of Woodward Boulevard and he was playing his harmonica and singing. And it was after that that Stevie met Berry Gordy, who then of course wanted to sign him at once."

Signing Steve to a contract was not all that easy. He was only eleven years old and therefore a minor. Not only did Gordy need Steve's parents' permission, but also the government had to agree to the child working. An official of the state of Michigan employed by the government had to act on Stevie's behalf and make sure that little Stevie would not miss lessons at school or work long hours in the studio; and he would also watch over Steve's earnings and hold them in trust for him until he reached the age of twenty-one.

So far there were no problems about rights and royalties, no hustles about percentages. In those days the recording industry was not as established as it is today and no one who worked on the contract on Steve's behalf gave much thought to the incredibly huge amount of money that could – and would – be made with Steve's records. Nor did anybody have the slightest clue that Stevie would soon be writing his own tunes. Although Stevie got only a tiny percentage in this first five-year contract (as well as the second five-year contract signed when he was sixteen) by the time he was twenty-one he had sold more than 30 million records, written lots of tunes and done lots of tours. All he got was one million dollars – but a lot of people in the music business still think that Steve was more than lucky. Elaine Jesmer:

"See, when Stevie started out he was a minor and with this he was fairly well protected by the government rules. Not only did the government see to it that he had four school lessons a day and that someone travelled with him, but they also supervised his finances. In Stevie's case the books were open to the government so nobody could mess around with them. A lot of other black artists ended up owing the company an awful lot of money and having no way to pay it back. They had contracts that for example guaranteed two releases a year, but then their records did not sell. Because releasing a record is not selling it. Selling it requires an expenditure in form of promotion and advertising or publicity. And if you haven't got that kind of thing going for you, then you might as well not have a record out. And if Motown had given them money and the record didn't do anything – then it was just too bad.

"Still, a lot of black kids fell for it. Because when Berry Gordy started his business black was *not* beautiful. And a black person had pretty good cause to feel that they had less of a chance than white people. At least in this country they did. Now it's almost gone to the other extreme where if you're black you're a minority with a better chance. It's just the reverse and just as prejudicial – America's way of handling social problems, if you want to call that handling. Anyway, what Motown did was kind of take advantage of this situation. They were trying to entice black performers to their company by saying nobody will do for you what a black company will do. That's a lot of bullshit. But a lot of black artists fell for it."

Jim Gilstrap: "Stevie did all right, because before he was of full age he had the government behind him and when he was twenty-one he signed a new contract anyway. The problem with Motown is, they even take your club money. That's in the contract. You don't have to sign it – but it's hard to get a contract at all. So people rather use this to start off and later hope to go to some other company. But first of all they give away their publishing and everything. And you're really selling your soul when you do that. But people do it. And get a salary. When you're hungry you do that and a lot of musicians are starving. But then they want to get away. Motown had such a lot of good acts. Big stars. But they have all left the company – like The Four Tops, The Miracles, The Isley Brothers, Gladys Knight and The Pips, The Spinners – and they've just lost the Jackson Five."

Billy Griffin: "You wouldn't believe some of the big artists who are really huge stars have record contracts which give them none of their publishing. But they signed long-term contracts when they started and a lot of times that's the only way you can get yourself exposed. At first. Take a record company like Motown for example. They say okay, we've got a lot of acts over here. And you don't have any other outlet for your material while they say you can write a song for Jermaine Jackson or Marvin Gaye or whoever. So you know that some qualified people will be doing your material and you will be getting exposed as a songwriter. So you've got to think twice before you skip a chance like this and rather go for it, get some exposure and after you've made a name for yourself as a writer then you can establish yourself in terms of publishing. It happens all the time. But then I guess this is just like any other business that you start in. You have to sacrifice something. Especially over here in America. It's so much bigger than Europe and there are many more artists trying to make it. Also in America you have to sell many more records to have a hit than you have to sell in Europe. So consequently you have to go through more turmoil to get your things going."

Pete Moore: "You must understand one thing about Motown. For many years the world looked upon Motown as being a family of young blacks trying to express their music to the world. But it wasn't that at all. It was *never* like that. Everybody always *thought* that Motown is just being a family. But Motown is a business. They operate as a business to get what they want to do, done."

Even Maureen Orth wrote in her on the whole pro-Motown *Newsweek* article: "Motown, run by Gordy and his family, acted as parents for its artists, who were often on the road. It controlled everything from their stage movements to their concert bookings and the copyright of their songs. Many of the performers were straight from the street and unschooled in finance. Unlike most white performers, they had no lawyers to negotiate their contracts and they accepted without question the royalties they received."

With Stevie being only eleven years old at the time, the

government official acting on his behalf was more interested to see that Stevie's education was contractually guaranteed than to bargain with Motown for royalties. That was none of his concern as long as Stevie got what was considered to be a fair share then.

Now that the contractual side had finally been settled, Motown could start working on Steve. The first two essential things were to find the right song for the child-act and at the same time create a marketable image for him. Stevie was put into the hands of various producers and, as Brian Holland, who was one of them, says: "He cut hundreds and hundreds of records."

Berry Gordy has always believed in competition. Norman Whitfield: "The amount of work given to a specific producer was like a see-saw in the early days. No one ever had an exclusive on a group. At Motown everything was based strictly on competition which kept a lot of energies in the production. Competition breeds champions, and this was Berry's philosophy – to keep everyone from becoming complacent by letting no one have an automatic exclusive on a group."

Stevie went into the studio and recorded endless tracks. Brian Holland: "They are all still in the can but probably won't be released ever, because for one reason Stevie's writing and producing his own things now which are more up-to-date type music." Also, Stevie will not allow it.

While Stevie was recording, Berry Gordy himself thought up an image for his eleven-year-old act. Gordy's first idea on how to sell Stevie was very much linked with the Ray Charles image. A Motown employee: "Motown did quite a heavy number on linking Stevie up with Ray Charles. But then the whole thing got too embarrassing and did not work. So they skipped it." According to some sources Gordy advertised little Stevie as Ray Charles' nephew. Aaron Fuchs' version in *Fusion* softens the story: "The link to Ray Charles was an irresistibly obvious one. Both were blind, black men, and passionate singers and instrumentally virtuous. Motown's publicity machine relished the comparison, doing nothing to discourage popular rumours that they were uncle and nephew (Wonder dismisses that campaign as 'a bunch of shit')." Also Stevie's first album was called *A Tribute To Uncle Ray*. (It was released on the same day as *The Jazz Soul Of Little Stevie*, six weeks after *Fingertips* had come out.)

Brian Holland, who produced Stevie on and off, remembers: "Well, first of all, at that time you can't talk about studio sessions as such. That was illegal. What we used to do was cut the tracks and then dub Stevie in later. But it was just amazing to watch him. That little one singing and doing such a great job. Also he was a very modest, shy person. And so talented! Every instrument that he found lying around in the studio he would pick up and start playing it. Which is really great. He was so easy to work with. He could catch on so quickly; very, very quickly. His ear was fantastic. Well, and then one day I came into the studio and he sat at the drums. Just practising, playing them over and over again. And it didn't take him long to get good at them either. The same with the piano. When I met him he could not play the piano at all – and all of a sudden he played it great. Whatever he did – Stevie always improved very fast."

Although Stevie had a natural talent for learning to play any instrument in almost no time, Brian Holland does not remember anything about two concertos that Stevie is said to have written by the age of ten or twelve: "I don't know anything about concertos," he said. "But I am quite sure that I would have heard them if they had existed at that time."

There are also many articles that not only try to make Stevie into another Wolfgang Amadeus Mozart but have Stevie spend all his time after school hours until late at night in the studio. Without his mother knowing where he was. Clarence Paul has been quoted as saying: "He'd come by at three every day after school and stay until dark. He'd play every instrument in the place and bust in on you when you was cuttin' somebody." But when I talked to Clarence he just laughed and said that the whole story, the *real* story was completely different. "Just think about it," he said. It is of course tempting to make up a lot of interesting stories now that Stevie is a star. A superstar. But when he was eleven, twelve and thirteen years old, he was just another one of Tamla's acts. And no matter how talented the little one was he certainly did not get away with busting in on other artists' sessions. It may be quite a cute thing to imagine the eleven-year-old buzzing around the studio all the time and being a nuisance. Only in reality little Stevie was not alone when he came into the studio. Brian Holland:

"His mother brought him into the studio. She always brought him. He'd never come by himself. She also was staying with him most of the time and then someone else would come and pick them both up. When you saw Stevie, you saw his mother around. All the time. She would not take anything for granted and just leave him alone. She really looked after him. They have always had a fantastic relationship. Steve loves his mother."

That Lula would accompany her son to the studio all the time was agreed within the family before the contract with Motown was settled. Stevie's mother and step-father wanted to be sure always to keep an eye on what was happening with the child: not to have had any influence over what Motown decided to do with him, but to be around in case Stevie needed Lula. After all, he was only a child and recording sessions were a stress he was not used to.

Also, Lula and her husband had rather mixed feelings about Stevie making records. On one hand, they were both glad that Stevie now had an opportunity to do the things he loved to do, but on the other they were both a little afraid of what would happen if Stevie did not live up to Motown's expectations and they dropped him. Stevie's step-father, who loved the eleven-year-old dearly, would have preferred to have Stevie finish school first, before getting into the music business. Both Stevie's parents knew how hard it would be – if the worst came to the worst – for the child to have one hit, catch a glimpse of the seemingly glittery, beautiful show-biz life, and then have to get used to an everyday routine and an ordinary job. Not that they doubted Stevie's talent, but the chances of a child star remaining at the top throughout his childhood and then continuing as an adult are usually very small. So the least thing

Stevie's parents decided that they could do for him, was to be there and give him moral support.

Stevie though, was "more eager than nervous" as he says and got used to the studio and all the people involved very fast. Most of the early songs that Stevie recorded in the Hitsville Studios (which later became the Motown Studios) on Woodward Boulevard, Detroit, were adult standards like *The Masquerade Is Over* and *Drown In My Own Tears*. The songs were about love (*Ain't That Love*) and lost love (*Come Back, Baby* and *My Baby's Gone*) which are to be found on the *Tribute To Uncle Ray* album.

Stevie's first single was a tune written by Clarence Paul *I Call It Pretty Music (But The Old People Call It The Blues)*. The session drummer on this blues single was no less than Marvin Gaye. But this was not the first track Stevie recorded. "The first thing I recorded was a thing called *Mother Thank You*. Originally it was called *You Made A Vow*, but they thought that it was too lovey for me, too adult." Motown finally changed the title again, called it *Thank You For Loving Me (All The Way)* and released it as the B-side on Stevie's sixth single *Castles In The Sand*.

I Call It Pretty Music was released on 16 August 1962 – and it was a flop. Stevie's second single, of which the A-side *Waterboy* was a duet with Clarence Paul (released on 3 October 1962) did not bring him fame either. Ronnie White: "Stevie didn't have it all that easy as people think. He made quite a few records that weren't successful." Even Stevie's first songwriting attempts did not make too much of an impression. Stevie:

"I wrote this song called *Lonely Boy*. I really liked it. It was about this girl neglecting me and the words went sort of:

> *You never see me passin' by*
> *You only turn your head towards the sky*
> *You only care, you don't care at all*
> *All you try to do is make me feel small*
> *I'm just a uhn uhn uhn uhn lonely boy . . ."*

Little Stevie Wonder was not at all a star at this time but

rather someone who was dragged along by the company in the hope that one day they would find the right recipe to sell him to the public. Other artists that Berry Gordy had signed by then were far more successful than the little nappy-headed boy.

The Marvelettes, who had come to Tamla via a talent contest at their Detroit high school, had provided the company with the million seller *Please Mr. Postman* in 1961. It was the first gold disc for Tamla and like another Gordy-written tune (*Money*) would be recorded by the Beatles at the end of 1963.

Mary Wells, who was produced by Smokey Robinson did well and gave Motown a string of hit records. Marvin Gaye's fourth release on Tamla, *Stubborn Kind Of Fellow*, had reached the Top Fifty as well as Eddie Holland's *Jamie* on Motown. The Contours, a group that had been introduced to Gordy by Jackie Wilson, gave him a number 3 hit – and a gold disc – with *Do You Love Me* (which was later covered in Britain by Brian Poole and the Tremeloes as well as The Dave Clark Five).

With *Do You Love Me* Gordy had brought another new label into the charts: the Gordy label. For some reason he liked setting up new labels which then, after they had been going for a little while, merged into the Motown Corporation. Like the Miracle label that Gordy had started in 1960 to which he signed the Distants, a group that he renamed the Temptations. Gordy had released a few Temptations records on Miracle, but as both did not seem to get anywhere he forgot about this label and put the group on to his Gordy label, where their first release *Dream Come True* turned into a substantial R & B hit in 1962.

By the end of the same year Tamla Motown had engulfed such labels as Harvey, Tri-Phi, Anna (although Gwen and Harvey Fuqua had had a few hits on their labels they had found themselves in financial difficulties that they could not cope with), Miracle and Melody. Gordy was beginning to do really well.

Not so Stevie. *Contract On Love*, his next single, did "make a little noise", as Brian Holland describes it, but nevertheless did not reach the charts. The sales figures were not really worth

51

looking at and Gordy, whose concept it was to make hit singles rather than build an artist, had to make a decision. He would either have to drop little Stevie or come up with an idea that would turn the boy's next single into a smash. Although Stevie's first records had been a loss for the company, Gordy could still not face the thought of giving up on the little boy. After all, the child was going down great in live performances and he was really talented. Apart from that Gordy, the business-man, realized that Stevie, now twelve years old, also had commercial value:

A child who was totally unspoiled and – despite his blindness – was such a happy, friendly, lovable and energetic person, just could not fail to reach people's hearts. If he was sold right. Again, Berry Gordy did some heavy thinking.

Meanwhile little Stevie was not worried about his records having flopped. For one thing, Stevie enjoyed the concerts that he together with other Motown artists would give from time to time and he just loved going into the studio where he was kept really busy recording lots and lots of songs. For another, he had enough self-confidence to believe that one day he would make it. Even though he was only twelve years of age, he had a determination that people older than him envied. Also, Stevie's family gave him a lot of moral support. No matter what other people said, Lula Hardaway, Steve's step-father and his brothers kept telling him how proud they were of what he did and how he did it. They loved his records. "It feels good to know that the people you love believe in you," says Stevie. And apart from his family the little nappy-headed boy was surrounded by many other people who believed in him. Brian Holland:

"When you listened to Stevie you just *knew* that he would break big. Not only because he had this really refreshing attitude toward music and would just sing and play along without worrying about how precise it was as long as it came from the heart. But also because already he had this stunning personality at this young age. Stevie made friends with every musician he met in the studio and they would take the time actually to show him the elementary techniques he had to know about the various instruments. Sometimes they would even teach him more difficult things to do."

Stevie became good friends with James Jamerson, a session bass player for Motown. And Benny Benjamin, Motown's first session drummer (who died of a stroke in 1969) became a close friend of Steve's and has also to be included in the list of musicians that Stevie admired most. Stevie: "We even played a session together later. The last song he played on was *What Does It Take To Win Your Love From Me*." Stevie refers to Benny Benjamin as having been "the Purdie of the sixties – although unfortunately unknown because studio musicians in those days would not get the recognition they are getting nowadays." (Bernhard "Pretty" Purdie, with whom Stevie compares Benny Benjamin, was born in 1939 and learned to play drums as a child. After having joined a few bands he made a name for himself as one of the top session drummers in the United States. He played on records made by James Brown, Tom Jones and Nina Simone, to name but a few, and is now the musical director of Aretha Franklin's backing combo.)

Here is a story that Stevie tells about Benny Benjamin: "He was one of the major forces in the Motown sound. Benny could have very well been the baddest – like Purdie. But also Benny would be messin' up all the time. Benny'd be late for sessions, Benny'd be drunk sometimes. I mean, he was a beautiful cat, but . . . Benny would come up with these stories like: 'Man, you'd never believe it, man, but like a goddamn *elephant*, man, in the middle of the road, stopped me from comin' to the session so that's why I'm late, baby, so it's cool!' But he was *ready*, man! He could play drums, you wouldn't even need a bass, that's how bad he was. Just listen to all that Motown shit, like *Can't Help Myself* and *My World Is Empty Without You Babe* and *This Old Heart Of Mine* and *Don't Mess With Bill* and *Girl's All Right With Me*, the drums would just *pop*."

Apart from his adult musician friends Stevie would make music with children from the neighbourhood and compose, or rather improvise, tunes on his harmonica, while other kids would clap their hands or play tin-can "bongos" to the beat

Stevie tapped with his feet. All of Stevie's energy went into making music and his aim was to be as good as he possibly could – and as an often reprinted Motown quotation on Stevie says: "I think whatever I would have dug doing at that young age I would have stayed with and probably wanted to do the best that I possibly could. I think that music was just the thing that I did get into because it was something that I dug."

Stevie also worked hard at school, because as much as he "dug" music and wanted to become a professional musician he also knew that a good education would help him along with whatever he would be doing later in life. Stevie lacked a little in spelling and in mathematics, but in other subjects he did quite well. His mother and step-father had taught Steve early that nothing comes from nothing and that they wanted their sons to grow into people who would not have to spend the rest of their days working the assembly line at Ford's. Fortunately Steveland's parents did not belong to the kind of black people who gave up before they had even tried. They did not accept that they were inferior because of their skin colour, but instead encouraged their children to learn as much as they could. "There may be times when people want to take everything away from you," they said. "But there is one thing they cannot take away: the things you've learned. So even if there's nothing else left you can always build something new upon the knowledge that is inside your heads."

Ironically enough though it was at school where Stevie received discouragement. The teachers wanted him to learn but for different reasons which had nothing to do with "thinking big". All they wanted was to give the little boy who was not only black – which was bad enough – but also blind – which in their eyes made his future lost – a solid enough foundation that would enable him to just do whatever little he could be doing anyway. "They must have had visions of me being a hawker, peddling with shoelace and pencils or haunting some street corner with a seeing-eye dog begging for money or at the best sitting in some busy place playing the harmonica and holding a hat for alms. But the more some people told me that I would

54

never make it the more determined I got – just to prove them wrong."

While Stevie's family gave Steve all the moral support they possibly could, and some of his teachers pictured his life gloomy, Berry Gordy was more convinced than ever that Little Stevie Wonder would be the next act in his company to make it big . . .

CHAPTER THREE

Hey, Harmonica Man

Berry Gordy sat in his office thinking what the hell was wrong with little Stevie's image. By now it was obvious that his first idea of linking Stevie up with Ray Charles had not worked. Gordy had already released three Stevie singles, he had had the press he needed, and despite all that nothing much had happened. Not in the charts, anyway – but in concerts with other Motown artists Stevie was the one who raised a storm within the audience. The kid had only to be seen to be loved.

Twelve years old, scrawny-shouldered, walking toward a spotlight that offered no solace, turning to an audience whose presence he could only feel, singing of beautiful things that he had never seen – it was enough for the audience to fall in love with the little boy. They loved him before he played, before he sang. And when he closed the show with a tune called *Fingertips* (written by Hank Cosby and Clarence Paul) the audiences went wild. Stevie on bongos, talking to the people: "I want you to clap your hands – come on, come on, yeah – stomp your feet, jump up and down do anything that you *want* to do!" Then Stevie playing the harmonica, then getting the audience involved again: ". . . ev'rybody say yeah . . . clap your hands just a little bit louder . . . ev'rybody have a good time . . ."

In his shows Stevie even announced *Fingertips* as being a track from his album *The Jazz Soul Of Little Stevie* which featured him on drums. But if people wanted to buy it they were in for a surprise: the album was not even released. Together with another longplay *Tribute To Uncle Charles* it gathered dust on Motown's shelves. Stevie needed a hit single before Gordy would take the chance to put an album out. And he needed a fresh image, a new name. Something more catchy than just "Little Stevie" as he was named on the instrumental jazz album.

Again, the stories on how Stevie got the stage name which would be his from now on until summer 1964, vary. Stevie is supposed to have said: "The name was given to me by Berry Gordy. They didn't like 'Steveland Morris' so they changed it." Alternatives, Steve says, were "Little Wonder" and "Wonder Steve". Stevie has also said that the name was given to him by Berry Gordy and Billie Jean Brown at Motown. But *Newsweek* gives the credit of having created the name to Clarence Paul: "People around the studio got to calling him the little boy wonder. Paul called him Little Stevie. One weekend, while dubbing his voice, Paul and two other producers decided that henceforth Steveland Hardaway would be known as Little Stevie Wonder."

Although this kind of decision certainly was not up to any producer to make, it sounds quite likely that the idea for his name came from what people called Stevie in the studio. "Little Stevie" because he was only five feet tall and weighed about a hundred pounds, and little boy "Wonder" – well, because he *was* a kind of wonder.

With Stevie having gotten his new name, Gordy set up a concert with Stevie and others of his artists and recorded the whole show. Stevie, the twelve-year-old genius, was the evening's sensation. He played drums on *La La La La La* (the B-side of *Waterboy*) and he did not have to ask the audience twice to join into the song. *Soul Bongo* (written by Clarence Paul and Marvin Gaye) features him on bongos and on his performances of the Ray Charles tunes *Hallelujah I Love Her So* and *Don't You Know* Stevie not only sings but also plays the piano. Clarence Paul: "He was spoiling the audiences already, when he was twelve." Brian Holland: "When Stevie got to *Fingertips*, the closing tune, people jumped up and down, clapped their hands and stomped their feet. They just went wild. The atmosphere was pure electricity, that's how great Stevie was. He had a rapport with the audience that was just unbelievable, they were really getting into it. At the end, it seemed, they were more exhausted by all the hand clapping stuff they did than Stevie was. This guy's always had this incredible amount of energy. God knows where he takes it from – but it's there – all the time."

To everyone's astonishment Stevie had also never had too much of a problem in getting his stage act together. He would move and dance on stage and his show would look right – although he did not have the advantage that sighted artists have who can watch their moves in front of a mirror and eliminate steps that do not look right. Other people would see for Stevie. He picked up on whatever moves they wanted him to do very quickly and take special care that he would not lose control over his movements and fall into "blindism". Stevie: "When you're blind you build up a lot of energy that other people get rid of through their eyes. Blind people have to work it off some other way and it is an unconscious thing. I, for myself, move my head around while other blind people keep rubbing their eyes, for example. Everybody developes their own blindism."

Having recorded this overwhelming concert, Gordy made a decision that was quite unusual: the next Stevie Wonder single would be released from this live show and he would also cut the tracks together and put all Stevie's songs that he had done in the show on an album (*The 12-Year-Old Genius – Recorded Live*).

Listening to the tracks, it had to be *Fingertips*. The standards were too adult (*Hallelujah I Love Her So, Don't You Know, The Masquerade Is Over* and *Drown In My Own Tears*), *Soul Bongo* was nothing to sing along with and *La La La La La* had already been the B-side of *Waterboy* and had not inspired any of the disc jockeys – as some B-sides do – to play the flip-side and make it into a hit.

However, *Fingertips* had a lot of potential. It was a new song and it also featured Stevie on the harmonica. (Although the publicity turned Little Stevie Wonder into a kind of monster when, talking about *Fingertips*, it said: "On this record and his subsequent hits he demonstrated his mastery of the piano, organ, drums and harmonica in addition to his unique vocal styling"). The audience's reaction made it even more lively. The track was too long, seven minutes, but this was the least of Gordy's problems. He just cut it in half – making the second part the A-side. On 21 May 1963, ten days before the album *Little Stevie Wonder – The 12-Year Old Genius* came out, Tamla Motown released *Fingertips Pt. II.*

Fingertips became a smash hit. Clarence Paul told me: "It got such a lot of airplay it was almost ridiculous. The single didn't even need Motown's publicity – the disc jockeys broke it. You just heard that Little Stevie Wonder on the radio all the time." Only six weeks after *Fingertips* had been released in the United States it went straight up to number 1 in *Billboard*'s "Pop 100" (which would not happen again until almost ten years later with *Superstition*). That was on 6 July 1963. One week earlier *Fingertips* had hit the top position in *Billboard*'s Rhythm & Blues charts, too. The single sold one million one hundred thousand copies and Motown awarded Stevie his first gold disc.

(Usually gold and platinum records are given by the Recording Industry Association of America. They certify a gold record for one million copes sold with singles and for one million dollars in sales for albums. Platinum is given for two million copies sold with singles and for two million dollars in sales for albums. As Motown is not a member of the Recording Industry Association of America Stevie's gold and platinum records are not listed in the official *Billboard* chart but only given to him by Motown directly.)

On 16 July 1963 Motown simultaneously released *Tribute To Uncle Ray* and *The Jazz Soul Of Little Stevie* and on 10 August Stevie received the *Billboard* award naming him the "Number One Artist in the Nation", which was printed for Stevie in braille. Little Stevie was a star.

The first consequence of his stardom was that most of his schoolmates were all of a sudden being really nice. Stevie: "You should have seen how friendly they all were – apart from the odd one who called me 'Wonders'. I hated that. After my first tour that guy even wanted to fight. He was a real bully, that dude, but I pushed him down the stairs." The other children – even the white kids – wanted to be his friends. Crowds of children gathered around him during the breaks between the lessons, and those youngsters who not only attended the same school as Stevie but were also in his class got envied most. Stevie:

"When *Fingertips* was number one I didn't realize and understand how many people had bought it. How much it all meant. How many other artists had broken their hearts and died trying to achieve exactly that." But something else he learned to understand very soon: it was the first time in his life that he experienced how much fame and so-called friendship are linked together.

Before *Fingertips* was a hit he had only been a nigger kid who was not worth knowing and whose ambition everybody had mistaken for a crazy idea. Now that Stevie was a star all the children curried favour with him. All of a sudden they wanted to walk with him – before they could not have cared less how their blind schoolmate found his way around. Now each and every one offered to take Stevie home – the ugly black ghetto Stevie lived in had turned into a sociable area. He got invited for lunches and dinners. His stardom made up for his black skin. Stevie's family experienced similar reactions. Thousands of white mothers envied Lula Hardaway the child that was a genius.

But there was also another side to it. Some of the black ghetto neighbours begrudged the Hardaways Stevie's success. Their jealousy made them feel even more inferior than they already did because they were black and poor and they would cut any member of the family whenever they could. In one way, Stevie's hit made life for his family harder. Stevie: "Whenever an artist had a record in the Top Ten people automatically assume that he's got plenty of cash. That isn't necessarily so." It definitely was not so with Stevie when *Fingertips* was number one. The Hardaways' financial situation had not changed at all. In 1963 they still lived in a house with no refrigerator – but how should they explain that to those of their neighbours who now thought that they had a fortune? And why should they defend themselves at all? From one day to the next everybody was watching them. Their privacy had gone.

Also Little Stevie Wonder was not only the talk of the town but also the focus of attention at Motown. Now they had to act really quick if they wanted to keep people's interest in Stevie. Because up to then all their artists had only been as hot as their last single. Tamla Motown's main problem was that eighty per cent of its income was made from singles. Although by the end of 1963 Gordy could claim to be the boss of the biggest independent record label in the world – the Motown group of labels had finished third in the year's single records sales in America after RCA and CBS – he was not completely satisfied. Gordy wanted to get a foot into the album market, but up to now the record-buying public had not gone for Tamla Motown's long players, which usually consisted of one or two hits and ten fillers. Gordy finally came up with an idea that he had gotten from Stevie's live recording and that would kill two birds with one stone:

He would put more emphasis on the "Motortown Revue", the travelling roadshow featuring various of his artists. The Motortown Revue had quite a lot of advantages. For one it would bring more than just one act – established artists as well as newcomers – to the big pop stadiums and expose them to a wider public than the black and Rhythm & Blues audiences. Also none of the acts would be on stage for too long – just enough for the audience to get to know them without getting tired of one particular act. Recording the show meant that the artists one after the other would sing their hits and Motown could put out hit- instead of nothing-albums.

So far Gordy had found to give the artist a chance of anything like self-expression undesirable. Smokey Robinson: "The artists – they don't have anything to do with it, really. The producer is doing the tune so they just go and sing it and fortunately for us we have artists who do not bitch about their songs." (Not until later, anyway, when Marvin Gaye and Stevie Wonder were the first to want more.)

By now Berry Gordy had quite a number of acts (apart from Stevie) that he wanted to feature: Marvin Gaye had scored a few hits for Tamla (*Hitch Hike*) and a new group that had been signed to the label had come up with a number of minor hits and needed exposure: The Supremes. The group consisted of four girls: Diana Ross (born on 26 March 1944), Mary Wilson, Florence Ballard and Barbara Martin, who had grown up together in a Detroit black ghetto and formerly sung as the Primettes before Gordy gave them a contract and renamed the group.

The Gordy label was also doing well with another all-girl group that Gordy had put together himself. Gordy had discovered that Martha Reeves (born on 18 July 1941), a lady who worked for him as a secretary, had a beautiful voice and he wanted to make use of it. Immediately he linked her up with two other girl singers, Rosalind Ashford and Annette Sterling and employed the three of them as session singers. The first record for which the girls did the backing vocals was Marvin Gaye's *Stubborn Kind Of Fellow* and the reaction to the girls' singing was so good that they were jokingly accused of having stolen the limelight on Marvin's disc. So Gordy turned the session group into a main act and named them the Vandellas. Their first recording, *Come And Get These Memories*, made the Top Thirty and their second single *Heatwave* got up to number 4. The Temptations on the Gordy label were not doing too well at this time so Gordy decided they could do with a little exposure, too. It was these acts and, of course, Little Stevie Wonder that the Tamla Motown boss wanted to see on the road. All the details had been worked out when Berry Gordy suddenly had to face another problem: the Board of Education did not want to permit little Stevie to go on the road.

Stevie had already toured America and Europe but the Board of Education had taken it as an exception and did not want it to become a habit. They wanted to see him at school and proposed that Stevie should postpone his musical career until he graduated in 1968. The special classes for blind children in the Detroit public-school system, so the Board of Education said, had no facilities to allow Stevie the extravagance of touring, missing lessons and then catching up with the educational subjects later.

While Stevie saw his dream of becoming a professional burst like a soapbubble ("I cried and prayed for a long time") Berry Gordy made every effort to get the Board of Education to change their mind. That involved lots of paperwork and gave Gordy a few sleepless nights – now that he had gotten *that* far with his child act he certainly was not prepared to take no for an answer – but it was worth it.

After a lot of hassle trying to find a way to get the permission for Stevie travelling, the little boy was finally enrolled in the Michigan School for the Blind in Lansing, Michigan. Dr. Robert Thompson, the school's superintendent, also recommended a private tutor for the time that Stevie was on the road: Ted Hull, a Michigan State University graduate holding a special degree for teaching the blind, was to accompany Stevie from now on. Half of the year, when Stevie was on tour, he would make sure that the minor had four to five lessons a day. The other six months of the year Stevie was to attend the school in Lansing with 265 other blind boys and girls, living on the campus.

The government wanted to see a chaperone, who would travel with Stevie and be a substitute for his mother because Lula had to stay at home and take care of her other children. Gordy named Motown administrator Ardena Johnston as Stevie's chaperone. The third person to be with Stevie all the time from now on was Clarence Paul, his producer and for a while his musical conductor.

Getting things together had taken quite a while and by now it was urgent for Gordy to have Stevie do a few concerts as long as he was still hot. Already another single of his had been released on 13 September 1963: *Workout Stevie Workout/Monkey Talk* had only reached number 33 in *Billboard*'s "Pop 100". *Fingertips* was still being played a lot in America though. (In England, where *Fingertips* had been released in August the single had not gotten anywhere.) Finally everything had been set up and Stevie did a few dates in the United States.

It was at the Uptown Theatre in Philadelphia that Stevie met Lee Garrett, another black and blind musician. Lee, who is seven years older than Stevie, remembers: "When I heard that Stevie was coming to town I definitely wanted to meet this cat. I lived in Philly then and I was doing some gigs myself singing with some band. The funny thing was, that when *Fingertips* hit the charts, lots of people mistook me for Stevie. Especially the audiences in parts of town where we had not played before. It's weird, I mean people should be able to tell whether someone is thirteen or twenty, but as soon as they saw somebody who was black and blind *and* singing, they thought it was Stevie. It even happens to me now – although I understand that we don't look alike at all.

"Anyway, I went backstage and I said to him 'Hi, I'm Lee, the other blind boy.' Stevie thought that was hilariously funny and started making jokes about it at once. Like he half-pushed me on stage and said 'This is Stevie Wonder' and then ran off into the wings to come back a few seconds later and say 'Oh, sorry, I'm Stevie Wonder. This is Lee Garrett who looks like Stevie Wonder' or 'This is Stevie Wonder who looks like Lee Garrett because he's older and he was born black and blind before I was' and all this kind of shit and he went on with it for ages. It was really funny."

Stevie and Lee were to become good friends a couple of years later and they would also be very productive together. Stevie's special kind of humour is also the subject of a story that Clarence Paul told me. And even today he can't think back to "what happened on that plane" without roaring and shaking with laughter.

"We were on that flight – I can't remember where we went to and when it actually happened, but I guess Stevie must have been around thirteen – when Stevie was in one of his silly moods. We had been joking all along anyway, but all of a sudden the plane had a turbulence and that was the cue for Stevie to really get going. He got up, went to the middle of the aisle and started screaming 'I'm a little black boy and I don't know nothin' but this is the day of judgement and I tell you you better start prayin' for your souls.'

"Stevie was only kiddin' but he did that whole number so well that it convinced everybody. People got down on their knees while Steve was goin' up and down the aisles screaming.

64

The most amazing thing is that nobody, none of the steward-esses or anybody stopped him. They just got a kick out of him. They did – but the passengers surely didn't . . . And after the plane had landed and we had gotten off Stevie told me that he thought this was black humour . . ."

Today Stevie has a different way of entertaining people on planes when he feels like it. Madelaine "Gypsie" Jones: "One day I was picking him up from the airport because it was one of the very few occasions that Stevie had flown from New York to Los Angeles just by himself. It was one of these non-stop flights on a jumbo. When the stewardess brought him out she kept thanking him and saying how much they had all enjoyed the flight and how wonderful everything was. It turned out that Steve had given a non-stop concert all through the five hours that it took the plane to get from New York to Los Angeles. He had just sat at the piano that they have on those gigantic planes and entertained all the passengers and all the crew with his music."

As a teenager though, Stevie had a very special kind of humour. No one was safe from his jokes and sometimes he would frighten hell out of everybody pretending to walk into a car or miss a step and fall down the stairs. Clarence: "It took me a while to get used to this. At the beginning when I travelled with Stevie he sometimes made my heart stand still with all the crazy stuff he did. But soon I got to a point where I didn't even consider Stevie blind any more. I just knew that he knew what he was doing."

Stevie's shows in the United States were going down that well, that Gordy did not want to accept not having conquered the British market. On 26 December 1963 he sent Stevie over to England to do some promotional spots on the television shows *Ready Steady Go* and *Thank Your Lucky Stars*. Little Stevie Wonder's appearances on English television helped *Fingertips* a little but the single still did not sell well enough to enter the charts. Gordy did not know that it would take another two years until a Stevie Wonder single would be found in the *Music Week* charts.

Two days after Stevie had left for England Tamla released

another Little Stevie Wonder album in America: *With A Song In My Heart*. For Motown, this album was quite a gamble – because just at the point when Stevie recorded it, his voice had started to break. Clarence Paul: "We had worked on the album and then left for a tour just before we were over-dubbing Steve's voice. When we came back his voice had dropped. Still – we dubbed it in, but the whole album is about half a step too high for Steve." As much as Berry Gordy was afraid that Stevie's singing career might have to come to an end, now that his voice had changed, Clarence Paul and Hank Cosby, who worked with Steve in the studio, were both quite confident that Stevie would get over his voice change without any problems. Clarence:

"I have been through this myself and I knew that the best thing for Stevie to do was to keep singing. With all the cracks and everything. Because eventually you know how high you can go before you crack. This is how a lot of duets came together. Stevie still did a good show, but ballads caused a little difficulty. So we did songs like *Funny How Time Slips Away* and *Blowin' In The Wind* together. People didn't notice Stevie's voice change too much when we got around tricky songs by turning them into a duet. Today Stevie can almost sing in some of the keys that he sang in ten years ago. And because he kept on singing his voice doesn't crack but he gets the high notes easily."

Hank Cosby: "Fortunately Stevie's voice changed gradually. Personally I think that his voice is not quite as good as it was when he was a kid, but then he is a much better singer today."

Stevie's fourth album *With A Song In My Heart* included standards like *On The Sunny Side Of The Street, Without A Song* and *Smile*. This longplay, unlike the first three, was not put out in Britain. To launch his artists in Europe Gordy had already decided to send his Motortown Revue over there in early 1964 and then see what would happen.

On 16 January 1964 Tamla released another Little Stevie Wonder single called *Castle In The Sand/Thank You For Loving Me (All The Way)* which at first did not take off at all but then entered *Billboard*'s "Pop 100" and slowly went up to number 52 on 29 February, from where it dropped again. Although this single was only a small hit for Stevie, it did something else for him. *Castle In The Sand* brought him into contact with movies and also to California for the first time in his life. Stevie:

"We did two movies out there: *Muscle Beach Party* and *Bikini Beach*. I loved California, and I was so excited to go there. Because all I knew about this part of America was that it is warm enough to grow oranges there. And I knew those didn't grow in Detroit. California was terrific. It was fun, fun, fun. I also enjoyed making the movies – although it was mainly me singing and playing music. You couldn't really call it a part."

Like Stevie, Berry Gordy was not worried too much about *Castle In The Sand* not being a smash, because he had other things to do. Gordy was working on final arrangements for his Motortown Revue – featuring Little Stevie Wonder along with acts including the Vandellas, the Miracles and special guest stars Georgie Fame & The Blue Flames – that was supposed to start in England on 20 March 1964. (The artists who went on the Motortown Revue in the beginning of 1964 also did a television show, a one-hour special for Associated Rediffusion called *The Sound Of Tamla Motown*. But, like the previous TV-shows that Stevie had done in England, it did not help to break his records.) Stevie was busy recording more songs at the studio and also getting dance lessons. Stevie:

"We had the Stevie Wonder Show and the Temptations and all other Motown stars toured on it. We used to do finales that were out of sight. Martha Reeves used to show me all the new dances to do. She would say 'Yeah, this is ba-ad, this will make you look sexy on stage.' I tried to do splits and I did the Hitchhike and all the latest stuff. Martha would always show me the baddest steps."

Clarence Paul also remembers that Martha Reeves had a special touch with Stevie. "The way she taught that kid to dance was just a smash. Martha would stand behind the little one, take his arms and while explaining the moves in words she would simultaneously do them with him. It was just like his body had become hers or the other way round. Martha and Stevie were good friends, too. He just adored Martha and she felt more like a sister toward him than a teacher." It did not take Stevie long to learn whatever step Martha showed him and no matter which place the Motortown Revue went Little Stevie Wonder was the star of the evening.

Clarence also remembers that Stevie always got that much into performing "that I almost had to carry him off stage. If it had been up to him he would have gone on forever." Ardena Johnstone, Stevie's chaperone, was so impressed by the little boy's stage appearance that Brian Holland remembers Ardena, after her first tour with Stevie, walking into the Motown office saying: "One day he'll be the biggest star who ever walked through these doors."

Stevie enjoyed travelling very much when he was a child. Clarence: "Everything new you do is always very exciting. If you have more or less lived in one place all the time and suddenly get the opportunity to travel a lot, then of course it is fun. Stevie didn't make any exception – he just loved getting on and off planes and even hour-long bus rides did not tire him. Instead of moaning he entertained everybody else who travelled with him. Like a private show that Little Stevie Wonder held for us and his adult colleagues."

But Little Stevie Wonder was to grow quickly. By the time he was fourteen years old he was six feet tall. So the next single that Motown put out on Stevie for the first time did not feature "Little Stevie Wonder" but only "Stevie Wonder". *Hey, Harmonica Man/This Little Girl* came out on 25 May in America and by 13 June had reached its highest position in *Billboard's* "Pop 100" making number 29. On 23 June Gordy released Stevie's fifth album *Stevie At The Beach*. This included Stevie's single *Castle In The Sand* (one vocal and one instrumental version) as well as his latest single *Hey, Harmonica Man* which was also from one of Stevie's beach movies. This album was not produced by Clarence Paul and Hank Cosby but by Hal Davis and Mark Gordon in California.

Even though Stevie had only come to fame one year ago, Scott St. James, who wrote the sleeve notes, talked about Stevie the child having "matured into the artist he is today".

Then he wrote: "The wonder of this child, still young in years, but mature in ability and devotion to his art, his disregard of the handicap of blindness, his presence, his personality, his vocal abilities, were amazing in themselves. Add to this the further wonder of his proficiency with the harmonica, and the public is presented with a truly unusual performer. Further add his familiarity with and mastery of the piano, organ, drums and bongos and the result is truly a 'wonder' in one so young . . . to illustrate the wonder of it all, the variety of his talent, and create the feeling of a Beach Party."

As much as this album was a Motown attempt to jump on to the Beach Boys' bandwagon, it failed to sell. The surfin' image just did not fit Stevie and his tracks *The Beachcomber, Beachstomp, Ebb Tide, Beyond The Sea* or *The Party At The Beach House* could just not get near Beach Boys' hits like *Surfer Girl, Surfin' USA, Fun Fun Fun* and *I Get Around* that had hit the charts in 1964.

Motown at this time was still trying to copy other people's sound rather than creating their own. The real Motown sound arrived in the second half of that year, and was mainly created by Holland-Dozier-Holland who then had found their own style of writing and came up with songs like *Where Did Our Love Go, Baby Love, Stop! In the Name Of Love* (the Supremes) and *Baby I Need Your Loving* and *I Can't Help Myself* (the Four Tops) to name but a few.

Pete Moore: "The Motown sound in the sixties was very much a pattern. The music was always different but the themes were all the same." Diana Ross: "Everybody liked it so much because it was a very sexy young sound."

On 14 September 1964 Motown released another single from the *Stevie At The Beach* album *(Happy Street/Sad Boy)* which since *Fingertips* was the first Stevie single not to come out in England and also the first record since *Fingertips* that did not get into the American charts. Then the Motortown Revue went on the road again.

By now the Supremes had gotten a string of hits and Mary Wells, who had been teamed up with Marvin Gaye as a duo all of a sudden felt neglected and left the company. (Ironically enough her biggest record ever, *My Guy*, came out in 1964.)

69

Gordy had also signed the Four Tops on a contract with his short-lived Workshop jazz label but then actually released their records on Motown. Another artist Gordy wanted to break was Kim Weston, whom he signed to Tamla in 1963 but who had not scored further hits since her debut record *Love Me All The Way* which had entered the Pop and the R & B charts. (In 1966 Kim married Motown executive Mickey Stevenson who moved to MGM.)

The Motortown Revues were very successful but they were also quite exhausting. Very seldom did the artists spend more than one night in one place, which meant a very tight schedule: arriving in one place, checking into the hotel, doing the sound-check, possibly a rehearsal, leave the concert hall late at night and either crash out at the hotel and get up early and to some place or even travel on the same night. Fortunately for Stevie he found it easy to cope with this hectic life, although he had at least four hours of school per day. Ted Hull: "We still managed to work our lessons in between the concerts and recording sessions."

With Ted Hull and Stevie were four print textbooks, five braille volumes, a cue board for arithmetic, a typewriter, tape recorder, braillewriter, slate and stylus for braillewriting, paper, a talking book machine, talking books from the Wayne County Library (C. S. Forester's *Age Of The Fighting Sail*) and a small organ which could be hooked into a car's cigarette lighter for practising and composing. Stevie's weakness was in spelling – that is why Ted Hull wanted to concentrate with Stevie on braillewriting and only taught him to write his autograph in longhand – and in maths. "But his interests in books were much higher than his reading ability," says Ted Hull, and names as Stevie's favourite authors Ernest Hemingway and James Baldwin.

When Stevie was not on tour but recording in Detroit he studied in an apartment that Ted had set up on the seventh floor of the Chatham Apartment Hotel. In the living room was a piano and a tape recorder for song composing, and Stevie also learned music reading and writing in braille. Ted: "But he didn't have to write down anything. He could invent a

70

tune one day, then spend a whole week without humming it again, and then nonchalantly remember and commit the notes to tape." But there was also a typewriter in the apartment and Stevie hated it. He had to sit there hour after hour typing five lines each of words like "authority, necessity, northwest, publish, beneath, appreciation, explained, bringing, inquire, cruel, improve, hotel, doubt and attending" with straight margins.

In Lansing Stevie learned even more instruments: "I was taught violin but I was never really good at it, and I learned to play bass. I played in the orchestra. I was a ba-ad bass player. I played it with a bow. I loved it, it was really nice."

In those years Stevie also developed the habit of turning the lights on and off when he went to the bathroom, and on tours Stevie even carried his own luggage at times. Ted Hull: "That was really funny, because the fan club couldn't find him and when someone told the girls that Stevie was over there with the bags in his hand they didn't believe him."

Stevie got used to the routine of travelling very fast and he did not mind that he had to take lessons while other artists could get a little more sleep or have a walk around town: "Shortly after you begin travelling you find that most hotels are made the same and you feel at home easily. I mean, you don't feel lost because you know where the bed is, the closet, the bathroom and the telephone."

There was also not much point in Stevie going shopping, because all that he needed was provided anyway and his pocket money was very little: $2.50 at the age of thirteen. His tutor, Ardena Johnston, once told a reporter: "Sometimes he spends it all, and then he whispers in my ear 'I'm broke.' I whisper back, 'I'm broke too.' We hope to teach him to use his money wisely, to avoid champagne tastes."

They need not have feared that Stevie would waste his money. For one, he was much more into milkshakes and soda-pops – and these, according to Clarence Paul, Stevie cheated out of his colleagues who had more cash than he. Also Stevie saved the money that he got to buy tapes and musical equipment. Clarence: "When he got a little older his allowance was

71

20 or 25 dollars per week. He wanted to buy microphones and tape recorders with it – but with that kind of money you don't get very far when you want to buy this sort of thing. So he saved it all and still conned hamburgers and milkshakes out of us. Like he would say 'Let's talk about this song we were going to do' and he would walk you up to the drugstore where you then would buy him what he wanted to eat or drink. He was the most beautiful little con-man I've ever come across."

All the rest of Stevie's earnings were tightly held in trust for him. Only his mother got an allowance to buy him clothes and whatever he needed for his tours and gigs. There were rumours that Stevie at the age of fifteen bought a house for his family in Detroit, but this is quite unlikely. But the Hardaways did move into a better area of town, to 18074 Greenlawn, which was more appropriate for the young star. Still – Stevie did not see too much of his home, because most of the time he was either in Lansing, in the Detroit Apartment Hotel or on tour. Clarence Paul tells a funny story about those early tours: "Ted Hull, was with us most of the time. He didn't only teach Stevie but he came along to gigs, too. And the incredible thing about Ted was that he was blind too. Well, not *really* blind, but as good as blind. But he refused to wear glasses. He just didn't want to admit that he couldn't see without them. Consequently he stumbled a lot and we all teased him a lot. Like we used to say, 'Hey, what's that – the blind leading the blind.' Two people in need of a seeing-eye dog. It was too hysterical watching one blind boy leading the other blind boy around. Fortunately Ted had a good sense of humour. Although he didn't laugh he never got angry. He just pretended not to hear. Like he was *deaf* as well . . ."

Still it was not all fun on the Motortown Revues or any other shows that black artists did. Elaine Jesmer remembers: "I've seen things happening to black performers you just would not believe. They were just beaten up in the South when they travelled together. That was not uncommon. It was not uncommon at all in the late fifties and early sixties. Like the road manager of the Four Tops was one of the victims of one of those nasty racial fights. It was on one of the Motortown

Revues that he got beaten up. It was a whistlestop – every night they'd be in a different city – and that night they had ended up in this little Southern town. The Four Tops had left Frazier – I think that's what his name was – to watch the bus. All of a sudden a bunch of redneck boys broke into the bus and they'd beat up this guy really bad. He crawled to the stage door and the Four Tops just looked at him – that was enough for them to draw their pistols and run outside. There were people killed in that fight. But it wasn't one of the Four Tops, I'm glad to say.

"I don't know if Stevie actually had to experience anything like that – because he was always fairly well protected by the government rules that made him have enough people around him to take care of him and drag him away in case something was about to happen. But it sure wasn't fun to be a black artist – or to be black at all – in those days."

As a matter of fact Stevie never had to face a situation where people attacked him physically but despite his young age he was very well aware of things that were happening around him. Nat "King" Cole was attacked by a gang of Southern racialists in 1956 when he was on stage in Birmingham, Alabama, playing to a predominantly white audience of 3000 people. Sonny Boy Williamson died a violent death in 1946; Sam Cooke was shot. Stevie also mentions Ray Charles as a victim of the hate that was going on: "People did him in. They knew like when he was on drugs. A lot of people would bust him, just to get money, or they would put him in jail in some of the Southern places just to get some bread."

This kind of thing happened to a lot of black performers. Elaine Jesmer told me: "At that time the police were always going after musicians to see if they had any dope. And often – even when they found no drugs – they would just bust you because you were black or because you were a musician. I've seen a lot of racism. A scene that I remember in front of my house was almost an everyday thing: I had an apartment in a white area of Los Angeles (Elaine is white) and one day Clarence Paul came to visit me. Around the time I was expecting him to turn up I heard some talk outside the house and I went out.

There was Clarence and there was a police car. I know that Clarence never was doing anything – they just wanted to hustle him.

"They saw a black guy driving in a white neighbourhood and when he stopped his car they just stepped in. They asked him what he was doing – as if they had a right to disturb him. When I got out of the house they backed back a little. And I remember Clarence saying 'Why me, baby, what did I do?' And I said 'You know why. Because you're black, that's why.' This is a police state. Especially California. They are power crazy. Do you know the only reason why the police in New York are supposed to be the friendliest? Because there are always so many people around everywhere that they just can't do the things the police can do over here where they can catch you without anybody watching."

Lee Garrett also recalls a scene where he got into trouble with the police: "Those two guys came up and they wanted to bust me for no reason at all – unless me being black was their reason. I hadn't done nothing and I did not see any point in going with them. When they started getting rough I just hit them back. Naturally I ended up in court. The funny thing about it though was that the judge didn't want to believe his eyes: There's this blind guy standing in front of him while the two policemen told him that I had attacked them. Mind you, I'd managed to beat them up quite a bit before they finally overpowered me so it must have been quite a weird thing for all the people in court to look at."

It was while he was touring, at the end of 1964, that Stevie Wonder started to write songs seriously. Clarence: "We would sit on a bus or in a car, touring, and we would just make up melodies and lyrics together. Stevie's composing was very instant, and that was the time for me to definitely foresee that one day, not too far away in the future, he would sing only his own tunes."

At this time, though, it was still out of the question for Stevie to go up to Berry Gordy and tell him that all he wanted to do from now on was his own music. Motown's recipe for success did not depend on any kind of artistic freedom. It is even said that the performers, as well as the writer/producers, were under the strain of constant competition. Groups had to compete for tracks. Writers would come up with a song and a track, and the artists would all sing over it, and the best would get a single released. Fortunately Stevie was not too much involved in that heavy kind of competition, because first of all he was different still being the youngest act, and secondly he just did not have the time to go through all that. Stevie had plenty to do at school and he did not hang out in the studio as much as he had done before. The newness of it all had faded. Stevie had been with Tamla Motown for over three years, and now was just another act of theirs. *Fingertips* had sold 1.6 million copies by now but no artist can live on one single's fame for ever. And although Stevie's other singles had not done too badly, other Motown artists were having bigger hits.

Also the Beatles had just begun to flood the American pop market with songs like *From Me To You, I Want To Hold Your Hand, A Hard Day's Night* and *Eight Days A Week*. So Stevie experienced what it is like to have had one number one hit and no other single to follow it up. Stevie:

"If you're not careful in this business your head can get really messed up. Some people are stars for six weeks at the most. It takes about two weeks to get a single recorded and out and another four weeks for the record to climb the charts. Then it comes back down. Within those weeks you can become a monster and think of yourself as the biggest star ever – but then you might never have another hit.

"What makes it worse is that within this time you may not have kept the same kind of rapport with the friends you had before and this short-lived success may destroy old friendships. Also new people you have met and taken for friends can turn out to be enemies. I went through that kind of experience after *Fingertips*. Everybody was about to kiss my feet and all doors were open for me.

"But I also remember that nothing is guaranteed. If you let that glitter go to your head it can kill you. While *Fingertips* was big I was big for a while. But then I didn't have a huge hit for a number of years and I learned something: That when you're hot you're hot and everybody does everything for you. But if you don't have a hit people are gonna look at you and say 'What do *you* want, kid?'

"Quite a lot of people lost confidence in me when they thought I was only a one-hit-wonder. Not so much Motown as people in general. There'd been great expectations of Stevie on drums, Stevie on keyboards, Stevie on this and that – while I found that I was becoming more and more myself. I would get ideas for tunes and spend a lot of time just making my music, messing around with a tape recorder and experimenting. There were a lot of things that I wanted to do musically that I wasn't doing. And I didn't want to get categorized – but everybody who stays with Motown for a long time does. I always had something more to reach for, although you never reach your final peak, I guess. Basically, no one really knew what I was going to do at Motown."

There was one man though, apart from Clarence Paul and Hank Cosby, who worked for Motown in 1964 (until 1972) and who has always given Stevie some kind of special support. This man is Gene Kee. He worked in Motown's artist department and in 1964 became Stevie's musical director. Gene's son Doug, who later handled Stevie's musical equipment for a few years, told me: "They had quite some difficulties with Motown, because nobody in the company really gave Stevie all that much support when he started out doing his own things. It must have been quite a tough situation for all of them to have been in: Motown wanted hits in their Motown sound, Stevie was already breaking away from that and my father, being employed by Motown but realizing that this kid who he worked with sure knew what he was doing, had to try and satisfy them both."

Going back to the end of 1964 and the beginning of 1965, Motown finally released an album from a Motortown Revue. *Motortown Revue Live*, including Stevie with *I Call It Pretty Music (But The Old People Call It The Blues)* and *Moon River* came out in England earlier than in the United States (U.K. release April 1965). This album sold rather well and did more for

76

Stevie than the album *Harmonica Man* (which was the British title for *Stevie On The Beach*) that had been released in January 1965 in Europe.

On 26 March, Tamla Motown put out another Stevie Wonder single *Kiss Me Baby/Tears In Vain* which was a flop in America as well as in England but nevertheless a milestone in Tamla Motown's European history.

It was Stevie's first single over there to be released on the Tamla Motown label. In the very beginning Motown material had come out in England on a variety of different labels – like Oriole and Fontana – and not had much sales impact. In 1963 EMI acquired the rights through their Stateside label and in 1965 the deal with EMI (and everywhere else in the world) was changed: Motown records were still pressed and distributed by EMI, but they appeared on their own Tamla Motown label.

In America Motown has its own distribution company, Hitsville, set up after problems with sub-contracted distribution. The question of how this was financed has given rise to music-business rumours – often repeated, never substantiated – of Motown links with organized crime. It is certainly true that American banks in the sixties were reluctant to lend money to black businesses; and it may well be that in desperation Berry Gordy turned to financiers whose funds came ultimately from less-than-respectable sources.

Anyway, while Berry Gordy jr. had prepared the ground for the Tamla Motown label to swamp Europe, Stevie used the time when he had no hits to develop his musical abilities even more. From what long-time friends of Stevie's say, he is totally self-taught, despite *Newsweek*'s claim that "he studied classical piano". In some articles Stevie is even said to have "made an amplifier and local A.M. radio station while at the Michigan School for the Blind". However, Clarence Paul says: "Let's put it this way, Stevie gave his mental assistance."

In those weeks when Stevie did not tour or work in the studio he stayed at the school in Lansing where he had found a new, favourite subject: sports. Steve: "I always participated in wrestling, that was a lot of fun. I also did a lot of other stuff that people thought I couldn't do. Like my brother and I rode a bike together. That was quite exciting."

Today Stevie prefers other sports. He roller-skates, swims, bowls and takes anyone at Air Hockey (played with a paddle and a puck that's kept afloat by air currents). Even though Stevie cannot *see* the puck, he can *hear* it. "Sound bounces off *everything*," he says. "It is only how much you *use* what you hear. Just try and put your hands right up to your ears then close your eyes and move your hands back and forth. If you really concentrate on it you will hear the sound getting closer and farther away. It's easy for me to locate things by sound, and you could do it, too. Only your hearing has become kind of spoiled because you never had to depend on it as much as a blind person has to. You'd be amazed if you knew how much of what you can *see* I can *hear*."

This is, for example, what Stevie wants to use as an idea for one of his next albums: "The sounds of the earth are something I'd like to put in rhythm. The sounds of birds, everything. I've been thinking about doing a complete acoustic album."

Stevie also "watches" television or movies a lot: "You can tell by the sounds and just from relating to the pictures to doing things in your own life. It all connects." Ira Tucker, Stevie's publicity manager since 1972, said: "When you go with Stevie to the movies the thing is, though, you got to be sure and keep him up on what's happening all the time. You sort of narrate things for him. But sometimes, you know, you can get so caught up in the flick yourself that you forget to keep telling him. You don't want to do that; it really makes him frustrated." Lee Garrett reduces the whole thing to a common denominator: "I'm sure that even every sighted person has watched television 'blind' at one time or another. Or have you never had the TV on and been in a different room? Television (although the name implicates it) and movies aren't all that visual after all. Just by listening to the sound you get a pretty good picture. You don't even have to have explained what's happening on the screen all the time.

"Even if a scene *is* visual and none of the actors talk, chances are, that you catch up with the flick. Steve and I have been to the pictures together a number of times. Just the two of us with nobody telling us anything. And believe me, we had a lot of fun and weren't frustrated at all!"

But back to 1965 and Stevie's next single. On 2 August Motown U.S. released *High Heel Sneakers/Music Talk*. (The B-side credits T. Hull, C. Paul and S. Judkins as writers/composers. Clarence: "It was one of them things that we made up riding on a bus. Stevie, Ted and I just grooved along doing some 'music talk'.")

High Heel Sneakers made it into the *Billboard* "Pop 100", but in September the record had reached its highest position, number 59. Apart from that *High Heel Sneakers* had also brought Stevie back into *Billboard*'s R & B charts and there it finally went to number 30 in October 1965. After this success Motown also released the single in England and sent Stevie with the Motortown Revue to Europe again.

They recorded the Paris concert and at the beginning of November 1965 Motown U.S. put out the album *Motortown Revue In Paris* with Stevie's *High Heel Sneakers* and *Fingertips* on it. Simultaneously the *Motortown Revue* album, which had been in Europe's record shops since April 1965 was released in the States (as *Motortown Revue Recorded Live, Vol. 2*). Motown put out also *A Package of 16 Hits* (including Stevie's *Come and Get These Memories, Contract On Love* and *Sunset*) and *16 Big Hits Vol. 3* (with Stevie's *Hey, Harmonica Man*). The fifth album finally was a special treat: a live-album, recorded three years earlier and called *Motortown Review At The Apollo*. In This New York performance Stevie Wonder sang *Don't You Know*. Aaron Fuchs wrote about this early live recording of Stevie's *In Fusion*:

"Unlike Michael Jackson (the Jackson Five), whose appeal could be geared directly to a youth market, from his earliest performances Stevie was getting a response from an older audience. The decade-old-album *Tamla Revue Live At The Apollo* offers germinal indication. Performer after performer, Diana Ross and Marvin Gaye among them, obligatorily try to elicit audience response with the *de rigueur* 'All right everybody, clap your hands' and 'Lemme hear you say yeah'. Enter the eleven-year-old Wonder, his voice high and squeaky, asking the crowd, 'Do you feel alright?' He asks again, and, still not satisfied, half-sings, half-speaks with a stacatto rhythm, 'I-Do-Not-Hear-You!' and breaks the hardened crowd up like no one else could that evening."

With those three live and two greatest hits albums Motown was now surer of getting some reaction from the album-buying public. People would rather spend their money on a longplay that had various artists and hits on it than on an album that was done by only one Motown act and that offered only one or two hits as bait. After all, there was no self-expression on the solo albums and also the time for concept albums (like, for example in 1967, the Beatles' *Sergeant Pepper's Lonely Hearts Club Band*) had not come yet.

While Motown was getting more and more commercial, advertising the Motown sound as *The Sound Of Young America*, Stevie was already beginning to turn away from them musically. He had bigger ambitions than to just sing other people's tunes and have a hit in the charts now and then. He wanted to be creative, not just a product selling a product. What happened with most Motown artists, Stevie says, was: "Holland-Dozier-Holland usually would sing the melodies (tunes they had written) themselves and say, 'This is how I want you to do it.' "

Now that Stevie was growing up fast he was aware of the fact that Motown would not always treat him as the child-exception. That he would get involved into the competition that the other artists were in already. But most of all, Stevie was seeking not only artistic, but at the same time personal, freedom. He wanted to get out of the ghetto for good, but he wanted to play things his way. He did not want to be anybody's puppet on a string.

Stevie making it on his own terms would reward those who had always believed in him, and it would also prove wrong all the people who had thought of him as a one-hit wonder. Now being black and blind had become more of a challenge for Stevie than ever before. He was only fifteen years old, but he had already experienced what it meant to grow up in a ghetto, he knew what it was like to be a star – to be loved and respected by everybody – for a little while to then be left alone again by people he thought had become his friends. At this stage, Stevie was extremely determined to escape all prejudices and pretences. And his music would help him to get wherever he wanted to.

The 15-year-old felt that he had a lot of music inside him, "And that music wanted out," laughs Clarence Paul. "He'd be making up those tunes all the time. He just sang whatever came straight from his head. And boy, did we dig it . . ." "We" were Clarence Paul, Hank Cosby and also Sylvia Moy, a lady songwriter working for Motown. They would either meet in the studio or they would get together at Stevie's home after he had finished his lessons with Ted Hull. And then they made music.

"It was like kind of a parlour game," says Clarence Paul. Writing songs was not considered work but fun. Any of the three would come up with either a little bit of a melody or a punchline for a lyric and then they would work on it. Sylvia Moy: "Stevie had developed his musical creativity long before concentrating on lyrics. So most of the time Stevie came up with a tune, sometimes a punchline for a lyric. I would write the words to it and Hank arranged the song." Some afternoons they would make up really silly things and "fall about laughing like we were crazy" as Clarence remembers. "But then that was a kind of brain-storming, if you know what I mean. Something always came out of the 'sessions' we did."

Even though Stevie's family did not have much money in those days, Lula would always try her very best to make Steve and his friends feel comfortable and welcome. "It was always friendly at Stevie's," says Clarence, "and whatever Lula had to give to her family she would always offer to her children's friends, too." Sometimes she would invite them to stay for dinner. "The Soulfood that Lula cooked was out of sight." Even if the Soulfood consisted of more greens and cornbread than ham or meat, Lula always managed to make the dinners so delicious, that nobody would realize that the meaty taste came from an odd slice of bacon more than anything else. Sometimes Lula would even succeed in talking her husband into giving some fresh bagels for the hungry bunch. And one of the biggest treats for Stevie was to get a soda-pop instead of drinking water or squash.

It was on one of those really groovy afternoons, that Stevie, totally happy with sweets, soda-pops, and Hank's and Sylvia's company suddenly clapped his hands, singing: "Baby, ev'rything is alright. Uptight, out of sight." With this, the punchline to *Uptight* was born. It sounded so great, the way Stevie did it, that Sylvia at once decided to write a complete lyric to the tune that Stevie had begun to make up.

But *that* had happened before, so neither Stevie nor the others guessed that they had just come up with the hit song which would start the world-wide Stevie Wonder phenomenon. No one – least of all Berry Gordy – had any idea what was to happen with Stevie and Motown from now on.

Everybody was in for a big surprise.

CHAPTER FOUR

Hey Love

Berry Gordy sat in his luxuriously furnished office on Detroit's Woodward Avenue and worried. Despite all the gold discs that he had decorated his office walls with, the Motown boss had a problem. As proud as Gordy was of million sellers like *Shop Around* (the Miracles), *Please Mr. Postman* (the Marvelettes), *My Guy* (Mary Wells), *Where Did Our Love Go, Baby Love* (the Supremes), *I Can't Help Myself* (the Four Tops), *Dancing In The Street* (the Vandellas) and Stevie's *Fingertips* he wished for another really big hit for Stevie. The wonder boy had not topped the charts for two years now and it was about time to get him back into the Top Ten.

The main problem with Stevie was, that unlike other Motown acts, he had not come across with a style that was distinctive as had the Supremes, the Four Tops and the Miracles. But those were adult acts who did not have to go through voice and image changes like Stevie. Although Motown had already managed to take Stevie away from the Ray Charles uncle-nephew image, away from the "Little Stevie Wonder" image and now had "Stevie Wonder" known as a successful live performer, the record-buying public had not adapted to it as well as the concert audiences.

Stevie had even gotten over his voice-crack and fortunately his singing had turned out – at least in Gordy's opinion – to be better than before. He also played instruments like the piano, the organ, drums and bongos and he was exceptionally good at playing the harmonica. His musicality came across perfectly when he did a live-show, but on recordings it did not matter too much to the listener how many of the instruments

Stevie actually played himself as they did not visualize it. His image was one that you could not pinpoint; and that made it so hard for Gordy to sell Stevie to a public that had not seen him live. Also at this point the 15-year-old was neither a child nor an adult. And being somewhere in between is always a difficult situation. The only thing that Gordy could do was find a musical direction for Stevie that would make his songs as much of a trademark for him as the Holland-Dozier-Holland songs worked for the Supremes and the Four Tops; and as Smokey Robinson's tunes did for the Miracles.

What Stevie needed urgently was the right song. Since his success with *Fingertips* he had more or less lived off the one hit. *Fingertips* was always the one single that popped up in people's heads when they thought about Stevie Wonder. And although four of his following six singles had gotten into *Billboard*'s "Pop 100" only *Hey, Harmonica Man* had made the Top Thirty. *Workout Stevie Workout* was number 33 and *Castle In The Sand* and *High Heel Sneakers* had only reached the Top Hundred. The fact that *High Heel Sneakers* had climbed to position 30 in the R & B charts was little consolation to Gordy. He wanted his artists to be the best.

Then came *Uptight*. When the Motown boss listened to that production he immediately knew that this was Stevie's next single. If *Uptight* failed to get into the Top Ten something in the music business was definitely wrong. This song had so much rhythm and so much drive, that people just could not ignore it. It had a great hook that you could sing along with and it was an incredibly good record to dance to.

On 22 November 1965 Motown released *Uptight (Everything Is Alright)/Purple Raindrops*. Ten weeks later the new Stevie Wonder single had jumped into the charts and got to number 3 in *Billboard*'s "Pop 100". Clarence Paul laughingly names this single as his nicest Christmas present in 1965, because "Even if I didn't have anything to do with actually writing the tune I was proud of being Stevie's teacher and having encouraged him to take up writing professionally."

Also in early 1966 *Uptight* went to number 1 in *Billboard*'s Rhythm & Blues charts and it was the first Stevie Wonder single to reach the *Music Week* charts in England, where the record had been released at the beginning of the year. When Gordy knew that *Uptight* was getting a lot of airplay in Britain he made a quick decision and sent Stevie to tour the United Kingdom.

It was a one-nighter tour Stevie left for on 21 January and it was only a short tour. Still *Uptight* got an even better push through Stevie's live-appearances and climbed to number 14 in the British charts. The audiences loved Stevie and he had always felt very warm toward them. "The people in England got really into my music. They were always screaming and the response that I got from them in my concerts was something that in America I had only experienced from black audiences so far."

At this point most of Stevie's fans were not even aware of the fact that Stevie had co-written his first world-wide hit: the writing credits were given to H. Cosby, S. Moy and S. Judkins. Why Stevie had used his full father's name and not his pseudonym, he cannot even explain himself. "Maybe I had not seen myself so much as a writer rather than a performer," he said once. "Or, I don't know. Actually, I had not even thought about it that deeply. At this time I don't think it was that important to me to make sure that everybody knew that I was writing. It was much more of a kick to see the song recorded and then watch the single shoot up to number one. It was enough for me to know that this song contained a part of me."

With *Uptight* Stevie had gotten new stardom, he did more television shows and tours than ever before and the number of Stevie Wonder fans increased rapidly. Still all this was no reason for the teenager to become big headed. Elaine Jesmer, who worked with Stevie around that time, remembers: "In those years I was doing the publicity for various clubs. And in doing publicity for them, I often ended up in doing the publicity for the acts that they had booked. That is how I met Stevie. He was performing in one of the clubs I worked for. But even though he was a star, he was such a modest, warm and friendly person and very easy to work with."

Strangely enough though, from this quiet and modest

teenager radiated such excitement that people just could not get enough of him. Elaine: "One day Ted, his tutor, asked me if I could take Stevie and him down to Watts. Stevie wanted to go there. At this time I had a little two-seater Mercedes 190 SL and while Ted sat in the front with me, Stevie was rolled up in a ball in the back. Stevie, a teenager then but already full grown, did not mind. He just laid there and he didn't say a word because he was so shy.

"Anyway, we got to Watts and we pulled up at 103rd Street and we just let him out. He just stood there and people started coming over. Stevie was just like a magnet. And the people would go up to him and they would touch him and he would touch them back. They didn't talk a lot, it was more like 'Oh my God, this is really Stevie Wonder.' The feeling from them to him and the other way round was just like magic. And I remember one little boy who was walking around the street corner and when he saw Stevie he stopped dead.

"He just looked at Stevie and his mouth fell open and his eyes got really big and then he looked at me and he wanted to say something but he couldn't. And I just nodded my head. The very second the boy turned around and took off. But then, about five minutes later he came back and he must have brought about twenty-five other kids with him – all between twelve and fourteen years old. And they were all over Stevie. It was an incredible scene. Everybody wanted to touch Stevie or take his hand."

Even when Stevie was at this young age his handshake had already had something very special about it. Elaine: "In the beginning it really freaked me out. I didn't know how he did it but when Stevie shook hands with you you immediately knew that this was more than a handshake. He is not like other people in terms of that. He really gets his first impression through touching. So when you gave him a limp handshake he would probably figure that you were limp minded. Although he would never say it."

To have Stevie hold your hand is an experience that you never forget. It is a feeling that is hard to describe: First of all, everything that happens when Stevie shakes your hand is entirely up to him. Stevie is directing while you are just part of it. But you only realize that after he has held your hand for quite a while – then you wonder why you did not just shake hands for a second or two, as you usually do, and let go.

All of a sudden you become aware that Stevie is holding on to you. But he does not grab your hand or tighten his grip – Stevie's handshake, although strong and firm, is yet light enough for you to withdraw your hand without any difficulty at all – if it were not for the magic that he has captured you with. It is not physical strength, but rather some kind of inexplicable attractive power, which makes you feel like you are connected with him totally.

Not just your hand but your whole body and your mind are touched with the vibrations that he gives out. And at the same time it is as though he can look right into you. All that make-up, and whatever else you put on – physically and psychically – to make a good impression, he strips off just by holding your hand. The weird thing about it is that you don't even mind, although with other people it makes you feel most uncomfortable when they seem to be able to look through you right from the very first minute that you say hello.

Stevie's handshake can last for minutes and gives you a very warm, comforting feeling. It is like somebody very close to you holding your hand: Your lover, your very best friend or your mother. Giving someone your hand for a longer time has something to do with trusting them, feeling safe. You would never dream of holding hands with a stranger for minutes – unless something clicks and you have fallen in love at first sight. But with Stevie it is not a sexual sensation, although it is definitely as intense.

It does not come as a surprise that everybody who has met Stevie experienced the same. Not only once, but every time they see him. Billy Griffin from the Miracles told me: "He has a way of touching – which I guess most blind people do – but with Stevie even this is still different. Take men, for example. Most men can't touch each other. They cannot hug you. But with Stevie he touches you and holds on to you while he is talking to you. And it's a great warmth that comes from him.

He can read vibrations from people. For him I think it is a
way of knowing how sincere a person is. He is so sensitive. He
can actually read the vibrations that you give out. Your
whole body and everything. That is stuff that *we* normally
don't think about. But he does."

Stevie, of course, is also extremely sensitive with voices.
"When you meet Stevie speak low" is the advice that Ira
Tucker jr., his publicist, gives every journalist that he in-
troduces to the musician. Ira: "Some people may go wild when
they find someone talking to them in a shrill or hysterical or
simply loud voice. Because they don't like the sound of it.
With Stevie, though, it is even worse: he doesn't say anything,
he doesn't complain, but sharp and loud, nervous voices,
actually give him a physical pain. Which is understandable –
if you think of how he can detect any flat note that only one
instrument in an orchestra plays. His ears are so sensitive,
it's almost untrue."

There is one noise that Stevie does like, though: His audiences screaming, stomping their feet and clapping their hands
when he performs on stage. "But that is a different kind of
thing," says Ira. "It is an audience reacting to him, not one
person shouting in his ear and half blowing his eardrums off."

Now that Stevie had come up with *Uptight* he had plenty of
this kind of beautiful noise again. His audiences had always
loved him. "But it is funny," he says. "As soon as you have a
number one everybody is going even more crazy over you than
before. If you just have nice songs that hang around somewhere
between 30 and 100 in the charts, people still dig your music
but you are no one to go totally wild about. But that is psychological, I guess. Especially when you're on tour with other
artists who happen to have a Top Ten hit in the charts at that
particular time that you do the show."

That this psychological aspect – as soon as you have one
hit record you are automatically a much better performer
altogether – can make all the difference is a phenomenon that
not only Stevie Wonder but every other musician or performer
has to go through on their way up. The Australian singer/
songwriter/performer Peter Allen, who at one time wrote a

number of songs with or for Helen Reddy (*Song For Jeffrey, Pretty Pretty*) and who penned *I Honestly Love You*, the hit that Olivia Newton-John won a Grammy with in 1975, told me:

"When you have a hit record in the charts it is much easier for an audience that you are new to, to really get into your performance and enjoy it. A hit song makes you kind of sociable. A million people have bought it so it's gotta be good and you've gotta be good because you wrote it. So the audience has a feeling of security that allows them to clap their hands and with this tell you that *they* like you, too.

"But if you haven't got a hit or an already established name and if nobody has told them that you're terrific, then it is like a comet, really. If they don't know you it's like everybody looks around 'cause they are not sure if they should like you or not and it is like 'What? Is there anyone else here liking him?' And you can't start at zero and take the audience right up with you but you have to start under that. You have to make friends with them really quickly and you have to let them know that you are nice and that you are good before you can actually start the show and take them with you somewhere else.

"Then eventually toward the end of the act people think 'Yes, we do like him,' but you really have to grab them by their throats and hit them over the head before they let their emotions go."

When Stevie toured with *Uptight* there was no doubt that his audiences loved him. They went wild over his performances and at the end of a show police were often needed to quell the enthusiasm. Stevie got hundreds and hundreds of fan letters and often his fans would not write to him but speak their messages on a tape and addressed it to either Tamla Motown or just "Stevie Wonder, Detroit".

Clarence Paul: "You would not believe how much love the kids put into their tapes. Many of Stevie's fans were around his age and they just adored him. Black or white – it didn't make no difference at all. They just *loved* Stevie and they also admired him for the courage that he had."

Some people admitted that they had thought of him as a

one-hit-wonder child star and *apologized* for that. Then Stevie received quite a number of letters from people that were handicapped in one way or another, thanking him for showing them that a physical handicap was no reason to give up on hopes and dreams.

The most touching letters and tapes were those in which other handicapped people told Stevie about things that they had done. But, they said, if Stevie had not encouraged them with his determination, they would not even have tried. Lee Garrett: "It wasn't necessarily anything that had to do with music but all sorts of stuff. Like a guy who had spent years and years in a wheelchair after an accident and through Stevie had found the willpower to want to learn to walk again. Or a young girl that was born with crippled arms but had begun how to learn to write and even paint with her feet."

It was mainly cheerful, happy mail that Stevie got from his fans. Obviously he got the odd begging letter now and then but Motown or Stevie's parents kept this kind of mail away from him. Clarence Paul: "Stevie didn't have much money himself at this time. But knowing him to be such a generous person he would have given most of what he had away to help other people." All the people who know Stevie agree to this.

The follow-up record to *Uptight* was a song written by Mickey Stevenson, Hank Cosby and Sylvia Moy. *Nothing's Too Good For My Baby/With A Child's Heart* came out in America on 24 March 1966. Just over two months later it was another hit for Stevie. The single was not as big as *Uptight* had been but it got to number 20 in *Billboard*'s "Pop 100" and went to number 4 in the R & B charts. (In England, where the single was released in April, it did not get placed.)

Motown found it was about time to release another Stevie Wonder album. Almost two years had gone by since they had put out *Stevie On The Beach* and there were hundreds of recently recorded Stevie Wonder tracks in the can.

But first of all five songs that had already been released on singles were to be on the *Up-Tight* album: *Contract On Love*, the third "Little Stevie Wonder" single that had failed to make it; *Music Talk* (the B-side to *High Heel Sneakers*); *Nothing's Too*

Good For My Baby and its B-side *With A Child's Heart*; and, of course, *Uptight*.

Three of the other eight songs to be on the album were, like *Music Talk* and *Uptight*, co-written by Stevie. Only this time he had put his stage name on the credits: *Hold Me* and *Pretty Little Angel* were two British-sounding pop songs and *Ain't That Asking For Trouble* had a little soul touch to it. *I Want My Baby Back*, *Love A Go Go* and *Teach Me Tonight* were the usual fillers, while the twelfth track on the album was an experiment.

Stevie had persuaded Berry Gordy to let him record Bob Dylan's *Blowin' In The Wind*. This song, which had been an American number 2 hit for Peter, Paul & Mary in 1963, had been part of Stevie's live-concerts for over one year now. Clarence Paul: "We did it as a kind of duet. For one, because we sang a lot together when his voice was changing and also, because Stevie used to forget the words of the song. So I said like 'How many years' and Stevie starts singing 'How many years can a mountain exist . . .' The song went down really well in the gigs that we did."

Still, for Gordy to let Stevie record *Blowin' In The Wind* was not only atypical for Motown – which most of Stevie's records had been anyway – but also for black performers: Stevie got involved with a song that like many other Dylan songs had become an anthem for white students involved in the civil rights and anti-war movements. Up to then those protest songs had been sung by white performers. Barry McGuire had had a huge hit with *Eve Of Destruction* (not a Dylan but a P. F. Sloan song). Tom Paxton and Phil Ochs were singing out against the Vietnam War. Their strength at this time did not lie in chart-topping recordings but live-concerts. Joan Baez was not only singing about war and peace but in 1962 had done three tours through Southern states that had maintained a strict non-discrimination policy. In 1964 she had begun to run a battle with American tax authorities by withholding that proportion of her taxes that was earmarked for arms and war. Peter, Paul & Mary had been the first to introduce Dylan's protest songs to a mass audience and Dylan himself had become hero of students and activists. *Blowin' In The Wind* was well known as a protest song about war and the missile crisis in Cuba:

> *. . . How many times must the cannon balls fly*
> *Before they're forever banned? . . .*
> *. . . How many deaths will it take till he knows*
> *That too many people have died?*
> *The answer, my friend, is blowin' in the wind,*
> *The answer is blowin' in the wind . . .*

Stevie, who had already developed a very strong sense of justice did not see any reason why, apart from commercial pop and soul songs, he should not sing about themes that he thought important. He was very much aware of the fact that he could not have knocked at Berry Gordy's office door, presenting him with a protest or political song that he had written. But he could suggest that he wanted to record a song that had already proved successful in his live shows and that also dealt with something that he was interested in. Later Stevie would write those songs himself, but for now he had to find a way to get Berry Gordy interested in taking the plunge of recording "that white stuff".

When Stevie first proposed to cover this Dylan song the Motown boss was not too happy with the idea. But then Stevie convinced him that Motown could not lose anything by giving it a try but instead make another revolutionary step forward in the black music business. Gordy finally agreed to Stevie's suggestion and on 4 May 1966 *Blowin' In The Wind* was released.

The next thing that happened was that the radio stations picked up on this track in the same way as they had taken to giving *With A Child's Heart*, the B-side of *Nothing's Too Good For My Baby*, a lot of airplay. (Three days before Motown got to release Stevie Wonder's version of *Blowin' In The Wind* as a single, *With A Child's Heart* entered *Billboard*'s R & B charts and got to position 8. That was three months after *Nothing's Too Good For My Baby* had been released and nobody had had the slightest idea that the B-side would also make the Top Ten.

Naturally, everybody involved was very pleased with the way things went and Stevie's success kept on.)

On 13 August 1966 *Blowin' In The Wind* got into *Billboard*'s "Pop 100" at number 9. The single was also another (Stevie's third) number 1 R & B hit and in the same month Motown put out the protest song in England where it got to position 29 in the *Music Week* charts. Stevie's *Up-Tight* album, which got to England in September, was his first one to sell reasonably well in Europe. In the United States this longplay did not do too well, but seven of the twelve songs had already been on five different singles of which four (excluding *Contract On Love*) had sold quite a number of copies – *Uptight* becoming a gold disc.

Berry Gordy was more than pleased. He had been proved right in sticking to Stevie when times had not been as good for the artist. Also other Motown acts crowded the charts. The Supremes had given the company more and more hits with *Stop! In The Name Of Love* and *I Hear A Symphony*. Jimmy Ruffin had a smash hit with *What Becomes Of The Broken Hearted*, the Miracles had had *The Tracks Of My Tears* and the Four Tops' *Reach Out, I'll Be There* was a transatlantic number 1. Junior Walker and the All Stars had had a number 2 hit with *Shotgun* and finally the Isley Brothers had gotten into the charts with *This Old Heart Of Mine* and *I Guess I'll Always Love You*. The Temptations were doing well with *Ain't Too Proud To Beg* and Marvin Gaye had scored a string of hit records.

Now it had been almost five years since Stevie had been signed to Tamla and Gordy was more than eager to get Stevie to agree to another five-year contract. He need not have worried: Stevie did not waste a single thought on whether to renew the contract or not. He did – although his fame had not only brought him joy but also a lot of problems. Lee Garrett, who had moved to Detroit and become friends with Stevie, remembers:

"It was neither easy for Steve nor for his parents or sisters that he was a star. Like some people in the neighbourhood got really nasty. They envied Stevie and his family so much, that they would try anything to make them unhappy. Especially the young ones, Larry, Timothy and Renee, who were then twelve, ten and four years old, had to suffer from some neighbours' hate. They did not have a chance to grow up like other kids. They either found themselves surrounded by children that wanted to get to Stevie through them or they would have vicious neighbours or even their kids say really terrible things to them.

"Especially after Stevie had recorded *Blowin' In The Wind*. It was as if singing black music wasn't good enough for that bastard anymore; as if he would rather be white than one of them niggers; as if money could obviously buy everything and Stevie would betray the black people with what he was doing. Some of the stuff they said was really heavy and the ones that had to suffer most from it were the family members. Because Stevie was either at school or on tour or in the studio or God knows where. So that also created some problems within the family. Although they all tried not to blame Stevie for it when the young ones came home crying . . ."

The irony was, though, that Stevie's family did not live in wealth. For one thing, Steve's earnings were locked away; anyway, Stevie's step-father would not have taken money from him. Still, the envious neighbours just could not get it into their heads that famous Stevie Wonder's family would more or less lead the same life as before.

They saw the nice clothes that Stevie had: silken stage suits and lace shirts. And even during the day he was dressed better than before. But they did not realize that Stevie's being well dressed had nothing to do with luxury but was a necessity for someone who was in the limelight even off-stage. And naturally Stevie's little brothers would "inherit" the clothes that he had grown out of, as is common in most families. Those neighbours forgot about the times when Stevie had worn Milton's and Calvin's worn-out shirts, pants and coats that Lula had tried to keep in shape, darning every little hole and preserving old clothes so that the younger boys could wear them later.

Stevie was of course aware of the fact that his fame caused a lot of problems for his family. "And believe me," said Lee

Garrett, "it did get to him. He wished so much that he could do something about it. But he knew that for the time being his hands were tied and the only thing he could do was to set his aims high, so that one day he would really have enough money to get his family out of all this hassle and away from those people who hurt their feelings.

"We often talked about the dreams that he had then. Most of them have come true, the one about his children and those regarding his music. He always told me that one day he would want to write all his own tunes and get the message of love, which he felt had been given to him, to other people. He also wanted to play as many instruments as possible and he dreamed about his own publishing and production company to take care of his business himself. Like he wanted to employ people that would do the things that he would tell them instead of all his life having other people to tell him what to do.

"Freedom, artistically and personally, meant the world to him. Then he could draw lines between the things that were important in his eyes and the things that weren't. He also wanted to make lots of money. But not so much for his sake and not just for the purpose of being rich. Stevie always said that he wanted to use some of the money to help other people wherever help was needed. He always despised people who had made a fortune but all they could do was think of luxury and their own comfort.

"Actually, money as such never meant anything to Steve. All he wanted it for was because of the things you can *do* with it in terms of making good use of it in every kind of way."

When Stevie was sixteen he had already learned a lot of things about the show business that were not glorious. He knew that it would be hard for him to be a successful musician and so-called star and at the same time lead a normal private life. It was pretty clear to him that he would have to differentiate between those people who wanted to be his real friends and those that would only want him for his fame. And this would not be an easy thing to do, because he loved people and he wanted to trust them. On the other hand he had to be very careful about the people he surrounded himself with.

Being blind you just do depend on others more than you would normally. And that meant that the chances of being taken advantage of were much greater. Stevie wanted to be a good person but he did not want to be anybody's fool. And for Stevie, who had already come to fame, it was much more difficult to become independent in little everyday things because there were always enough people around him to do things for him. Lee:

"From when he was thirteen he never actually had to find out things about life. Like where to – physically – go. People would walk him. They would do anything for him. He never had to hit his head against a wall because other people would see to it that he didn't. He never had a chance to do things in private, find out things about himself. There were always people around him. Always. When he dropped something there was always somone to pick it up. And if Stevie picked it up himself he did it for fun, for the kick of it. But he never had to.

"For me all those things were a necessity. I had to run into walls, I had to find the things that I had dropped, I had to learn to cook for myself. At times that was very hard but today I am glad that I had to go through all this, because I can live by myself and I don't have to put up with having people around when I don't actually feel like it. I have learned to dress myself. Like all my clothes have little tags in them that tell me in braille which colour they are, so I don't have to depend on anyone to put the right clothes together. I also go for a walk on my own and I haven't got a cane or a seeing-eye dog.

"Steve has seeing-eye people that go with him all the time. Also Stevie never had to make a decision on his own. There are plenty of people who do it for him. He knows how to think but he doesn't have to use it. Which is convenient for him in one way – because all the energy that he has can go into his music. On the other hand, though, he is at the mercy of the people he is with. And not all of them are his friends."

Despite the fact that there would always be people around him that would not have the best of intentions as far as Stevie was concerned, he decided to choose this way of living rather than spend a lot of time getting Lee's kind of independence. All that Stevie was ever interested in was his music. That was the only thing he really took the time and the patience to learn all about. It was all he ever wanted to do. Elaine Jesmer: "Even when Stevie was only a teenager music was the only thing that was important to him. Music is just like food to him. He lives, breathes, thinks music. All the time."

Lee: "Even when he told me about his plans for setting up his own organization one day, he made it quite clear that he would only deal with the creative side of the music business. The only thing that made it important to him to have his own companies was that he then could employ people to deal with the business side of it in a way that he wanted them to. He also said that, as much as he admired me for having as much independence as a blind person can possibly have, he could not be bothered with all those everyday things.

"And Steve was not even being ignorant, he had only set his priorities. In most matters Stevie was an extremely serious person, you would never have thought of him as the 15- or 16-year-old-boy that he was. But then again, he could just forget about the heavy talks that we had and change into a real young rascal."

Then Stevie would be prepared to do any kind of silly stuff that you proposed to him or he would come up with funny ideas himself. Like Stevie and Lee would sneak out at night and go to town where they would have a beer in a pub. Only: Stevie was not used to any alcohol at all and he would almost fall off his feet after two glasses of beer.

They would walk along the streets and chat up young ladies who mostly were no ladies because otherwise they would not have been out there in the night all by themselves. They would talk and joke with them until the girls got fed up with it.

Or they would go to some street corner and while Stevie played the harmonica Lee would sing, pretending they were street musicians. Lee: "People would look at us and say: 'Neither of them is Stevie Wonder.' We did some really crazy stuff."

It was also through Lee that Stevie found his first girl. Lee: "Well. Stevie was about fifteen at the time and I must have been around twenty-two. Being seven years older was quite an age difference then – especially when it came down to girls. While Stevie was a boy I was a man – and I was telling Stevie something about girlfriends that I had had.

"I've always liked ladies very much and I've never had any problems in finding a nice girl for myself. You might ask yourself what makes a black and blind guy that attractive for a woman, but still – there is obviously something to it. Apart from being a musician, which always makes it easier to meet friendly ladies, they obviously seem to think that a blind man is more sensitive and treats them with more tenderness. Anyway, whatever the reason may be, it was no problem to find girlfriends.

"Stevie then of course was at an age where he also got interested in ladies, but he wasn't quite sure how to go about it. First of all he was really shy when it came to meeting girls and secondly, he was Stevie Wonder. Being a star it is much difficult to be certain that she really likes *you* and not just the guy who tops the charts. He could have had any of those hundreds of girls who queued up at the stage entrance after he had finished a gig, but he didn't want that.

"So one day I introduced him to a 20-year-old ladyfriend I had and left the two of them alone. He told me they went to the girl's place. Her parents were both working during the day. So the next day when I met Stevie I asked him 'How did it go, man?' and I found out that all they had done all afternoon was to just sit there, listen to the radio, talk a little and drink soda-pops.

" 'Well,' I asked him, 'didn't you kiss her?' Almost embarrassed, Stevie admitted that he had – but only after the girl had more or less taken the initiative. 'And then?' I said. 'Nothing,' was the answer. I couldn't believe it. 'Man,' I told him, 'this was the opportunity of a lifetime! I introduce you to a beautiful woman who takes you home with her. More than that, she knows all about love that you want to know about it. Why the hell didn't you . . .?'

" 'Oh no,' Stevie burst out. 'I can't do that *nasty* thing! That's how you make babies! ! !'

"You should have seen Stevie telling me that. I bet his facial expression must have been like if he got the shock of his life. How could anyone dare to suggest that he, this nice young boy, would do something *nasty* as that! Well, then I had a long talk with him explaining that making love isn't at all nasty. In fact I told him that it would be much better for him to get his first impression of it with a lady who is already experienced. First, because she could gently teach him all about it, and also because she would know how to take care of it that he would not 'make a baby' which he was so afraid of.

"As Stevie had really fancied the lady who I had introduced him to, I arranged another meeting for them. They secretly went out together for a couple of weeks before anything 'happened'. But then he came up to me and said: 'I've done it.' Well, I won't go into it too much, but one thing was for sure: Stevie had definitely discovered that making love was not nasty at all . . ."

With Stevie's new love of girls he had also gotten a few more problems. One of them was, that it was almost impossible for him to develop any long-term relationships: Stevie was on the road most of the time. Another thing was that he had to keep those little love affairs secret – with his fifteen or sixteen years his parents would very clearly have told him that he was not to get involved into any 'intimate' relationships. Problem number three was, that the females that Stevie met were either ladies who he worked with and for whom he was just the young boy; or fans of his, to whom he was the star. Both these kinds of ladies were not suitable for love-affairs.

The chances of Stevie meeting a nice young girl outside the music business were zero. And another reason for Stevie to give up almost as soon as he had started to think about girlfriends was that he was just too busy. His music still took precedence over anything else and he would rather compose songs about girls than actually being with them. Clarence Paul:

"Stevie seemed to go through a period where every song he got an idea for was a love song which had the name of a girl for a title. But Sylvia changed it when she wrote the lyrics to his tunes."

1966 was a very creative year for Stevie. Most of the songs that he wrote at this time were co-written by either Hank Cosby and/or Clarence Paul and Sylvia Moy. It was also in this year that they came up with *My Cherie Amour*, a tune that was to be a big hit for Stevie three years later. And from now on with the exception of three singles (of which two were Christmas records) – Stevie would at least be involved in writing the B-sides for his singles.

One of those B-sides was *Sylvia*, the flip-side to *A Place In The Sun*. Hank Cosby: "Stevie had met a girl called Sylvia. Funnily enough though she was one of the few ladies that Stevie did not fall in love with at this time. But we had this love song, and our Sylvia had worked on it, so we decided let's give it her name."

A Place In The Sun was released on 24 October 1966 in America. Six weeks later it had entered *Billboard*'s "Pop 100" where it got to number 9 and in the R & B charts it brought Stevie up to position 3.

A Place In The Sun was a tune written by Bryan Wells with lyrics by Ronald Miller. Miller, who according to his own words was then "a 31-year-old Jewish failure" had been signed to Motown as a writer in 1961. Before that he was a pizza salesman who sang in clubs at night. Ron: "When I came to Motown everybody there was making money with stuff that I had written when I was thirteen. You know those lyrics that are simple and easy. I hated the stuff that was supposed to make people cry and laugh. Those nothing lyrics."

But then, when Ron heard Stevie sing *Blowin' In The Wind* he started to believe in songwriting again and with Stevie in mind wrote *A Place In The Sun*. Ron: "This song was about the kind of philosophies the little kid believed in." And it also followed up the socially critical direction that Stevie had entered with Dylan's song:

Like a long lonely stream I keep runnin' towards a dream
Movin' on, movin' on . . .
Like a branch on a tree I keep reachin' to be free
Movin' on, movin' on.
There's a place in the sun
Where there's hope for ev'ryone
Where my poor restless heart's gotta run . . .

Altogether now five Stevie Wonder singles had made the R & B Top Ten in 1966. Two of them topped the charts (*Uptight* and *Blowin' In The Wind*), *A Place In The Sun* reached number 3. *Nothing's Too Good For My Baby* had been a number 4 and *With A Child's Heart* had reached position 8.

That was reason enough for *Billboard* magazine to cite Stevie Wonder as one of the nation's Top Single Artists in 1966 in their year-end wrapup edition. A special issue of it was printed for Stevie in braille.

The only "flop" that Stevie accounted for was a Christmas single that came out on 22 November. *Someday At Christmas/ The Miracles Of Christmas* failed to make the Top 100. But that did not particularly upset anybody at Motown. It just irritated Gordy a little, for the A-side had been written by the same team that had penned *A Place In The Sun* and it too was sympathetic to the anti-war movement in a way:

Someday at Christmas men won't be boys
Playing with bombs like kids play with toys.

For some reason, though, Stevie never had any notable success with Christmas recording. A long play *Someday At Christmas* was released a year later and did not sell. Nor did another Christmas single that was taken from this album and put out in 1971, *What Christmas Means To Me/Bedtime For Toys*.

Still Berry Gordy could be happy with what Stevie had achieved in just one year, despite the fact that he had remained a singles artist.

On 9 December 1966 Motown released the Stevie Wonder album *Down To Earth*. It had four hit songs on it, but only one, *A Place In The Sun* was Stevie's. *My World Is Empty Without You* had come to fame with the Supremes. Dylan's *Mr. Tambourine Man* had been a hit for the Byrds and *Bang Bang (My Baby Shot Me Down)* had been written by Sonny Bono and was one of the golden greats for now his ex-wife Cher.

Three other tracks were co-written by Stevie: *Thank You Love* (ten years later to be revived in *Summer Soft* on *Songs In The Key Of Life*), *Be Cool, Be Calm (And Keep Yourself Together)* and *Sylvia*. They were love songs, as were *Angel Baby (Don't You Ever Leave Me)*, *Down To Earth* and *Hey Love*.

Apart from those tracks the album contained *The Lonesome Road*, a gospel song; and *16 Tons*, a blues that had been a number 1 hit ten years ago for Tennessee Ernie Ford and in the same year a number 10 hit for Frankie Laine.

By contrast with the other Stevie Wonder albums Motown had put out in the previous three years, this one had not even the hint of a concept. It showed no direction, it had no personality. The *Up-Tight* album had at least had some of Stevie's singles, including a few hits. *Down To Earth* sounded like a Motown attempt to let the disc jockeys pick whatever musical direction on the album they liked best.

At the end of 1966 Motown and Stevie had agreed to another five-year contract. Again it was controlled by the government as far as Stevie was concerned. It was the last Stevie Wonder–Tamla Motown contract that Berry Gordy signed with a smile on his face.

The next five years would bring a lot of changes, which would show their results on Stevie's 21st birthday.

But Gordy did not have to worry yet. Five years was a long time. Not only at Motown: the next few years were to change America's and Britain's music scene faster and more often than ever before.

Where I'm Coming From

San Francisco, California, was the city where in January 1967 the first major free outdoor festival, the Human Be-In, took place. San Francisco with the hippie-culture and drug-scene that had slowly developed within the last few years, had gotten ready to swamp the rest of America and Europe with new philosophies and a new type of music.

The surf sound that had come from Los Angeles in 1961 and that had survived until 1966, had now to give way to another kind of Californian music. Instead of California beaches, girls, cars and fun, fun, fun it was now California flower-power, magical mystery tours, acid trips and psychedelic pictures. It was also the height and the end of the short-lived British Pop Boom.

1967 was the year when the Spencer Davis Group had a hit with *Gimme Some Lovin'*, the Easybeats had *Friday On My Mind*, the 5th Dimension went *Up Up And Away*, and the Hollies sang about *Carrie Anne* and *King Midas In Reverse*. It was the year when Engelbert Humperdinck's *Release Me* took over from Tom Jones' *Green Green Grass Of Home*, the Small Faces sang *Itchycoo Park*, Van Morrison raved about a *Brown Eyed Girl* and the Troggs about a *Wild Thing*. It was also the year when for the first time a session group, the Monkees, came to fame with *Pleasant Valley Sunday* and the two Neil Diamond compositions *I'm A Believer* and *A Little Bit Me, A Little Bit You*.

While light-hearted and carefree music was on its way to conquer the charts, Berry Gordy decided that Stevie Wonder's next single should be *Travelin' Man*. Not a happy song at all, but about an "uninspired, tired-out travelin' man", written by Ron Miller and Bryan Wells. Ron: "*Travelin' Man* was a song Bryan and I had written as a B-side. The actual song that we had thought of as Stevie's follow-up single was a tune called *Yester-Me, Yester-You, Yesterday*. But Gordy didn't give that song much chance and put it in the can. There it caught dust for almost another three years . . ."

Travelin' Man/Hey Love was released on 9 February 1967. Four weeks later the A-side was number 32 in *Billboard*'s "Pop 100" and number 31 in the R & B charts. That is as far as the travelin' man got. Still, considering that at this time the flower-children had gathered together and started to tell the world where happiness was at, Stevie was lucky that this single got into the Top Fifty at all.

And while Berry Gordy was trying to figure out what had gone wrong the disc jockeys in the radio stations showed him: They turned the B-side into the A-side (as they had done with *Nothing's Too Good For My Baby/With A Child's Heart*) and gave Tamla another hit in April. *Hey Love* got to number 90 in the "Pop 100", but the R & B charts declared it a number 9 hit in early May. By now Gordy could be positive that love had found its way back into songs. Protest and fighting, wondering and searching for the true reason of life were not important any more. As long as everybody just loved one another, hate and wars would stop automatically. That, at least, was what the new Californian music taught.

Jefferson Airplane, a group that had become synonymous with the San Francisco Sound (Jorma Kaukonen, Jack Casady, Paul Kantner, Marty Ballin and Grace Slick) had had a Top Ten hit with *Somebody To Love*:

> *. . . don't you need somebody to love*
> *don't you want somebody to love*
> *wouldn't you love somebody to love*
> *you better find somebody to love . . .*

Eric Burdon & the Animals (John Weider, Vic Briggs, Danny McCulloch, Barry Jenkins) had hit the charts with *Good Times*:

When I think of all the good times
I've been wasting having good times . . .
When I was drinking, I should have been thinking . . .
When I was fighting, I could have done the right thing . . .

The Beach Boys (then Brian, Dennis and Carl Wilson, Mike Love, Al Jardine) had adapted to the new Californian Sound and sang about *Good Vibrations*:

I'm picking up good vibrations
She's giving me excitation . . .

The Tremeloes had a hit with their optimistic *Even The Bad Times Are Good* and the Young Rascals with *Groovin'*.

The bands and their fans had started to grow what was then considered to be long hair. They wore hippie outfits, which was any kind of loose, colourful clothes. Jeans, wide shirts and blouses. The girls put on long skirts, not elegant, but comfortable. Their parents did not understand it, but at least this kind of revolution was a peaceful one. So far. The big fights between the generations started when the minors moved into communes or wanted to get married young. Love, the theme of the flower-children only included love for their parents as long as they did not try to stop their children from whatever they wanted to do. If the parents did not agree to it, their young ones went their own ways without their blessings.

This time Motown's timing was just right for the new Stevie Wonder single: *I Was Made To Love Her* (written by Henry Cosby, Lula Hardaway, Stevie Wonder and Sylvia Moy) tells the story of a young man who would not give up his loved one:

You know my papa disapproved it,
My mama boohooed it,
But I told them time and time again
I was made to love her
Build my world around her . . .

I Was Made To Love Her/Hold Me was released in America on 18 May. Seven weeks later it was number 2 in the "Pop 100" and topped the R & B charts. In England this was Stevie's first single to get into the Top Ten. By the middle of August it had reached position 5 in the *Music Week* charts. (*A Place In The Sun* was number 20 in January and *Travelin' Man* had gotten to position 50 at the end of April.)

As far as Stevie was concerned, Berry Gordy did not have to worry any more. The Miracles were also doing well with *The Tracks Of My Tears* (written by Pete Moore) and Marvin Gaye and Kim Weston were also doing well: they had had a huge hit with the duet *It Takes Two*. Although Kim left Motown for MGM the same year, Gordy was not troubled but teamed Marvin up with Tammi Terrell as well as using him as a solo artist.

Gordy's main problem was that white artists like the Rolling Stones (who by then had had hits like *Get Off My Cloud, Paint It Black* and *Ruby Tuesday*) and the Animals were getting the white audiences with their Rhythm & Blues. Black Blues had a hard time getting into the charts – especially the kind of black music that Motown provided the market with. All of a sudden Gordy realized that Stax Records, another black label that had started in Memphis in 1958, was getting more attention than he did with Motown. Now Stax – the label that Gordy had not taken too seriously – had black acts that were more successful than his. They came up with a funky soul, the sound was rough and had intensity.

Wilson Pickett had hits like *Mustang Sally, Soul Dance No. 3* and *Funky Broadway*. Booker T and the MG's had *Groovin'*, Otis Redding had had hits like *I've Been Loving You Too Long* (1965) and now *Fa Fa Fa*. Sam & Dave had been in the charts with *Hold On I'm Coming* and Percy Sledge (on Atlantic) *When A Man Loves A Woman*.

There were also three lady singers that were outselling Gordy's stars: Dionne Warwick (then on Scepter) who had scored her first big hits in 1963 *(Anyone Who Had A Heart)* and 1964 *(Walk On By)* and now with *I Say A Little Prayer*. Nina Simone was in the charts with *Ain't Got No – I Got Life* from the musical *Hair* and also a song called *Young, Gifted And Black*. The one lady that got to Gordy most was Aretha Franklin (on Stax). She had taken over from Diana Ross as the Queen of Soul, and her hits were enormous: *I've Never Loved A Man (The Way I Love You)*, *Respect*, *Natural Woman* and *Chain Of Fools* to name but a few.

Gordy gave his three top groups a front by changing the billings to Smokey Robinson and the Miracles, Martha and the Vandellas and Diana Ross and the Supremes in 1967. It did not work. People did not merely want a lead singer. They wanted a different kind of music.

At this point Gordy decided that it was time for him to activate the new Soul label that he had formed in late 1966. The first group he had signed to it were Gladys Knight and the Pips. Although their first record *Just Walk In My Shoes* (produced by Harvey Fuqua and Johnny Bristol) had been a hit, it was an anonymous one. Now Gordy went on the whole hog. He did not have anything to lose by trying. Their next record initiated the Memphis Sound that Stax was so successful with. It was *Take Me In Your Arms And Love Me* which was written and produced in the typical Holland-Dozier-Holland style, and then a Whitfield tune *I Heard It Through The Grapevine* – which one year later would become Marvin Gaye's biggest hit so far. Gordy found Whitfield the best bet for Gladys Knight and the Pips and this team succeeded in producing a string of hit records together – although Gladys was not the rival to Aretha Franklin that Gordy had hoped for.

But the funky Soul Sound was only one new musical direction that Gordy had to face. The harmless "make love-not-war" songs had not bothered him too much – but already the flower children of San Francisco were getting more and more specific.

For one, songs about the city itself swamped the music market. That was a thing that Motown could certainly not compete with. You just could not imagine black artists singing songs *San Francisco (Be Sure To Wear Some Flowers In Your Hair)* by Scott McKenzie. Or *California Dreamin'*, *Monday Monday* and *I Saw Her Again* like the Mamas & Papas (then John and Michelle Phillips, 'Mama' Cass Elliott and Denny Doherty). Donovan's tribute to the flower-power was *Mellow Yellow* and

Sunshine Superman, the Move did *Blackberry Way*, *Flowers In The Rain* and *California Man*.

San Francisco had become the American dream. But this dream did not come all by itself. In 1967 LSD was not illegal in California and apart from its apostles like Ken Kesey – who later wrote *One Flew Over The Cuckoo's Nest* – and Timothy Leary who advertised it, drugs had found their way into songs. Eric Burdon & The Animals sang in *San Franciscan Nights*:

> *Strobe light beams, creates dreams*
> *Walls move, minds do too*
> *On a warm San Franciscan night . . .*

Jefferson Airplane were even more direct in their hit single *White Rabbit* from their album *Surrealistic Pillow*:

> *One pill makes you larger*
> *And one pill makes you small*
> *And the ones that mother gives you*
> *Don't do anything at all*
> *. . . And you just have some kind of mushroom . . .*

The drug and psychedelic scene was something that Motown definitely would not get involved with yet. Only few black artists like Otis Redding and Jimi Hendrix joined the flower-children at the Monterey Festival (near Los Angeles) in June 1967.

Redding's raw, sexy soul fit into the type of music that was played there (Redding, the same year voted the World's No. One Male Singer by *Melody Maker*, died in December 1967, when his aircraft plunged to the bottom of the frozen lake Montana). Jimi Hendrix, who the year before had formed the Jimi Hendrix Experience (with Noel Redding and Mitch Mitchell) was bringing new elements into Rhythm & Blues. By this time his album *Are You Experienced* had come out. Monterey also saw the Who (Pete Townshend, Roger Daltrey, Keith Moon and John Entwistle) who had already made a name for themselves with *My Generation* (1965) and now sang about the sexual fantasy *Pictures Of Lily* and had their *The Who Sell Out* album in the shops.

Country Joe and the Fish played acid rock. Their songs on the long play *Electric Music For The Mind And Body* dealt with themes like love (*Grace*), social satire (*Not So Sweet Martha Lorraine*) and drugs (*Flying High*). The Doors came up with *The End* and *Light My Fire* from their debut album *The Doors* and a psychedelic album *Strange Days*. Grateful Dead was another well known acid rock band. They had just signed with Warner Brothers and released their first album *Grateful Dead*. Cream (Eric Clapton, Ginger Baker and Jack Bruce) were in the charts with *I Feel Free*, *Fresh Cream* and had released their long play *Disraeli Gears* with songs like *Strange Brew* and *Sunshine Of Your Love*.

Pink Floyd were getting it together and had had a first success with the bizarre single *Arnold Layne* as well as their first album *The Piper At The Gates Of Dawn*. Procul Harum had an enormous hit with their mystical single *A Whiter Shade Of Pale*. The Rolling Stones sang *We Love You* (with John Lennon and Paul McCartney doing back-up vocals) and the Beatles had come up with *Sergeant Pepper's Lonely Hearts Club Band*, a mixture of youth and drug culture, electronics and mysticism. Lennon, Starr, McCartney and George Harrison had gotten involved with the Indian Maharishi and brought the sitar into their music. They were also openly admitting taking drugs and their acid song *Lucy In The Sky With Diamonds* was one of the album tracks. Drugs and Eastern religion, Hinduism, had become the big cult. Psychedelic light shows and electronic sounds were beginning to dominate live-concerts.

Then came the day when drugs were declared illegal in California and a lot of drug busts took place. Still, the bands' philosophies remained the same. But now instead of propagating them openly the happy hippie flower power generation escaped into the underground culture.

Stevie Wonder did not come in touch with the psychedelic scene too closely. Within the Motown Young Sound of America the world was still in perfect order. Drugs were something that did not exist within the Motown music and nor did electronic sounds. If the artists smoked pot or tripped on LSD they did not admit to it. Nevertheless, it was almost inevitable that many people at least tried some kind of drug – including Stevie.

In her *Newsweek* article, Maureen Orth gave Motown credit for keeping Stevie out of the drugs scene: "To Motown's credit, it took pains to keep him away from drugs. Today Stevie is still very down on dope, especially for musicians." But it is not owing to Motown that Stevie did not get involved in the drug scene. The true reason for Stevie not taking drugs is simply that he does not like what they do to him:

"I smoked grass twice. The first time it was quite nice, but the second time it scared me to death. Things just got larger. It was something new and different, but I found that I'm busy enough checking things out all the time anyway so that I don't really need it."

According to his friends, Stevie hardly even touches alcohol. Doug Kee told me: "Stevie's just naturally high. He doesn't need to *get* high. I don't know what kind of vibe he is on but it's all right. He doesn't even drink alcohol, apart from a glass of wine or a can of beer occasionally. But if he does drink another one or two he goes out like a light. So there's no point for him in drinking. The same with dope. He has experimented with it like everybody else has I guess, but it is just not his kind of thing."

Gypsie Jones comments: "He's told me that he thinks that drugs would destroy the character of his music. He'd be tripping out on himself too much and not on the things around him, which is quite logical. And anyway, Steve doesn't need that kind of trip. He's tripping on his music."

Although Stevie is not into drugs himself, in 1972 he gave a benefit concert in Michigan, together with John Lennon, to raise money for John Sinclair, who had been sentenced to 20 years' imprisonment for possessing *one* marijuana cigarette. Gypsie: "Steve was really upset about this kind of injustice. He felt that it was just ridiculously crazy to give Sinclair that much time for just one marijuana cigarette. He said it was such an irrelevant thing to do – especially when on the other hand someone, who killed thousands of people in Vietnam, is set free. Steve hates injustice."

As little as Stevie was affected by the drug culture in 1967, he *was* influenced by the new kind of music that had come up. He listened to everything that was going on. Stevie liked Johnny Mathis (who is said to have become the first black American millionaire) and he loved Otis Redding, especially Redding's posthumous hit *Sitting On The Dock Of The Bay*. He admired the Beatles – and still does – although he will not admit to his writing having been influenced by theirs:

"I just dug more the effects they got, like echoes and the voice things, the writing, like *For The Benefit Of Mr. Kite*." Stevie also does not agree on the comparisons that have been made between him and the Beatles. "If I could be as inspirational as the Beatles, I would be very happy. I will always admire the Beatles – individually as well as a group. But I'm not going to compare myself to them – they made an impact on *all* music. They are, in fact, my all-time favourites, and the thing I really like about them is they were very, very modest and they were nice enough to include people they had admired throughout the years and to acknowledge it. They brought all different cultures together. They made white Middle America wake up about those old black artists – the Beatles brought them to people who had never heard of them. And it gave those artists – who were sometimes starving – some money."

But not only does Stevie admire the Beatles, they also acknowledge him to be one of the greatest musicians of our time. Paul McCartney, who dedicated his album *Red Rose Speedway* (1973) to Stevie, is supposed to have said: "When Stevie sings he puts a little sunshine into all our lives."

Stevie also listened to Sly Stone a lot. There he does admit to having been influenced by Sly's funkiness. "You can hear it in *Uptight*," he says. Other musicians that Stevie listened closely to were groups like Pink Floyd and later to Emerson, Lake and Palmer and The Headband, consisting of the American Robert Margouleff and the British Malcolm Cecil who would work with Stevie in years to come. For the time being Steve did not make any use of the great new musical influences, but just stored everything in his mind.

His third single in 1967 (release date 14 September America

and Europe) was in the usual Motown groove. *I'm Wondering/ Every Time I See You I Go Wild*, both sides co-written by Stevie, got to position 12 in *Billboard*'s "Pop 100" and also entered the British *Music Week* and the American R & B charts. In England the single did not get any further than number 22 while it made place 4 in the R & B charts. *I'm Wondering*, again a love song, dealt with the problem of having a new girlfriend who has just broken up with someone else:

> *I'm wondering, oh yes I'm wondering*
> *If I can make you love me more than you loved him . . .*

It also features Stevie on harmonica.

Just a month before Stevie's *I'm Wondering* came out, Motown had released another non-selling Stevie Wonder album. *I Was Made To Love Her* included Stevie's version of Otis Redding's *Respect*, of the Temptations hit *My Girl*, and Ray Charles' *A Fool For You*. Only three of the eleven songs had been co-written by Stevie: The Title track, *I'd Cry* and *Every Time I See You I Go Wild*.

By the end of 1967 Stevie had already written hundreds of songs. Hank Cosby: "He'd write five or six songs a day, around 25 a week. The only trouble was Sylvia could not keep up with writing lyrics to Steve's tunes. He would say 'Have you done this and that one?' and Sylvia would go 'You only gave that to me yesterday and I've another 30 tracks lying here . . .' It was then that Stevie started also to put lyrics to his tunes, but most of them ended up on a shelf in Motown."

Most of the songs that Stevie wrote happened when he was on the road. Stevie: "If you keep your life happening then there's no problem with writing on the road. It only is a problem when you look at it as a problem. But even when you're touring you can keep your life in order and do the things you want to do." Ronald Miller credits Clarence Paul and Hank Cosby for Steve's working discipline: "A raw talent is basically a God-given thing. But it means nothing unless you use discipline and develop a technique. Anybody can sit down and write a hit song once – but day in day out you better have some technique. And Stevie was all feeling and emotional. Hank and Clarence channelled it. They made the kid work. They took him and treated him like a professional. They made him work like a professional, and collectively put out some wonderful things together. Clarence's church background and Hank's jazz background helped Stevie a lot."

Although Stevie was already stockpiling innumerable tracks that he had written or co-written, Gordy would not allow Steve to put his own album together but rather tried to find a successful mixture of styles that he thought were *in*. Stevie had to sing everything from Holland-Dozier-Holland numbers to Ray Charles, Smokey Robinson, Ron Miller and Otis Redding tunes. This recipe turned out to be poor bait for the album-buying public.

But if Steve did not sell albums, he made enough money for Motown with hit singles. According to a sales figure given by Motown Stevie had already sold over six million records within those first five and a half years. It you take the 18 singles that had been released in this time (of which three were gold) and Stevie's nine long plays, this figure looks all right. Stevie was also earning considerable money for the company on the many tours, even world tours, that he did. Although Stevie's last singles had been doing well, it was another five months until Motown released the next. There are rumours that Gordy wanted to concentrate on his other acts first, and also that he was waiting for clues to the direction America's music would take.

On 19 March 1968 Stevie's *Shoo-Be-Doo-Be-Doo-Da-Day*/ *Why Don't You Lead Me To Love* was in the shops. In the beginning of June this soul single was number 9 in the "Pop 100" and another number 1 hit for Stevie in the R & B charts. In England the record reached position 46. Again Motown made Stevie's fans wait half a year – until September – before his next single came out.

In between, though, Gordy started an experiment: Under the name of Eivets Rednow he released the single *Alfie* at the end of June. The David/Bacharach tune was played on the harmonica by Stevie. The long play *Alfie* which came out in November (on the Gordy label) was all instrumental and had standards like *Ruby, A House Is Not A Home, Grazing In The Grass* and a Medley of *Never My Love/Ask The Lonely* plus four Stevie Wonder compositions on it: *Which Way The Wind, Bye Bye World, How Can You Believe* and *More Than A Dream.* The latter, the B-side of the single, was co-written by Hank Cosby.

Some people knew at once that Eivets Rednow could only be Stevie Wonder. They knew the way Stevie played. Besides they only had to read this obviously strange name backwards (and look at the credits of the songs which said Stevie Wonder) to figure it all out. Some other people did not think that Eivets Rednow was just another pseudonym for Stevie. This is a story that Stevie tells:

"There was this cat in the airport that came up and said 'Hey, man, these whites are taking over everything. I heard a kid today, man, played *Alfie* just like *you*, man!' 'Oh,' I said. 'This cat named Rednow?' 'Yeah, that's it,' he said. 'Oh, man,' I grinned, 'that cat is – well, don't worry about him . . .' "

No one had to worry about Eivets Rednow. The cat did not make it. Neither the single nor the album got anywhere near the charts. "Which is a pity, really," says Doug Kee whose father was involved in making the album. "It is a great instrumental album and everybody who worked on it was convinced that it could have sold – if Motown had done some promotion on it." As it happened Motown had not, but Stevie didn't mind too much. For him it had been a lot of fun making the album – for the first time on record he experimented with the clavinet, an instrument that would be one of his favourites soon – and also he had enough other things going for him with the other Stevie Wonder recordings that came on the market.

On 14 September *You Met Your Match/My Girl* was released. It was co-penned by Stevie and his mother Lula Hardaway. Steve: "We wrote this tune when I was on tour in Japan and my mother accompanied me. She was great at thinking up punchlines and we wrote quite a few songs together."

A week after release *You Met Your Match* got into the "Pop 100" but it only went up to number 35. In October the single was number 2 in the American R & B charts whereas in England it was a flop. This time it was only four weeks before the release of Stevie's next single.

For Once In My Life/Angie Girl, the first A-side *not* written by Steve since *Travelin' Man*, brought Stevie into the "Pop 100" and the R & B charts both at number 2. In England *For Once In My Life* went to position 3. Surprisingly enough this Ron Miller–Orlando Murden tune was a hit that almost had not happened for Steve. Hank Cosby: "When I first discussed that tune with Stevie he hated it. It had already been recorded by 40 other artists and not become a hit. But finally I convinced Steve that he should give it a try – and he did. Ron went crazy, though, when he heard what Stevie had done to his song . . ."

Ron Miller: "I wrote *For Once In My Life* like a Tony Bennett ballad. It was beautiful. And then – along comes Stevie. He put a harmonica solo in it and he put the tempo up and made a whole different song out of it."

Steve: "*For Once In My Life* was a great tune, but it lacked excitement. The other interpretations were beautiful – but too old fashioned. I wanted to do the song the way I felt it. You know the bit when I go 'wow'! That is after the music starts you become aware of the mood of the song – and then you just have to go 'wow'."

By now this song has more than a hundred cover versions – and although this tune was not written by Stevie, whenever the song is sung by someone else you think of it as Steve's. In November Motown put out a Stevie Wonder album *For Once In My Life*, and this, for a change, had some of his recent hits on it: The title track, *Shoo-Be-Doo-Be-Doo-Da-Day* and *You Met Your Match*. This album also included *I Don't Know Why*, another song for which Stevie's mother was mentioned in the credits and which was to be his next single – but not until early next year.

At the end of 1968 Berry Gordy could look back on quite a good year: Stevie had gotten his fourth gold record (*For Once In My Life*), Marvin Gaye had sold a million with *I Heard It Through The Grapevine*, Diana Ross and the Supremes had topped the charts with *Love Child* and the Temptations had had a Top Ten hit with *Cloud 9* (with Dennis Edwards from the Contours – David Ruffin had left the band in 1968).

The enormous success of *Love Child* and *Cloud 9* had shown that Motown, although slow in making changes, had managed to adapt to the change of attitude within the audiences. Black had started to become beautiful. It was not black ghettos any more, but black pride and black power. *Love Child* had shown pride instead of shame of ghetto illegitimacy. *Cloud 9* was a song about drugs. Although the lyrics did not glorify drugs they at least did not condemn them:

> *Cloud nine . . .*
> *A million miles from reality*
> *You can be what you want to be . . .*

Norman Whitfield, the then only Motown producer with an interest in giving his productions a psychedelic touch, had been responsible for this single. Whitfield was the one who tried to catch up with what happened around Motown more than any of the other producers. The Holland-Dozier-Holland sound had almost worn itself out by now. Their records did still sell, but despite this, Gordy decided that Whitfield should work more and more on his most important acts. Finally Brian and Eddie Holland as well as Lamont Dozier left Motown at the end of 1968 to form their own company.

It was also in 1968 that Gordy signed the Jackson Five (Michael, Jermaine, Jackie, Marlon and Tito Jackson), a group discovered by Diana Ross. The youngest of the five, Michael, was born on 29 August 1958 and the eldest, Jackie, was born on 4 May 1951. The Jackson Five, Gordy had decided, would be the first black child group to win international chart success. On balance, the Motown boss was satisfied with 1968. But 1969 would be even better.

It started out with Stevie's single *I Don't Know Why* which was released in America and Europe on 28 January. It took two and a half months for the single to reach the charts. In the United States it went to number 39 in *Billboard*'s "Pop 100".

On 7 March Stevie left Detroit for an 18-day tour through

the United Kingdom. The result was that within the next month the single got into the *Music Week* charts. Funnily enough, though, it was the B-side *My Cherie Amour* that was getting more and more airplay. While *I Don't Know Why* reached position 14 in the British charts and number 16 in America's R & B charts, *My Cherie Amour* got to number 4 in *Music Week*, *Billboard*'s "Pop 100" and the R & B charts. But although *My Cherie Amour* had been more of a success than the original A-side, *I Don't Know Why* was quite a significant record for Stevie: It was the first single A-side to be released that Stevie had written all by himself.

Stevie's tour through Britain was a huge success. His concerts were sold out and his fans recognized each tune before he had even started singing it. Again, Stevie would have liked to stay longer and see more of Europe, but his audiences in the United States were waiting for him.

When he came back to the Motown office in Detroit, they had a surprise for him: Stevie had an invitation to the White House in Washington. The President's Committee on Employment of Handicapped People wanted to present Stevie with the Distinguished Service Award.

"Stevie was really nervous," Lee Garrett told me. "Steve kept saying that he didn't know what to say to them. After all, he felt that he hadn't done anything really for anybody yet. Even when he was just about nineteen he would have liked to donate some money to organizations that would help blind people. But as you know he was not in command of what he earned until he was of full age. Anyway, we all told Stevie that he wouldn't have to worry about it and that he had done a lot for other handicapped people already by showing them that with willpower one can overcome a handicap."

The big day was 5 May. Stevie met President Nixon in the White House Rose Garden. Although the musician could not see all those beautiful flowers, he could smell them. Stevie gathered that it had probably been the idea of Nixon's publicity department to arrange their meeting in the Rose Garden, where the spring air was filled with a lovely scent. Nevertheless, he thanked the President for the joy that the roses gave him.

Then Nixon congratulated Stevie for being selected to receive the highest honour that the Committee could give. Lula Hardaway, who had accompanied her son to the White House, was so touched by the whole event, that she could hardly say a word when the President greeted her, too. Later in the afternoon the Secretary of Labour, George P. Shultz, presented Stevie with the Distinguished Service Award.

Within the same month Stevie got another surprise: *My Cherie Amour* was selling so well that he got another gold record. This was Stevie's fifth, but before the year was over there would be another one: *Yester-Me, Yester-You, Yesterday*. This song, which was written by Ron Miller and Bryan Wells had been in the can for years and like *Blowin' In The Wind* and *I Don't Know Why* it was to be on an album before Motown released it as a single.

The longplay *My Cherie Amour* came out on 29 August. Including the title track five songs had been co-written by Stevie: *Angie Girl* (the flip-side of *For Once In My Life*), *I've Got You, Give Your Love* and *Somebody Knows, Somebody Cares. Yester-Me, Yester-You, Yesterday* from the album was put out as a single on 9 September. In November it hit the "Pop 100" at position 7, the R & B charts at number 5 and in England it was a number 2 hit.

1969 had been a terrific year for Motown. In England it had been their best so far. They had 26 hits in the U.K., their tours had been sold out: Stevie's, the Four Tops, Junior Walker and Edwin Starr to name but a few. Marvin Gaye and Tammi Terrell had had smash hits like *Ain't No Mountain High Enough* and *The Onion Song. Dancing In The Streets* by Martha and the Vandellas had been successfully re-released and Marv Johnson scored a hit with *I'll Pick A Rose For My Rose.* The Jackson Five's first single *I Want You Back* had topped the charts immediately, the Temptations had a number 1 with *I Can't Get Next To You* and the Miracles were doing if not fantastically at least quite well.

There had also been some changes: Martha and the Vandellas had to take a break caused by the illness of Martha and Diana Ross left the Supremes to pursue a solo career. She was replaced by Jean Terrell. Also Motown's studio drummer Benny Benjamin had died of a stroke. This event was one that overshadowed the joy of the good things that had happened a little.

1969 had also been a year of more significant changes within the American and British music scene. The Beatles had definitely broken up. John Lennon had married Yoko Ono and shocked the world with a three-day love-in in an Amsterdam hotel. He had also released his first solo single *Give Peace A Chance*.

The Woodstock Festival had been the biggest open-air festival ever. 450,000 people had attended it and according to an investigation by the *Variety* magazine the promoters had sold 1.4 million dollars' worth of tickets of which they paid the artists 150,000 dollars. The festival had been filmed and recorded live – which meant that the promoters would make even more money. Still – the press played Woodstock as more or less a *free* festival and three days of love and peace. The artists included Joni Mitchell, Crosby Stills Nash & Young, Jimi Hendrix and the Who.

The same year had also brought Altamont: a festival where a young black was knifed by a Hell's Angel in front of the stage when the Rolling Stones were performing.

Jane Birkin and Serge Gainsbourg had released their most spectacular erotic single *Je T'Aime Moi Non Plus*, Jethro Tull was making it big with *Living In The Past* and Peter Sarstedt's *Where Do You Go To My Lovely* was one of the best remembered records of the year.

Alice Cooper had started to tour the country with his outrageous and violent shows. His stage act contained the simulated killing of a baby and chicken blood ran all over the stage floor. David Bowie had found first success with his *Space Oddity* album. White Rock had become more and more visual and the Glitter bands were on their way up.

Gordy had gotten himself ready for the challenges that the seventies would bring. In late 1969 he founded his Rare Earth label with which he intended to get into the white rock scene.

For Stevie the new decade began with another big honour.

On 10 January 1970 he was presented with the Show Business Inspiration Award 1969 by Fight For The Sight, an organization that promoted research into eye diseases. Stevie was given the award by the newspaper columnist Earl Wilson on the Merv Griffin Show for his "compelling achievement in the world of entertainment". The plaque was inscribed: "To Stevie Wonder for assisting the cause of research for the conquest of blinding eye diseases and inspiring all who look to The Fight For The Sight with hope for a brighter tomorrow." Other show business personalities that had been honoured with this award before were Bob Hope, Sammy Davis jr. and Danny Kaye. A month later the citation from Fight For The Sight was read into the U.S.A. congressional record.

On 13 January Motown released Stevie's single *Never Had A Dream Come True* (Moy-Wonder-Cosby) which got into the America "Pop 100" at position 26. In the R & B charts it went to number 11 and in England it made number 6.

Also in January Steve gave two live concerts at Detroit's Roostertail Club where both performances were recorded live. As usual Stevie's concerts were sold out and for those people in Stevie's neighbourhood who had helped the little nappy-headed boy years ago on his way up, it was one of the biggest events ever. Former teachers and schoolmates came to see the star and also, most of Motown's artists were in the audiences. The album *Live!* came out on 3 March and apart from Stevie's hits included tracks like *Alfie, By The Time I Get To Phoenix* and *Everybody's Talking*.

On 9 March Stevie made a personal appearance at the Eye Institute of New York's Columbia Presbyterian Medical Center, which examines and treats thousands of under-privileged youngsters with eye problems. The children could hardly believe that Stevie had really come to visit them. Their affection towards the star was overwhelming. They hugged and kissed Stevie, they sang some of his tunes for him and told him that he was their biggest idol. Stevie stayed there all afternoon and before he left he gave out hundreds of his records for the young patients to keep.

One week later, Stevie gave his first headlining appearance at

New York's Copacabana Nightclub. A dream that every artist dreams had come true for him. But happy though he was to top the bill at the Copacabana and stay there for two weeks, the event was overshadowed by the tragic death of Tammi Terrell.

Tammi, who had been Marvin Gaye's singing partner since 1967 had died of a tumour in the brain. Stevie: "Tammi's death was so terrible, because it was so unnecessary. She was so young – only twenty-four and she was such a lovely person. We had become real good friends. It hurts so much to lose a friend to death and there is nothing that you can do about it. I often wonder, why it is that good people have to lose their lives so young.

"I'm not even talking about people like Brian Jones, Brian Epstein, Janis Joplin, Jimi Hendrix, Jim Morrison, Marilyn Monroe or Mama Cass who died of an overdose or something like that. I am talking about people like Otis Redding, for example. He was only thirty-six when his aircraft crashed and he and members of his band were killed. Sam Cooke, who was only thirty-three, Little Walter was thirty-eight, and King Curtis was only thirty-seven when he died. Clyde McPhatter was only thirty-nine and Benny Benjamin was only in his twenties when he died."

Benny's death was the first experience Stevie had of the death of a close friend. It happened in 1969, and upset Stevie a lot. Strangely enough, Benny's death had been something that Stevie had foreseen. Stevie: "It doesn't mean that Benny's death hurt me less, but I took it more calmly when I got the message. Somehow I had been prepared for it. It was less of a shock." In an interview with *Rolling Stone* Stevie talked about Benny Benjamin's death in length:

"I had a dream about Benny Benjamin. I talked to him a few days before he died; he was in hospital. But in my dream I talked to him, he said 'Look, man, I'm . . . I'm not gonna make it.' 'What, you kiddin'!' The image . . . he was sitting on my knee, which means like he was very weak. And he said, 'So, like I'm leavin' it up to you.' That was like a Wednesday, and that following Sunday I went to church and then to the studio to do a session; we were gonna record *You Can't Judge A*

Book By Its Cover, and they said, 'Hey, man, we're not gonna do it today, Benny's just died.' "

Tammi Terrell's death gave rise to a wave of sadness. Her audiences reacted with sincere sorrow. Marvin Gaye was so shaken by this event that a few months later, after he had recorded a song called *The End Of Our Road* he quit touring for almost a year. It was the unnecessary nature of Tammi's death that made it so hard to bear for the people who loved her. It was said that Tammi could still be alive if Motown had shown more personal interest in the singer instead of letting her tour when she was ill. Elaine Jesmer:

"Tammi was on the road long after she had become sick. And she was sick. The cancer of the brain gave her headaches all the time. But at this point no one knew what made her so ill and nobody sent her to a doctor. Instead she had someone travelling with her. And even that was billed to her. Motown didn't pay for it, although it was a Motown employee. Tammi was taking all kinds of pills to kill the pain. And by the time she collapsed on stage it was too late. The cancer was so far gone that the doctors couldn't remove the tumour. Half her brain was practically gone.

"If Tammi had seen a doctor earlier instead of being on the road all the time, maybe it could have saved her life. But she felt responsible for Motown in a way that she promoted her and Marvin's records by touring. But Motown did not feel their responsibility for her and let Tammi act in their interest. So she paid for it with her life. To some extent, anyway."

As tragic as Tammi's death had been for everybody at Motown, for the others the show had to go on. On 3 June 1970 a new Stevie Wonder single was released world wide: *Signed, Sealed, Delivered I'm Yours/I'm More Than Happy (I'm Satisfied)*. This song, which turned out to be the biggest record for Stevie (it became platinum) was written by Stevie Wonder, Lee Garrett, Syreeta Wright and Lula Hardaway. Lee:

"That was really funny how we got this biggie together. At this time I was a disc jockey for a Detroit radio station and before I found a flat, Stevie had invited me to live with him and his family. The first few weeks were a bit weird, because Lula knew me as a friend of Steve's but at the same time she was very suspicious of me. She thought that I was a singer who hadn't made it; that I had now taken a job in Detroit to be close to Stevie and try to take advantage of him. There were so many people who tried to get things out of Stevie. Especially when we started writing together Lula freaked a little. Up to then Steve had mostly stuck with Hank and Sylvia. Now he and I would sit there and make music. Only when Lula joined us, she realized that I had no intentions of clinging on to Stevie's fame and then Lula accepted me.

"Anyway, quite a while before we wrote *Signed, Sealed, Delivered, I'm Yours* Stevie had met Syreeta Wright, who was a secretary at Motowns and had also recorded one single which didn't get anywhere. They had talked a bit in the office or the studio and he had started to like her. Steve also thought that she had some musical talent. So we just decided to invite her over to Stevie's place when we were doing some writing. That way he would kill two birds with one stone – give Syreeta a chance to develop her interest in music and it would give Steve a chance to get closer to her. And that was exactly what we did: asked Syreeta to come over.

"I had teased Stevie about her a little. That's how we had come up with the line *Signed, Sealed, Delivered I'm Yours*. Well, so he just asked her, if she could write some lyrics round it. Finally the four of us, Lula, Syreeta, Stevie and I finished the song."

Around the same time this team also wrote *It's A Shame* which was a million selling hit for the Spinners on Motown in 1970.

At the beginning of June *Signed, Sealed, Delivered I'm Yours* topped the R & B charts and in the middle of July it had gotten up to number 3 in the "Pop 100". In England it made position 15. But there was even more to this single for Stevie – apart from being the biggest hit. It was the first Stevie Wonder production to become a million seller (although it was not the first production of his own to be released).

Stevie took his first step into record production with *You Met Your Match*, on *Greatest Hits Volume 2. (I Don't Know Why* is sometimes said to be his first production, but the album credits Hank Cosby.) Before Stevie's first *important* production – which

Signed, Sealed, Delivered I'm Yours undoubtedly is – had come out, Stevie had also been given a try at producing other artists.

During his 1969 trip to Britain, Stevie confessed that he would like to spend more time in the studio with a view to recording other artists. Soon afterwards he produced some sessions with some groups on the new Rare Earth label and he had also done sessions with Syreeta, who then recorded under the name of Rita Wright. Stevie is also said to have done some production work on Martha Reeves but it was never released.

Although Stevie produced all his own records after *Signed, Sealed, Delivered I'm Yours* he admits to not having been looked upon as a top producer immediately. Talking about a production he did on David Ruffin a little after *Signed, Sealed, Delivered I'm Yours* Stevie says: "I would get the product to Motown and nobody would listen and I'd say, 'Fuck it,' and I wouldn't worry about it . . ."

A few things did not come off, but Stevie did have some success with others. He did *It's A Shame* for the Spinners and also their follow-up *We'll Have Made It*, which was not as big as the first one.

In August, Motown released the *Signed, Sealed And Delivered* album, from which Stevie's next single came. But just before the record company put out Stevie's next million seller, Stevie requested a few weeks' holiday:

On 14 September 1970 Stevie Wonder married Syreeta Wright in Detroit's Burnette Baptist Church. After the wedding ceremony the newly-wed couple gave a reception which they left early. While the wedding guests carried on celebrating, Stevie and Syreeta boarded a jet to Bermuda.

Fifteen days later, when Stevie and Syreeta had come back from their short honeymoon, Motown released *Heaven Help Us All*, a song written by Ron Miller, who co-produced this track. Ron: "*Heaven Help Us All* was kind of an ego trip for me. It was the first song where I had written the music *and* the lyrics. That is why I wanted to stick with this song until the end and co-produce it. When I think about it today, if we had to do it again I would leave Stevie to it. I think he would have made an even bigger hit out of it, if he had produced it the way he wanted to.

"But then as I said, this song was very much of an ego trip for me. See, when I came to Motown I had no idea about production. I couldn't tell a trumpet from a trombone. Then I learned it. And I also taught Stevie a lot of what I had learned. We worked together very closely. In the old days it was me who taught him the songs. There was no way for us to do all the stuff in braille. So I took the time to speak the words from a mike into his earphones before he had to sing the line. Yeah, we really worked together very closely."

Aaron Fuchs even credits Miller to some degree with having influenced Stevie's writing around 1970. He wrote in *Fusion*: "With the recording of *Heaven Help Us All*, Wonder moved closer to the soon-to-prevail quasi-religious song of consolation. This tune and Stevie's own *Never Had A Dream Come True* are both particularly important in the lyrical implications of paranoia (or maybe it was a painfully acute sense of reality) that was to signal an onslaught of romantic fantasy in black music. In *Never Had A Dream Come True*, a song about an escape in a dream, Wonder sings:

> *We're as free as the wind where true love is no sin.*
> *Therefore men are men and not machines . . .*

The sudden shift of that last stanza is matched by *Heaven Help Us All* with:

> *Heaven help the child that never had a hope*
> *Heaven help the girl that walks the street alone*
> *Heaven help the roses when the bombs begin to fall*
> *Heaven help us all . . .*

With this song Stevie got his eighth gold single. By the end of October it had reached position 2 in the R & B charts and in November it got to position 9 in the American "Pop 100" and to number 29 in the British *Music Week* charts.

In October Motown U.K. put out the Stevie album *Live At The Talk Of The Town* that had been recorded the same year when he was in London.

1970 was the second year for Steve to be awarded two gold singles; and it was the year in which Motown officially acknowledged Stevie as a man. At the time Stevie worked at the Copacabana Nightclub Motown had released a new Stevie Wonder biography, called *Stevie Wonder . . . The Man*, in which Berry Gordy had said "If you liked the boy, you'll love the man."

To make sure that Stevie's adult image would take over Bobbi Amato (Motown International) had sent out a memorandum to all international licensees on 30 April: "We ask you to notify all newspapers, magazines, etc. in your area that new photographs are available and instruct them to DESTROY any photographs of Stevie Wonder that they may have in their files..."

With Stevie, Motown had taken off to new heights and 1970 had also been another good year for Motown altogether. Apart from Tammi Terrell's death, which gave a bitter taste to the year and kept Marvin Gaye away from the music scene, Gordy could be satisfied.

His new Rare Earth label had taken off splendidly. The group Rare Earth had scored a few Top Ten hits. Among them *Get Ready* and *(I Know) I'm Losing You*. The Jackson Five had topped the charts with *ABC, The Love You Save* and *I'll Be There* – all three singles to become gold discs. *Reach Out And Touch* had been a Top Twenty hit for Diana Ross and her *Ain't No Mountain High Enough* was a gold record. Gladys Knight and the Pips had done well with *Make Me The Woman That You Go Home To,* David and Jimmy Ruffin had teamed up as a duo and gained a few small hits, Smokey Robinson and the Miracles had achieved British success with a 1967 track *The Tears Of A Clown*. The Spinners had been in the charts with *It's A Shame* and *Message From A Black Man* and Edwin Starr with *War*.

But, as good as things were looking for Gordy and his companies at the end of 1970, it was the last year in which things would run that smoothly. With the beginning of the new year a great number of excellent composers and lyricists would come up. Some of them were just starting, others had been in the business longer but were now getting established. The standards they were setting would be high. Also artists that were big already would still be getting more and more fame.

Like the Who, whose rock opera *Tommy* had shown Pete Townshend to be one of the best writers of our time. 1971 would bring their album *Who's Next*. The Rolling Stones had just put out their album *Get Yer Ya Yas Out* (September 1970) which was to be followed by *Sticky Fingers* in April.

Single members of beloved groups that had broken up released successful albums: George Harrison, Paul McCartney, Ringo Starr and John Lennon from the Beatles; David Crosby, Stephen Stills, Graham Nash and Neil Young (ex-Crosby, Stills, Nash & Young); and Simon & Garfunkel, who had split after their most successful relationship (*Bridge Over Troubled Water, The Graduate* etc.) and were now recording solo albums.

Bread would release *Manna* and James Taylor's 1970 album *Sweet Baby James* would be followed by *Mud Slide Slim* and *One Man Dog*. Rod Stewart had become a star and 1971 would bring his long play *Every Picture Tells A Story*. Van Morrison would release *His Band And Street Choir* and *Tupelo Honey*, Harry Nilsson *The Point* and *Nilsson Schmilsson*. Loggins and Messia would put out *Sittin' In* and Carole King her much talked-about *Tapestry* and *Music*. Neil Diamond would come up with *Stones*, Kris Kristofferson *The Silver Tongued Devil And I* and Gordon Lightfoot would break with *If You Could Read My Mind* and Don McLean with *American Pie*.

There would be Black Sabbath, Santana and Chicago. 1971 would also be the year of the rock musical *Jesus Christ Superstar* (Helen Reddy topping the charts with *I Don't Know How To Love Him*). But most important of all, Elton John was on his way up. In 1970 he had swept into the *Billboard* album charts at number 17 with *Elton John* and he would do it again with *Tumbleweed Connection* and *Madman Across The Water* plus the Soundtrack *Friends*. In the year to come Elton John would have four albums in the American Top Twenty simultaneously. With this he would be the first artist since the Beatles to have achieved that much success. Elton John's music and Bernie Taupin's lyrics would make it hard for anybody to reach their standard.

127

1971 was going to be a hard year. Especially for Stevie, whose aim it was to get acknowledged as a singer, songwriter and producer as well as being a musician playing a variety of instruments.

After a long discussion, Berry Gordy had finally given Stevie the go-ahead to write, sing, and produce as well as partly play his own album. This was an experiment that Gordy was not too happy with – especially after Marvin Gaye had come up with the same idea and was about to put an album out that allowed him the artistic freedom that he had wanted (*What's Going On,* 1971). But then Gordy had decided – for once – to let Stevie have his own way. The last thing that Gordy worried about was a financial loss: he was sure that he would find the minimum of one hit amongst the album tracks as Stevie had already co-written eight out of seventeen hit singles (since *Uptight*). Even if Gordy did not like Stevie's production he could always get someone else to re-produce the track that would be chosen as a single. Apart from that there were hundreds of Stevie Wonder tracks in the can that Gordy could always fall back on. Also up to now Stevie's albums had not sold too well anyway so that there was no album-buying public to be terribly disappointed.

The only thing that worried Gordy was that Stevie had developed too much desire for artistic freedom. It seemed that the older Stevie got the less he was willing to submit to Motown's rules. Still – one way of showing Stevie where he belonged was to let him do his own album. If it had some hits on it and if it sold – great. If not it would be proof that Stevie could not do all the things that he thought he could. Then Stevie would have to realize that he needed Motown to guide him.

The reason for Gordy's careful psychological approach was a simple one: in only a few months from now Stevie would turn twenty-one. The contract needed re-negotiation, as Stevie could then act on his own behalf. The rick of upsetting Stevie now was one that Gordy would not want to take. After all, Steve was one of Motown's hottest acts and any other record company would sign him without making too many demands.

The idea of Stevie leaving Motown to find artistic freedom elsewhere was one that Berry Gordy did not like.

While Stevie was working on his own album, Motown released a track from Stevie's *Signed, Sealed, And Delivered* album: The Lennon/McCartney song *We Can Work It Out* which had been a Beatles single release in December 1965. Stevie's version of this, almost an "oldie but goldie", came out on 18 February. This track, which is said to be the first one on which Stevie played all the instruments himself, reached America's "Pop 100" at number 13 and went to position 3 in the R & B charts. In England the single got to position 27. In summer the B-side of this single *Never Dreamed You'd Leave In Summer* also got into *Billboard's* "Pop 100" at number 78.

12 April 1971 was the big day: Motown released *Where I'm Coming From*. It had taken Stevie and Syreeta almost one year to write hundreds of songs from which they picked those for the album. Since *Signed, Sealed, Delivered I'm Yours* they had more or less been working on songs together. Stevie had arranged, recorded and produced the tracks and then together with Motown finally selected nine of them to be on the album. When *Where I'm Coming From* came out, Motown sent out promotional postcards to the press and to radio stations. On the back the cards said in big letters "Open Your Ears" and the front was all black with just a small photograph of the album cover and a few lines printed in white in the top right hand quarter:

"Listen.
Stevie Wonder sees more
than you and I.
He sees with his heart.
His soul.
His mind.
Listen.
Hear what Stevie Wonder sees.
Where I'm Coming From."

But that is about as far as Motown's promotional support on the album went. Stevie: "If it had been pushed there wouldn't have been all the fuss about *Music Of My Mind* later. Because people would have been prepared for it. Motown felt uneasy to touch social and political themes."

Where I'm Coming From contained a wide range from protest songs to the discovery of sublime love. Nevertheless critics declared it a "premature" album. They said it was "inaccessible", they spoke about "an utter lack of temperance" or just called the time that Stevie wrote it in his "creative lull". It is of course very easy to listen to *Where I'm Coming From* today (especially after having heard Stevie's follow-up albums) and put it down. Admittedly I also prefer to listen to Stevie's later albums but one has to consider the time and the circumstances at which Stevie and Syreeta wrote and produced this album.

For one thing, the musical changes since Stevie had first listened to, then sung and later written music had been enormous. At the same time America's young generation had started and experienced a lot of changing attitudes. Within the last ten years black people had not only become accepted but beautiful. The aggressive age of Rock-'n-Roll had given way to an almost apathetic hippie culture. Love and peace is all nice and easy when you've smoked a joint. There had also been the high time of politically engaged artists like Dylan and Baez. Vietnam had become the concern of America's youth because thousands of them had been sent over there. Many had not come back and the ones who survived were lucky if they found their way back into life.

Then there was another phase of aggressive music. The Stones sang about violence and Alice Cooper practised it on stage. Not for real, of course, but it looked real and it was supposed to. Sex was not talked about quietly any more but also had come into the open. Either in an aggressive way as Jagger put it to the Stones' audiences, or provocatively, like James Brown with his *Sex Machine*. Elvis and Tom Jones had started to wiggle their hips, and even nice housewives were trying to get on stage and rip the clothes off their idols. John Lennon and Yoko Ono had shown naked behinds on an album cover. Eastern religion had made a great impact on music and attitudes of people. Psychedelic sounds had swept America and now transvestite songs were coming up (David Bowie, Lou Reed). The music and its audiences were open to everything. There was no direction and there were thousands. But one thing was clear to Steve: "People are not interested in 'Baby, Baby' songs any more. There is more to life than that. I also think that singles are very important but I don't want to rely on singles only. There are some rock artists who don't want to do singles at all. I don't mind – as long as they come off an album but for me they are generally only one page in the book."

Yet Motown had been influenced very little by all these different images. Stevie and Marvin Gaye were the only artists who had had the real urge to get out of the stagnating Motown Sound and develop their own. Stevie: "With Marvin and me the same thought was in both of our minds. That was that we wanted to go to another place, musically. There was something else we both had in our heads other than doing one part, things that didn't give us full musical expression. Marvin is a very talented man. He is a very brilliant man and he does what he believes and what I believe. As long as you don't do things that hurt people in terms of expression, you've gotta do what you've gotta do."

Stevie was also going through tremendous personal changes. Not only from a poor black and blind ghetto child to a financially secure star but also from a child to a man. The first of the two is hard enough to go through and still stay sane. And growing up alone is not easy either. To find out who you are and what you want to get from and give to life. And Stevie was signed to a company that did not help its artists to find self-expression, but rather dominated them.

All these things should be taken into consideration when we judge the first album that Stevie and Syreeta did on their own, even if *Where I'm Coming From* does have too much of a preaching or prophetic touch in some songs. *Look Around*, for example, where Stevie sings:

> *We are idle strangers married to our dangers*
> *Into space we change our ways.*
> *Flying to our heavens we are all together*
> *Into hell we chase the light of day . . .*

In the chorus he calls:

> *Look around and you'll see ruins of the human history . . .*

In the next track, *Do Yourself A Favour*, Stevie reaches almost messianic heights. He speaks of:

> *Isolated junk yard letting out the garbage*
> *Eating through the core of life . . .*

and

> *Let the devil step right in Lucifer's your only friend.*
> *Ain't a soul goin' pity you.*

In the chorus he warns:

> *Do yourself a favour educate your mind*
> *Get yourself together hey there ain't much time.*

In interviews regarding heavy tracks like those from the album, Stevie said: "I want peace for all people." And he went even further by stating: "Sometimes I wish that I could have been all the soldiers that were killed in Vietnam, yeah, I guess you could call it a sacrificial wish."

The third cut on the first album-side is a love song called *Think Of Me As Your Soldier*. And somehow the other social meaning that Stevie may have intended to put over with this song seems to have been overrated by critics:

> *Think of me as your soldier*
> *The man whose life is for you*
> *And the sweet love that's greater than time has known . . .*

The last cut on the second side of *Where I'm Coming From* goes over almost seven minutes (6.58) and is called *Sunshine In Their Eyes*. It is a song about the children of the second class and it contains lines like:

> *A lonesome tear, a hungry face*
> *A barren of pain of dream unchanged*
> *Oh, I can't wait until the day*
> *There's sunshine in their eyes . . .*

Syreeta joins in at times with lines like "most of the news is bad" while Stevie goes through the whole story with the mother being worried because she thinks the world comes to an end. The father is extra-careful, because his brother's son has been robbed and there's also hardly any money to feed the baby. The song has heavy orchestration and a children's choir. Aaron Fuchs' comment in *Fusion* on *Sunshine In Their Eyes* was: "Regardless of the underlying philosophy, it has all the impact of a charity ad that dares you turn the page" and this sums it up.

The best "social" track on the album is the opening number on the second album side. *I Wanna Talk To You* is a dialogue between Stevie and a member of the older generation. It has a kind of gospel feel to it – the (young) one who has nothing talking to the (old) one who has everything:

> *C'mon gimme a little room now*
> *Do you have to take it all*
> *Yeah, that's the way it is I guess*
> *When you're born with nothing at all . . .*

Compared to the gentleness of Stevie's later dialogues of conflict like *Superwoman* or *Big Brother* this song is full of bitterness. It has been said to be Stevie's most severe putdown and it ends with Stevie saying: "I don't wanna talk to you."

One problem with the song is, though, that the words that the member of the older generation speaks (the voice being on one colourless level) are extremely hard to understand. But this is something that quite often occurs in Stevie's songs, especially the later ones. Jim Gilstrap, a one time member of Wonderlove says: "With Stevie's lyrics I often don't understand the words he sings. Only when you read them you all of a sudden go 'Yeah, man, is *that* what you mean! I dig it'."

Apart from the social-critical songs *Where I'm Coming From* contains a number of love songs. Syreeta Wright, who co-wrote all album tracks, names *Something Out Of The Blue* and *Take Up A Course In Happiness* as her favourites. Syreeta: "When I heard the melody of *Something Out Of The Blue* it

133

instantly reminded me of a poem I had written. So I changed it around to fit the music. My favourite line in the song is the opening line:

> *I opened my mind, peace I could not find*
> *Then something out of the blue said I needed you.*
> *Time swept me way merged me into pain*
> *Then something out of the blue said you need me too . . .*

"This is something which happens to all of us at times. That we are going through very traumatic experiences where we're nothing but the pain that we are feeling."

Take Up A Course In Happiness is another song where Syreeta heard the melody first and it inspired her at once to write a lyric for it. Syreeta: "The chorus was the thing I wrote first. The lines just came to my head the moment Steve played the melody:

> *Take up a course in happiness*
> *Take up a course to clear out your mind*
> *You will show yourself how to smile . . .*

"Afterwards I wrote the verses around it."

Take Up A Course In Happiness is a happy "get yourself together" song. No matter what happens, don't let it get you down. It is very close to the kind of *Raindrops Keep Falling On My Head* or *Singing In The Rain* feel.

Never Dreamed You'd Leave In Summer was the flip-side to *We Can Work It Out*. Syreeta: "This song is basically about two people being together and obviously one wants to leave or has left with the intention of maybe coming back – but they never do. This is something that I think everybody should think about when people break up: why didn't that relationship work? What within me made it not work. Because it is too easy and comfortable to do to always blame the other person . . ."

Never Dreamed You'd Leave In Summer is a song that does give an indication of the direction in which Stevie would be able to go and it would fit on any of his later albums very well. The lyrics Syreeta wrote match the soft, melancholic melody Stevie composed splendidly:

I never dreamed you'd leave in summer
I thought you would go then come back home
I thought the cold would leave by summer
But my quiet nights will be spent all alone . . .

The time that Stevie put this song out it was also recorded by Joan Baez and Three Dog Night.

If You Really Love Me, the last track on the album, gave Stevie another gold disc when it was released as a single. The lyrics, Stevie says, came from his and Syreeta's experiences and were written entirely by Syreeta:

If you really love me won't you tell me
Then I won't have to be playing around

If You Really Love Me was the only big hit on *Where I'm Coming From.* But regardless of the fact that the album did not make any impact, Stevie and Syreeta still like it. Stevie: "I believed in it. It was an important step forward for me. It also showed me some of my faults – but If I had to do the album again today, I would probably only remix some of the tracks."

Syreeta: "The thing is that Steve would have eventually broken off and done his own thing anyway. And the reason that it happened at that time is not just me. But people who loved him generally, like his family, all wanted him to reflect himself. Because when you are with someone then you know their genius, you know their actual potential that nobody else sees. So I think just the support of people who were close to him at that time probably helped him to make up his mind that he was going to do his own thing right then and there. And I still think that *Where I'm Coming From* is a good album that showed some of the direction in which Stevie was to go soon."

Between the release date of the album and that of *If You Really Love Me* as a single (22 July 1971), fell Stevie's 21st birthday. According to the calendar, 13 May 1971 was a Thursday.

For Motown it might as well have been a Friday 13th.

CHAPTER SIX

Music Of My Mind

The 21st birthday, or whichever one makes you adult, is
something very special for everybody. One day you are a
child: the next, an adult – at least on paper. All of a sudden
you have all the responsibility for yourself and for whatever
you do. And if you haven't realized that until then, you will
definitely know on the day you come of age.

On birthday parties like this the other "grown-ups" usually
give speeches telling you that you are now accepted as one of
them. They tell you how nice it is to be your own master and
at the same time they talk about the difficulties of responsibility. That you better think twice before you make an important decision and how hard it is from now on to get out of
trouble once you have got yourself into it. If the congratulator
wants to be really nice to you he will make sure that in him
you have a friend. Someone you can always turn to for advice
as he is quite a few years and many experiences ahead of
you.

Berry Gordy and his Motown executives were really nice.
On Stevie's 21st birthday they praised him for how bravely
he had taken up the battle with life, how he had overcome his
handicap; and how many people there were in similar situations
to whom Stevie had given strength. And, of course, how
much Stevie had achieved for himself and Tamla Motown
already.

They told Stevie that he was an important member of the
big, strong Motown family who had helped conquer the
world's music scene. How long ten years can be and how quickly
time flies once you can look back on something. And Stevie

and all the rest of his Motown brothers and sisters could look back on many a success, starting from when Gordy had signed the little nappy-headed boy to his company, which then had been in its youth itself.

They recalled how everybody had believed in Little Stevie Wonder who had then rewarded their belief with *Fingertips*. They talked about *Uptight*, the first hit that Stevie had co-written with Sylvia and Hank and how beautiful it was that they had become such good friends. They also mentioned other people who had helped Stevie along the way like Clarence Paul, Ron White, Ted Hull, Ardena Johnston, Brian Holland, Ron Miller, Gene Kee, Martha Reeves and everybody else.

They thanked Stevie's parents for having supported their son in so very many ways, and they said how glad they were that Stevie should have found the most lovely and loving wife in Syreeta. They joked about Steve having taken the efficient secretary from Motown but that on the other hand he had given them another star with Syreeta. They said how well the couple worked together and how happy everybody could be. Then they put figures to the success that Stevie had gained over those last ten years:

Motown had released 27 Stevie Wonder singles plus the one as Eivets Rednow. Out of these Stevie had had one number 1 in *Billboard*'s "Pop 100". In the same charts two records had reached position 2 and another 2 position 3. Six singles had been in the "Pop 100" Top Ten, four in the Top Thirty, another four in the Top Fifty and three in the Top Hundred.

In *Billboard*'s R & B charts the result had been even better: Six number 1 hits, three number 2 hits, two records went to number 3 and 4 each and one to position 5. Two more singles had gotten into the Top Ten and the Top Twenty, one single had reached position 30 and another one position 31.

In England Stevie had had records reaching numbers 2, 3, 4, 5 and 6. Four singles had made *Music Week*'s Top Twenty, three the Top Thirty. Altogether Stevie had been awarded with eight gold discs and one platinum record so far.

The albums that Motown had released on Stevie over the

years counted up to 15 (plus *Alfie* on the Gordy label) and Stevie's hits were also presented on 27 compilation or Motortown Revue albums. The records that Stevie had sold added up to more than thirty million.

All this, Gordy and his executives said, was very impressive. At the same time, though, it would belong to the past. Stevie now had to look toward the future. And Tamla Motown would be only too pleased if the success that Stevie Wonder and the company had had together would continue in the years to come. Now at twenty-one Stevie could re-negotiate the contract with Tamla that had brought them both so much success. Not only because the second five years were almost up but because the contract that had been signed on his behalf was not valid any more. Stevie was now responsible for himself.

The conditions that Motown offered, and that he had been tied to for the last ten years, were not anything like what Stevie wanted. So Stevie just told Motown that he appreciated everything they had done for him so far very much, but for the moment he was not interested in re-negotiating anything. Instead, he wanted two things.

He wanted the money they held in trust for him.

And he wanted out.

There was no point in trying to convince Stevie to do anything else. With exception of the receipt for his money he would not sign anything. Not now, anyway. He told Motown that he needed some breathing space and that he and Syreeta were going to New York. He would also let them know when he was ready to talk business again.

There was nothing much Gordy and his executives could do – apart from freak. Nobody in the organization believed that a nice friendly guy like Stevie could come up with a decision like that. None of the other artists – apart from Marvin – would have dared to disagree with anything that Motown proposed. And with Marvin Gaye it was still a different kind of thing: his marriage to Anna Gordy put him in a better position (they are divorced now) and also he had gotten a lot of money from Motown, when he mentioned that he would like to leave. Elaine Jesmer: "They got him for eight million dollars. For a star like Marvin this is a nice cheap price . . ."

Diana Ross was getting better treatment, too, not so much because she had asked for it but rather because Gordy had declared Dianne (which is her real name) his special protégé. Gordy in fact even made Diana Ross head of Product Evaluation at Motown at one time. That was when she was pregnant with her first child and waiting to begin the movie *The Lady Sings The Blues* – Motown's first step into the movie business. Dianne held the position as the head of Product Evaluation for almost one year. In this time she had power over the vice-president in charge of deciding which tunes became singles, which singles got released where and when.

Apart from Diana Ross and Marvin Gaye only Smokey Robinson, one of the many vice-presidents at Motown, held special position. But he had had that to begin with, anyway. Other than that Gordy had never shown the slightest interest in even discussing contracts with his artists. If they did not like what he offered, that was their problem. He would rather drop the artist than agree to a compromise.

With Stevie, though, the situation was different: not only because Stevie had been making lots of money for the company so far, and not only because Gordy knew that Stevie had even more potential than he had shown already. There was also a question of prestige. It would be the most embarrassing thing for Motown to lose Stevie now. A big artist turning his back on the company as soon as his 21st birthday had arrived would cast a bad reflection on the company. So all Gordy could do for now was to hope that Stevie would not take too long to come back and that they would find a reasonable agreement. Other than that Gordy could only grin and bear it and pay Stevie out.

The childhood earnings amounted to one million dollars. Stevie took the money, took Syreeta, and the two of them left for New York. They moved into a residential hotel and concentrated on a new kind of music they had been wanting to make for so long. Stevie: "Even though I had done more or less my own thing with *Where I'm Coming From* it didn't look like I was getting a chance like this again. Admittedly the album didn't do too well but I didn't feel like going through all this hassle with other producers again. Because I knew that I just wasn't produced right. It came to a thing where I was going 'dit-dit-dit-dun-da-dun' for three minutes until they shouted *cut* and 'That's enough, fade it out, fade it out, fade it out, *fade it out*' and I couldn't deal with that."

Stevie also said that when he left Motown in 1971 "I wanted to do an album with the money I had accumulated. But this time it wasn't so much a question of where I was coming from but rather where I was going to. I had to find out what my direction and my destiny was. And there was no way that I could just go on from where I had stopped with Motown. It was a completely different thing that was in my head. I don't think you can *gradually* leave a kind of music. You can't mix one concept with another. It has to be an abrupt change where you say 'Okay, this is what I want to do from now on and all the other stuff belongs to the past.' "

For Stevie, this mainly meant getting away from the Soul tag: "The whole thing is so ridiculous anyway. A lot of people say soul is dying – and have the wrong idea about soul in the first place. To them it's a black singer who screams a lot. But to me soul is the way an artist expresses his inner self. It's being able to do anything with feeling and with sincerity. How much of what you're doing is part of your life. A lot of people have soul: the Beatles, Aretha."

When Stevie worked on his new songs, he did not have any recording contract at all. The business side did not interest him at this very moment and he was not going to deal with it anyway. Instead he hired Johanen Vigoda, a top showbusiness lawyer in New York, who also worked for Jimi Hendrix and Ritchie Havens. It was through Ritchie (who had come to fame with his versions of Beatles songs like *Strawberry Fields Forever, She's Leaving Home* (1968) and in 1971 with *Here Comes The Sun*) that Stevie met Vigoda, one of the very few white people that work with Steve.

Vigoda is said to be one of the toughest lawyers in the music scene. Ken East, head of Motown London: "Johanen thinks very commercial. You never get to any kind of deal with him concerning Stevie if they don't get the biggest slice of the cake." When Stevie had written *He's Misstra Know-It-All* some people assumed that this was a song about his lawyer:

Playin' hard, talkin' fast
Makin' sure that he won't be the last
He's Misstra Know-It-All
Makes a deal with a smile
Knowin' all the time that his lie's a mile . . .

But Stevie said: "No, Vigoda and I are friends. Though neither of us is gonna take no bull. I ain't gonna take nothing of him. I'm gonna check and make sure everything is all right. But aside from all that I've come to know of him as a friend. That song (from *Innervisions*) is just about the coolest guy with the biggest mouth . . ."

An ex-Motown employee's description of Vigoda was: "He is of average height, slim and looks quite sporty. His dark, slightly waved hair looks always a mess and most of the time he wears a blue cap. You could perhaps call him handsome, if it wasn't for his eyes. They are like steel. There is no sign of affection in them, ever. I've never seen him smile with his eyes. The skin of his face reminds you of tawed leather and you can't guess his age. Vigoda could be anything from 35 to 45 years. And he always gets what he wants."

This description of Vigoda fits quite well. When I was supposed to meet him in the coffee-shop of the Los Angeles Continental Hyatt House Hotel I could spot him at once. The ex-Motown employee was right: You could call Joha en handsome – only there is no way that you can get through to him. You might as well talk to a wall.

Mind you, he is very nice, very charming, very gentleman-like and at times you could really think that you are conversing – provided you like small talk. He does not drink alcohol – at least not very often – and that is why he does not meet you in the bar. He does not drink much coffee either. Instead he prefers milk or soda water: "With this kind of hectic life I lead," he told me, "that is the least I can do for my health."

He talks about everything you don't want to talk about. His messed-up love-life, for example: "See, I'm in love with this woman and we broke up because my job takes most of my time. But what can I do – once you've committed yourself to work for Stevie that's it. He keeps me up most of the time. But I guess, it's either one or the other, business or private life . . ."

He is angry that his car broke down: "In the middle of the bl . . . road (Vigoda does not seem to swear with women around). Now I have to take it to get repaired and I also have to get to New York in a hurry. What an unnecessary pain in the *neck*."

He mentions friends from England: "Do you know Clive Davis [head of Arista Records]? He's such a great guy. And Dave Most [Mickie Most's brother who runs RAK publishing and promotion]? What a good promoter and *so* talented!"

Vigoda likes sunshine best, but if it has to be rain then he definitely prefers the rain to catch him when he is in England: "When it rains in New York, everything you get is a lot of dirt upon you. Even London isn't that bad. But the English countryside is the most beautiful. The air is so fresh and clean, you can *breathe*. I just *love* England. It's outtasight . . ."

Most things are "outtasight" for Johanen Vigoda, he uses that phrase in every second sentence. But no matter how much he talks he never speaks about Steve. For obvious reasons he is not inclined to give any information about Stevie's contracts with Motown. But he doesn't like to talk about Steve at all: "See, I only *work* for him. Like when he whistles I've got to be there. He often rings me up at five or six o'clock in the morning. That is when he is awake and when I should be asleep. But Steve doesn't care. He tells me what he wants done and I have to do it. But I can't really tell you anything about him. He's a great musician, that's all I know . . ."

The way Johanen Vigoda gets what he or Stevie wants is, he just ignores any kind of subject or proposal that he does not like. I can very well imagine him dealing with Motown on Stevie's behalf. He does not negotiate: he tells you his client's needs.

With Motown he did exactly the same thing that Motown

had done with their artists so far: you agree to my demands – then we get along fine. If you don't – that is your problem. I can easily go some other place . . . But before Stevie hired Vigoda at the end of 1971 he only thought about his new album.

First of all, he brought his favourite instruments more into his music: the clavichord and the clavinet, with which he had been experimenting since 1968. Stevie: "With the stuff that I am recording and that I do in my live shows I am always a year ahead of my last album. Like in 1969 I had recorded some clavinet sounds on tape and put it through the speakers in my show. It blew people's minds . . ."

The clavinet is a funky electronic harpsichord of which Stevie gives the following description: "It is a keyboard instrument that produces a sound like that sort of reminiscent of the guitar – or at least that is the effect that I try to get. It's a very delicate instrument and one that if it's played properly can produce very interesting sounds. Almost like a synthesizer in that you have to learn its character. It's no good just playing it as you would play an organ."

Stevie also brought the Arp and Moog synthesizers, machines which can electronically produce almost any sound desired, into his music. What had really turned him on to experiment with synthesizers was Walter Carlo's *Switched On Bach* and the Headband's *Tonto's Expanding Headband* album. Ritchie Havens brought Stevie together with Robert Margouleff and Malcolm Cecil (the Headband) who then introduced Stevie to the synthesizer and worked on the Moog programming for him.

Before Robert and Malcolm had formed the Headband and founded Centaur Music, their own production company, Robert Margouleff had worked as a singer under Leonard Bernstein, Aaron Copeland, and Eugène Ormandy, and studied under a scholarship with the Boston Symphony at Tanglewood. He had also worked as a lighting and stage designer consultant with La Mama and as a film maker he had shot the critically acclaimed but financially suicidal *Ciao Manhattan*. All that he was left with after the creditors had moved in was an electronic machine that could make music.

Cecil was an actor-bass-player in the London West End productions *The Connections* and *The Establishment*. He had played bass with Stan Getz, Roland Kirk, Ginger Baker and John McLaughlin at Ronnie Scott's Club in London and with the BBC radio orchestra. He had also founded the Jazz Couriers and before he went to America to team up with Margouleff, he had toured and made studies of the music of Africa as well as the Far East. By the time that Malcolm and Robert met Stevie, they had been working together for about one year. Apart from recording their own music the two synthesizer experts worked as an independent engineering/production support team for other musicians at the Electric Lady Studio in New York City. They had engineered and/or provided the Moog for artists such as T. Rex and Ritchie Havens.

Stevie had a very simple reason for wanting to use the synthesizer in his music: "It is not that I had gotten tired of strings or horns or anything. It's just that the Arp and the Moog give you another dimension. They express what's inside your mind."

Malcolm Cecil explains: "By using the synthesizer you get rid of all the people standing between the artist and his music. Like without it Stevie had to have someone who arranged his songs for him. So Steve told him what he wanted and the arranger put down what *he* thought that Stevie had played. When the music came back from the copyist the musicians who played it interpreted what *they* thought the arranger had written down. This way it was really hard for Stevie to get the sound that *he* had wanted originally."

The way that Stevie created the music that came from his mind was mainly through experimenting. He would just sit and play the synthesizers, which were new to him, until the sound that came out of them was right. Steve spent endless days and nights at the Electric Lady to get well acquainted with the Arp and the Moog that he wanted to use on his next album. Once he knew what kind of effects he could produce with those machines, how far they would allow him to simulate other instruments, Stevie could concentrate on writing songs.

"I think in the first week we recorded close to 35 tunes," remembers Malcolm Cecil. "We came upon a very nice thing where everybody's juice sort of helped the project. It was a good recipe. Robert understood Stevie's vocal direction, I was understanding more his rhythm direction. It was a very nice flow. We worked through work days, holidays, thanksgiving, the whole lot. It was a lot of playing around – including good times and hard times the same. We layed down close to a hundred tracks before the album was finished. Most of them are still in the can – and a lot of good ones I can tell you . . ."

Being blind was not a handicap for Stevie when he was learning how to play the synthesizer, as he had never considered it as a drawback: "Physical blindness is not a handicap. The only handicap is that people don't seem to be able to communicate. They have certain prejudices because of a colour or because of a person being from a different place. And I think these are things that cripple all of us within the mind."

In one way though Stevie admits that not being able to see has influenced his *writing*: "In a way I have to use my imagination to go places, to write words about things that I have heard people talk about. But in my music and in being blind I'm able to associate what people say with what's inside of me . . ."

Also, being blind, Stevie is not so much exposed to things that happen around him that could take his mind off work. Billy Griffin: "If we do a studio session and a beautiful girl walks into the room, immediately our mind is off the project. With Stevie this kind of temptation is milder. Before he can fancy a girl he has to talk to her first."

Jim Gilstrap: "Stevie is not hindered by all the things there are to see around you. I mean when I'm working and all of a sudden I see something, anything around me, that catches my interest, then I can't concentrate on music as much as before. Especially in summer, you see the sun, people getting their bathing clothes together, open cars and all the stuff that has a lot of fun to it. So you rather join the happy crowd than sit in a studio. With Stevie it's different. Of course he realizes that on a beautiful day it is more fun to be outside but he does not get tempted as easily as we do."

Lee Garrett: "You could say that being blind makes the music better. Because being blind makes you more patient. You take more time to experiment with your ear. Also you enjoy things much more. You don't rush things."

Stevie certainly did not rush making his album. He and Syreeta kept writing one song after the other. Nine of them were to be on his *Music Of My Mind* album and another six songs came on Syreeta's album *Syreeta* (one song, *I Love Every Little Thing About You*, was on both). When Steve writes songs, he usually gets the melody – or at least a very definite idea for the melody – on tape. It is Stevie either playing any of the instruments he masters or just Stevie singing. The lyrics are generally put down later – by him or songwriting friends of his. The words in his songs mostly deal with things that either he or people around him have experienced. Stevie:

"It is really important that you deliver the song the way you meant it to be. That you find the right words to say what you want to say. That your lyrics mean something to you. I have found out that the only way that I can write a good song is to write from experience. Things that have happened. And I also think that the number one thing in music is emotion. That has to be the main ingredient.

"Songs have to come from your mind and from your heart, not from trying to get a sound together that sells. I think, that as long as you are honest in everything that you do, no matter if you write songs or books or if you paint, people will feel it. They know within their hearts what is for real and what is not."

Stevie also claims that he can *see* the instruments he hears: "When I hear music I can *see* it, each instrument has its own colour. The piano for instance is brown, and I can see each instrument playing its own part. It's like a puzzle and when I fit all the pieces together, that's my high."

As weird as it may sound, there is indeed such thing as "colour sound" as well as there is a "colour taste" which are the two most common forms of an inborn blending of senses which is clinically called *synesthesia*. *Dorland's Illustrated Medical Dictionary* defines synesthesia as "a secondary sensation accompanying an actual perception: the experiencing of a sensation in one place; also the condition in which a stimulus of one sense is perceived as sensation of a different sense, as when a sound produces a sensation of colour."

According to *Viva*, "Lawrence E. Marks, Ph.D., Yale, suggests that there is some mechanism of the human nervous system that connects all the various senses to each other, and that most people are capable of some degree of synesthesia. But so far science has been able to learn very little about synesthesia, and no one has been exactly able to pinpoint just where it originates and what it is."

Approximately eight per cent of the population are born with synesthesia and it looks like Stevie is one of them. He does not promote this gift of his by having it publicized. Which is understandable: when people find that someone is synesthetic, their reaction is that they think he is wrong in his head or messing around with drugs.

Stevie's blindism is reason enough for others to offer him drugs or mistake him for a junkie and with synesthesia the association to several of what are called the "consciousness-altering" drugs is somehow justified: synesthetes are born on a permanent trip.

Synesthesia is neither imaginary nor voluntary and although the synesthete is said to be able to control the sense-mingling to a small degree, it is always there. Someone born with a colour hearing cannot separate the sound of a song from the visual pattern it produces. He is even thought to be able to tell the difference in two different singers or groups singing the same song by the way it *looks*, not sounds, because the *look* of the two is different.

Voices make a different pattern, too. It can either be very light or very dark, colourful, wide or narrow and it can have a deep or any other texture. Stevie's amazing gift of recognizing people by their voice – even years after he has first met them – may very well be connected with a certain pattern rather than just the sound.

Colour hearing is supposed to be a gift 90 per cent of the time and a nuisance the other 10 per cent. For Stevie, it could be a 100 per cent a gift: even though he cannot see with his eyes it must be a tremendous sensation for someone who is blind to actually *visualize* colours in his mind. It seems also much easier for synesthetes to detect flat notes because of the disturbance they cause in the colour pattern. Which looks like it is a gift for musicians. Also synesthesists do not rely on the sound but on the *picture*. *Viva* gave some examples of what music can look like:

"Oriental music is black and white with occasional strands of pink, or threads and blocks of luminous green. Elton John, singing *Daniel*, is misty grey moving and blending with soft gold, with star bursts like a gone-to-seed dandelion with orange and red-orange scattered through it.

"Rachmaninoff's *Rhapsody on a Theme of Paganini* – the part toward the end – that's deep, deep purple, a thousand light years deep, stormy, thundering, building like a thunderhead, then into blue – an almost black blue that shines in the dark like lights on water. Then gold against the blue background – swordlike shapes, soaring, flying shapes, transparent almost, nebulous as mist, then more and more solid, gold-edged with gold, climbing, free-moving. Turning now, the shapes falling again, settling. Green in there now, coming down. Settling, with the piano, in a blue and green pool, calm and still.

"Music may set off a giant moving canvas of colour, pattern, texture and perspective. Probably the closest the general public has come to *seeing* it is during the beginning of Walt Disney's movie *Fantasia*, where the music was co-ordinated with screen images of colour and movement. This is as near as most people can get, although it lacks the depth and scope of a full-blown synesthesia 'trip'.

"Colour-hearing synesthetes agree on what they see only in the most general terms: high-pitched notes are light in colour and generally small in size and deep tones are darker and bulkier. Many synesthetes see percussion as red, but the Disney artists drew the drum solos in *Fantasia* in brown and oranges. Another synesthete describes percussion as 90 per cent black and white – very geometric and exact, in outline, shape and movement.

"Some synesthetic descriptions have become part of our language and are common to everyone. People who say they have no synesthesia still know what you mean when you say a sound, or a note of music is *bright*, that the notes of a flute are *silvery*, and a French horn or an unusually mellow voice has a *golden* sound."

Maybe that this is where Stevie has his very distinct ideas of colours from. "Purple," he says, "sounds just *crazy* to me and brown is a little duller than green, isn't it? I think of clouds as white, and a cloud to me is something that is invisible yet visible – though you can't see through it. It's fluffy, it moves around, but it is still a sheet that covers. A black cloud is heavier in texture, and the wind might have a little more trouble getting through it. Black is mystical, it's magic – to me it's the colour of curiosity. A lot of white people don't understand black people because they relate black to things they commonly know. If you have never seen a black person before, you might think of black magic or the things that leave you curious.

"Red, to me, is fire – something that is burning. Shimmering flames, sparkling, the hottest hot. Blue is very, *very* cool, distant . . ."

While Stevie was creating his new music, Motown released the single *If You Really Love Me/Think of Me As Your Soldier* from *Where I'm Coming From*. This was in July 1972. In September the song had gotten to number 8 in *Billboard*'s "Pop 100" and to position 4 in the R & B charts. (In England Motown had put out *Never Dreamed You'd Leave In Summer* as the A-side with *If You Really Love Me* as the flip-side. Only when *Never Dreamed You'd Leave In Summer* did not enter the charts Motown finally released the American single in January 1972 in Britain where it got into the *Music Week* charts at position 20.)

If You Really Love Me turned into another gold disc for Stevie. On 21 October Motown also put another Stevie Wonder *Greatest Hits* album out. Volume 2 included all of

Steve's hits since *Travelin' Man* with the exception of *I Was Made To Love Her* and *I'm Wondering*.

A little later Stevie's lawyer and Motown finally got to agree the new contract that Johanen Vigoda had worked out. This contract is said to be 120 pages long. It almost goes without saying that it was in Stevie's favour. He got the things he wanted:

Artistic freedom was one point. Stevie now gained the right to record wherever, whenever and whatever he wants to. He also formed his own production company – Taurus. Stevie has the choice of musicians he wants to work with – in the studio and on concerts – and chooses the tracks to be on his albums. Doug Kee:

"Before, Motown picked his material and said what was going to be on an album. But it was important to Stevie to be in full control of his own creative thing and do whatever he wanted to do, not what some executive who sits in an office and is half tone-deaf decides. Like they listened to Steve's stuff and said like 'This tune is all right' and the only thing they based their decisions on was the media charts. Then they would put this and that out because they thought it was commercial – according to other hits that they saw in the charts. Not because the tune was *Stevie's*."

Stevie was also allowed to form his own group which he called Wonderlove.

Personal freedom was another thing that Stevie had asked for and got. Now he could set up his own management and promotion office. From now on Motown had nothing to do with the bookings of concerts any more. It is entirely up to Stevie to say when he wants to go on the road, where he wants to go to for how long and for how much money. Doug:

"Stevie also names the support act. The same with the promotion. Motown can *propose* to him but they cannot actually tell him what he *has* to do. Motown doesn't do anything but put the record out. That's virtually all they do."

But the most important thing for Stevie was that he now set up his own publishing company – Black Bull. Before Stevie was 21, Gordy's publishing company Jobete owned all the rights to Steve's songs. Now Stevie owns at the very least half the rights. Motown London's press officer Bob Fisher told me that Jobete and Black Bull have "split publishing" which would mean that they go fifty-fifty. What happens is, that of each record *sold* the publishing company gets a certain percentage which is laid down by government rules. In the United Kingdom it is six and a quarter per cent, in France it is eight and in the United States it is two cents per track.

Out of this percentage the publishing company has to pay the composer(s)/lyricist(s) – which is generally 50 per cent of the publisher's income on records sold. Even if more than one publishing company is involved with the copyrights of a song, the writer's share cannot be touched. The publishers would have to come to an agreement only concerning their half.

Discussing Stevie's contract with people in the publishing business, it seems very unlikely, though, that Stevie should split his publishing with Jobete. It is more likely that Jobete only administer Black Bull for less than half of the publisher's earnings. The guessed rate is that 75 to 80 per cent go to Black Bull and the rest to Jobete.

All this does not sound like one could make a fortune with publishing or writing, as for example with one copy of *Songs In The Key Of Life* sold (21 tracks) the publisher would only get 42 cents. Out of which 21 cents go straight to the composer/lyricist to share between them. The other 21 cents go to the publisher.

But there are more sources for publisher and writer to make money on. A bigger slice comes from performances (radio and TV plays, stage, clubs etc.) where the royalties are higher. The amount of money paid depends on the size and nature of the premises. The BBC, for example, pays a percentage of its income from broadcasting receiving licences and a commercial radio station pays a percentage of its advertising revenue. In Britain this money is collected by the PRS (Performing Right Society) which then divides it among the composer, lyricist and publisher interested in each title. In America it is BMI and ASCAP.

According to the PRS rules the usual division of royalties

is two thirds to the writer and one third to the publisher, but this agreement can vary as long as the publisher does get *no* more than 50 per cent.

The writer also gets 10 per cent of sheet music (of the market selling price of a single song copy or a proportionate royalty concerning song books where more than one writer's work is included). But the writer does not receive a fee from the use of lyrics in magazines or newspapers. In England magazines usually pay around £40 to £50 per lyric to the publisher(s).

Huge money, though, can also be made on artist royalties. People just starting in the business usually get around 3 to 5 per cent on records sold. But this percentage is negotiable and can, for example, increase automatically within the year following the contract or even in proportion to the amount of records sold. The usual superstar rate is said to be between 12 and 20 per cent. People like Elton John and Paul McCartney for instance, can get an artist's royalty rate as high as 21 per cent.

When Stevie re-negotiated his contract with Motown in 1971, rumours were that he would be on a 20 per cent basis.

The publishing percentage Stevie got from his first two five-year contracts with Motown was also a secret. But it cannot have been much. One million dollars is very little indeed as payment for the numerous tours that Stevie did in those years, a record sale of around 30 million copies and for writing and co-writing the A- or B-side of 17 hits in the American charts including gold discs, plus a lot of album tracks.

In the beginning of 1972 Stevie Wonder presented Motown with the tapes to his new album. And only those. Stevie had selected the cuts and he was not willing to have anybody try and change his mind on the tracks by playing all the songs that he had recorded to then.

Six of the tracks were written by Stevie, the other three by Stevie and Syreeta. Stevie had recorded the album at three different studios: Media Sound and Electric Lady in New

York; and Crystal Industries, Los Angeles. Stevie had produced the album in association with Robert Margouleff and Malcolm Cecil who had also done the engineering and Moog programming.

Most of all: Stevie had arranged the songs himself and performed almost all of them. Using multi-tracking, he built up the sound layer by layer, playing drums, piano, organ, Moog and Arp synthesizers, harmonica, clavichord, clavinet and the bag (a throat sound amplifier made by Kustom).

There are only two tracks on which Stevie does not play all the instruments (*Superwoman* contains a guitar solo by Buzzy Feiton and *Love Having You Around* a trombone solo by Art Baron). It was virtually the work of one man – except that, contrary to the credits on the album sleeve which do not mention any backing vocalists, Stevie did not overdub his own backing vocals. Jim Gilstrap: "I sang on the album and like the other session singers I thought it was a bit weird that Stevie did not mention us."

It had taken Stevie more than six months to get the album as perfect as he had wanted it to be. And before it made any money, it had cost him a lot. Steve is said to have poured a quarter million dollars of his own money into studio time. But to him this album was the most important thing and well worth it.

It was called *Music Of My Mind*.

Motown was not too impressed with the album when they first got it, but they had agreed to release it. And Stevie, the "one man band" is supposed to have told them: "I'm not trying to be different, I'm trying to be myself. For the first time I've been able to express exactly what comes from inside my mind."

Earlier in 1972, just before *Music Of My Mind* came out, Stevie had toured England and talked about his album. In the interviews he did Stevie gave the impression of not being too sure about his audience's reaction either:

"If people don't want to accept what I'm doing now I'll drop the name Stevie Wonder and just become part of Wonderlove and concentrate more on production. I'm not just going out there to make money. We'll just have to give it time and see how it goes. Attitudes might change.

"Or maybe I'll end up writing for people, which is fine. Because as long as I'm part of creating something new that's fine with me. I mean this isn't exactly criticism but James Brown said he'd retire four years ago and like he's been going on stage and doing the same thing over and over again since. Me, I'd get tired of that. Because after a while people are bound to say 'Man, I'm sick of that shit' and James is going to have to deal with people not coming to his shows. I really couldn't do the same thing for the next two years. Not now – I really couldn't."

On 3 March 1972 *Music Of My Mind* was in the shops. Within a few days it was the most talked-about album around, and every radio station had picked up on it. People called it the most spectacular release since the Beatles' *Sergeant Pepper's Lonly Hearts Club Band*. Today *Music Of My Mind* is considered the blueprint for Stevie's subsequent albums.

The music of Stevie's mind showed him as a great personality with a lot to say. "He builds his world in sound" was written in the sleeve notes, and:

Stevie draws his vision
from the world of pure vibration,
which is music, feelings, energy . . .

This man is his own instrument.
The instrument is an orchestra.

Within the line of top artists, this album had put Stevie in a different class. And while Keith Emerson (ex Emerson, Lake & Palmer) is declared to play the synthesizer "as technically as hell", Stevie Wonder plays it with emotion. *Melody Maker* wrote: "It's almost tactile the way he forces those electronic circuits to emit soulful, moving, tremendously delicate melodies. Wonder's main contribution is that he's made the synthesizer a living instrument, feeling his way into the physical attributes of the machine."

Music Of My Mind, "a gift to the spirit from one who really

154

cares", is an album of mainly love songs. The opening track *Love Having You Around* has a powerful soul-beat and optimistic lyrics that fit a happy, loving mood:

> *And when the day is through,*
> *Nothin' to do, just sit around groovin' with you,*
> *And I say it 'cause I love having you around . . .*

The electronically distorted background voice, which Stevie used as a gimmick in this opening cut, was produced with the bag.

I Love Every Little Thing About You is another happy love song. But it starts more gently to then develop into a powerful beat. It is also the song that Syreeta sings on her first album, but the arrangements are totally different.

Happier Than The Morning Sun is Malcolm Cecil's favourite tune on the album: "It is simple. No heavy production, not too many waterfalls." Stevie plays the clavinet most beautifully, and the soft melody turns its lyrics, which could easily sound like *Kitsch* if they were put to music in any other way, into a most lovely love song:

> *I'm happier than the morning sun*
> *And that's the way you said that it would be*
> *If I should ever bring you into my life.*

Keep On Running is a knock-out. This track begins with a kind of ominous tangle of electronic squiggles, piano, nervous cymbal clashes and dark bassy threats as Stevie sings:

> *Something gonna get you*
> *Something gonna grab you*
> *Something gonna jump out of the bushes and grab you . . .*

After two verses the song becomes faster and Steve repeats:

> *Keep on running*
> *Keep on running from my love . . .*

It is incredible how Stevie chases you with the synthesizer; how a beat on the drum symbolizes you stumbling and falling, getting up again and keeping on running . . .

Evil is supposed to be the fastest song that Stevie ever wrote: "I wrote *Evil* in the studio the day after Memorial Day (which is England's Remembrance Day) straight away. It took me about three or four hours to write the song, record it and finish it totally." Stevie co-wrote this song with Yvonne Wright (no relationship to Syreeta) and it is one track on the album that is not about the love between two people:

> *Evil, why have you engulfed so many hearts . . . Evil*
> *Evil, why have you destroyed so many minds . . . Leaving*
> *Room for, darkness, where lost dreams can hide . . .*

In this song Stevie is referring to the "spiritual blindness" that he so often talks about in interviews. On the other hand, *Evil* is just an accusation – Stevie does not provide a solution.

The other four songs on *Music Of My Mind* are love songs which have more of a personal touch than people realized when the album first came out. In *Girl Blue* Stevie sings:

> *Thoughts of love are in your mind,*
> *Yet splintered hopes push them aside.*
> *A look at life is what you need to try . . .*

Seems So Long has lines like:

> *And now I feel it's not fair*
> *for me to fall in love*
> *The truth is the real me you must uncover . . .*

In *Sweet Little Girl* Stevie sings:

> *Sweet little girl, you know your baby Stevie's true,*
> *Your love is driving me crazy, crazy, crazy,*
> *Girl I'm in love . . .*

And *Superwoman*, the track that was chosen as the single (it got into the "Pop 100" at number 33, in the R & B charts at position 13 whereas in England it did not reach the charts) summed it all up:

> *Mary wants to be a superwoman*
> *But is that really in her head*
> *But I just want to live each day to love her*

For what she is . . .
Mary wants to be a superwoman
And try to boss the bull around
But does she really think she'll get by with a dream . . .

Malcolm Cecil: "I remember Ewart Abner at Motown running up and down the corridor and asking 'Who is this superwoman Steve talks about?' Well, now we all know . . ."

The superwoman Stevie's friends believe to be Syreeta. And although in some interviews Stevie had said: "When you get music and you get creativity and you get love together, it is the best thing that can happen to you" he now changed the last words of this statement: " . . . and you get love together, it's pretty heavy."

Just about the time that *Music Of My Mind* came out, Stevie and Syreeta had been married for one and a half years. And then their marriage broke up.

CHAPTER SEVEN

To Know You Is To Love You

The end of Stevie's and Syreeta's marriage was a surprise for most of their friends. Doug Kee: "Whenever I was around, the vibe was cool. Everything seemed to be perfectly all right. Even after their divorce the vibe was cool."

It was not that Syreeta and Stevie had fallen out of love. The two of them are, in fact, still the best of friends and if ever one of them would need help – the other would be around in no time. From what Stevie's friends have told me, the main reason their *marriage* came to an end was a very obvious one:

Both of them, Syreeta as well as Stevie, had great ambitions. They both wanted to make a career. Only: Stevie had already gotten much further in making his dreams come true while Syreeta had only just started. It would, of course, have been very easy for Syreeta to cling on to Stevie's fame and use him as a stepping-stone. Instead Syreeta wanted to make it on her own terms.

Syreeta Annette Wright spent her childhood in Pennsylvania where she was more or less raised by her mother and grandparents. Syreeta's father had died when she was a young child.

"As soon as I could talk I also started singing," she says laughingly, when she talks about the old days. Syreeta was brought up religiously and the first tunes that she sang were those she had listened to in church. "When I was four years old I used to sing the *Lord's Prayer* and my mother would hold her breath until I made the high notes. I always started out about eight notes higher than everyone else. Fortunately I still have that range."

When Syreeta was in her teens, the family moved to Detroit

but Syreeta was enrolled into a private school in South Carolina. "My mother wanted to give me the best education possible." In this school Syreeta started writing poetry and she was also introduced to all kinds of music. Syreeta: "The school opened my eyes to the many possibilities there are in life. It was then that I knew that I wanted to become a professional singer. But I had also been taught the importance of having an ordinary job first, so that I would always have something to fall back on if a career in show business did not work."

Syreeta was very ambitious. She finished school with good notes and then went back to Detroit. There she joined Motown as a secretary. "If I have to work in a normal job to be able to live I decided it might as well be a job with a record company. At least that brought me nearer to the music that I loved so much."

Her intention to become a singer was not a well-kept secret at Motown, and she was lucky enough to get the same opportunity that Motown had given Martha Reeves years ago: they used her to do backing vocals on studio sessions. Syreeta: "They even cut a solo single with me under the name of Rita Wright. I was also supposed to do an album. But when my single *I Can't Give Back The Love I Feel/Something On My Mind* (both Ashford & Simpson tunes, release date 11 January 1968) flopped, they got off the idea. The general opinion was that I sounded too average and didn't have my own style."

Nevertheless Rita Wright did more sessions, trying to find the right tune and the right direction. Some of the productions were done by Stevie. Syreeta: "This is how we met, but it took a little while until we fell in love." Apart from solo recordings Syreeta worked as a session singer and a secretary at Motown and she also wrote a lot of poetry: "It helps you to sort yourself out. When I was at school I had written a lot of poetry, mainly about things that I didn't understand. By writing them down, formulating them, I could put things in perspective and then figure them out for myself."

Syreeta, who had always been more interested in things happening around her than in just the relationship of two people, wrote many poems about her favourite subject:

"Something I was most curious about was how the universe revolves and that type of thing."

Syreeta's poetry was always very private to her and she would not share it with anybody except for her mother at times. But when she and Stevie grew closer, Syreeta felt that she could trust him and showed Steve some of the things that she had written: "One of the poems was called *Where Is The Man*. Steve said that he loved it and insisted that we would put music to it. We actually did as a matter of fact. But then it turned out to be something very personal and we never cut it."

Instead Stevie invited Syreeta to take part in working on his songs. Syreeta: "I got all butterflies, not really believing that he was all that serious about it, but he was." They co-wrote *Signed, Sealed, Delivered, I'm Yours, It's A Shame* and many more songs. Some of them are on Stevie's album *Where I'm Coming From*.

While working together more and more frequently it did not take Syreeta and Stevie much longer to find that they had fallen in love. Syreeta: "I think the reason for Stevie to trust me was that he could feel that I was in love with *him*. Not with the *star* that he was. I have always admired Steve, but even then I had never gotten so far that I would fall off my feet when given a chance to meet him. To me he was a great musician who I respected to find that he was also the most lovable man."

They got engaged and on 14 September 1970 they married. The wedding ceremony was outrageous. All their friends turned up to congratulate the couple – including Berry Gordy, the Motown boss himself.

"Stevie was so nervous that he was 40 minutes late for the wedding. Believe me, I was getting nervous, too. But when he turned up he explained what had happened: while dressing for the ceremony poor Steve had developed a sudden nose-bleed . . ."

Then Stevie was rushed into the side door of Detroit's Burnette Baptist church, where Syreeta was waiting for him. Again everybody was wondering if Stevie would really make it: the crowd of fans that had gathered almost blocked the entrance...

Meanwhile Syreeta's and Stevie's parents had lit the candles that signified the start of the ceremony, officiated by the Reverend J. A. Caldwell, pastor of Burnette church. Stevie's valet and cousin, John Harris, acted as their best man and John's wife Darlene as matron of honour.

Berry Gordy, who had been in Los Angeles on business, had especially flown into Detroit to personally give the couple all his best wishes. Mr. and Mrs. Berry Gordy sr., his brother Fuller and his sisters Gwen Gordy Fuqua and Esther Edwards, senior vice-president of Motown as well as her husband, State Representative George H. Edwards, were also there.

After the brief wedding ceremony the newly-wed couple and their three hundred guests had lunch at Detroit's posh Mauna Loa restaurant. Syreeta: "It was such an amazing day. Everybody was just high on our happiness and Steve and I were above the clouds anyway. Spiritually and in the other sense. Because while all our guests were celebrating our wedding Stevie and I had gotten on a plane that brought us to Bermuda." There the couple spent their honeymoon. They came back to work on the first album that they had co-written.

"While Stevie and I worked on *Where I'm Coming From* we had a lot of serious talks about the future, his and mine. We both knew that Steve had to break away from Motown's control completely in order to be as creative as he wanted to be. I felt the same for myself."

It was after Steve's 21st birthday that he and Syreeta really started writing the kind of music they wanted to. But that was also when their problems started. Jim Gilstrap, who worked as a session singer with both of them at the time:

"The thing with Stevie is that he'd be in the studio most of the time and then, when he comes home, first thing he does is sit at the piano. And his woman, she wants to be with her man. Not just listen to his tapes and him playing music all the time. How can a woman cope with that, day after day? And also when he finishes work he's tired and out. Steve only sleeps a few hours per day and when he's awake he makes music. A woman needs more attention than that."

Syreeta herself said: "He gets up with his tape recorder or going to the piano and he goes to bed the same way. And in between that he's in the studio . . . " And Stevie was once quoted as having said: "Writing songs for me has no certain space or time. It doesn't matter when or where. I compose a song when I'm eating or drinking or *even when I make love* . . ."

But it was not only a lack of attention. Much more weighed the fact that Stevie already had a career to build another one upon while Syreeta was in her beginnings. She did go to the studio with Steve, but most of the time they worked on his new album. Not on hers. And even when they recorded Syreeta's first solo album it was mainly the work of Stevie:

Three of the nine tracks that were on the *Syreeta* album were written by Stevie. Another three tracks the two of them had co-written, one was the Lennon/McCartney title *She's Leaving Home*, another was by Smokey Robinson/Robert Rogers *What Love Has Joined Together* and only one song on her album was written by Syreeta alone.

Apart from guitar (Buzzy Feiton), bass (Scott Edwards), drums (Keith Copeland) who were Wonderlove members and strings (Julian Gaillard Orchestra) Stevie played all other instruments. *She's Leaving Home* he even played all alone. On three tracks Stevie, who had produced the album in association with Margouleff and Cecil used his Wonderlove singers Linda Tucker, Lani Groves, Gloria Barley and Jim Gilstrap for backing vocals.

Stevie had also together with Yusuf Rahman and Trevor Lawrence (who played bell tree on one track) arranged the music. The album was recorded at the Electric Lady, New York, Chrystal Industries, Los Angeles and the Olympic Studios, London.

Whatever way you look at it, Stevie dominates the album. On *To Know You Is To Love You* (Wright/Wonder), a song that was also recorded by B. B. King, Stevie even sings the first verse.

Also the first cut on the *Syreeta* album is a Stevie Wonder tune that he did on *Music Of My Mind: I Love Every Little Thing About You*. No wonder that the critics wrote "With his songs and arrangements and even his voice in the backing it sounds like a Stevie Wonder album with a girl singer."

The next track, *Black Maybe* (Wonder) deals with the colour problem.

> *You've seen the way they've done your boy in*
> *And your boy's still down after 300 years . . .*

but then reveals black pride:

> *Black maybe it's time to wake up and come around.*

The next song is one of my favourite tracks on the album. It is a happy, straightforward love song, but it has a different twist to it. *Keep Him Like He Is* was written by Syreeta and Stevie:

> *God looked on this tired earth*
> *And planned a major change*
> *And after many tries he smiled*
> *To see you standing there . . . Saying*
> *I'll keep him like he is . . .*

The last cut on the first album side is the one that Syreeta wrote. *Happiness* is another love song but comes close to the usual cliché with lines like:

> *In My heaven here on earth I found my paradise*
> *All the laughter in my heart I credit to your smile.*
> *Happiness is seeing all the stars in your eyes*
> *Happiness is knowing you are loved . . .*

Syreeta's interpretation of the Beatles' *She's Leaving Home* is excellent. And Stevie, playing synthesizer, also experimented with the bag and makes better use of it than on his *Music Of My Mind* album. Stevie: "This throat sound amplifier creates an emotion in that the voice is low. And it frightens you a little. I was just playing the Arp, not really singing, but playing the notes and moving my mouth." With the bag Stevie imitated the parents' voices in the background

> *We gave her most of our lives*
> *Sacrificed most of our lives*
> *We gave her everything money could buy . . .*

while Syreeta performs the song with tremendous feeling.

What Love Has Joined Together is an old Smokey Robinson/ Robert Rogers song and *How Many Days* (Wonder) sound also like you have heard it all before. With this tune you get the idea that it is quite an arbitrary mixture of various melodies and lyrics that Stevie put together (everything from *Blowin' In The Wind* to *I Could Have Danced All Night* from *My Fair Lady*):

> *How many years must a girl be lonely*
> *Before she ever finds her goal*
> *How many days must my heart be broken*
> *Before you come home again . . .*

The ninth track finally deals more or less with the same theme as *Something Out Of The Blue* that Syreeta and Stevie had written for the *Where I'm Coming From* album. First you are lonely, then love brings you happiness: *Baby Don't You Let Me Lose This*:

> *And now the days don't seem so all alone*
> *You brought me back to life again*
> *Now I have somewhere to belong*
> *You brought me back to life . . .*

This first album was not as well accepted by the critics as Syreeta had hoped for. Today she calls it "a bit ahead of time" but nevertheless declares this LP a big step forward in her own career. Stevie, on his side, thinks that his association with the album might have led to the critics' not accepting it. "I told Motown I did not want Syreeta's album to be promoted as a husband/wife thing, because I didn't think that would be good for her. But what can you do? Once people knew that I was involved they thought that that was the interesting thing to write about."

Stevie *could* have done something about it by using a pseudonym – if he really wanted to avoid this association. But he didn't, and Syreeta was the one who was least upset about Steve's involvement being known. "Why shouldn't I work with someone who is a great, great artist and settle for second best just because this artist happens to be my husband? That, I think, would have been the most ridiculous thing to do. Even if Steve and I had not gotten married I would have liked him to help me with my album. He has also written songs for other people and produced others than just himself or me. And whoever he worked with is as proud of that as I am."

The main difficulty, Syreeta and Stevie's friends assume, was what Stevie talked about in his song *Superwoman*:

> *Mary wants to be a superwoman*
> *And try to boss the bull around . . .*

Stevie, the bull (his birthsign is Taurus) did not want to be "bossed" around. In many interviews Stevie said about the break-up of his marriage: "Syreeta is a Leo and, well, Leo and Taurus are both very strong signs and they both want to lead."

Syreeta, although very loving, wanted a partnership more than a male-dominated marriage. She did not want to submit to Stevie but lead her own life. Stevie for his part needed a woman who fitted more into the old-fashioned husband/wife picture. Syreeta: "The problem with Steve and I was that our needs at that particular time were different. They were different to the extent that we just did not complement each other. It had nothing to do with did we love each other or didn't we.

"It just had something to do with the fact that what he needed I could not give him and what I needed he could not give me. And love had nothing to do with it. We didn't know enough about being alive on this earth. We hadn't lived long enough, we had no experience that could have helped us out at that time."

When they knew that their marriage would not work out, Syreeta was independent enough within herself to be able to leave Stevie. She did not want a man in order to feel secure – socially or financially. She only accepted living with someone as long as it was good. And because she loved him. And as a woman in love Syreeta was like any other woman: she wanted her man to not only work with her or she with him – but to just be together at times and have some privacy.

Syreeta rarely had Stevie to herself. Not only because he was in the studio so much but also because he had a number of girlfriends. Doug Kee: "See, there you've got Stevie the superstar. He was really burning at this time – he still is – and going to a lot of places. And all the women just throw themselves at him, which makes it very easy to say yes and very hard to say no. At least to say no all the time. I don't know if anyone in this world would have that much strength and you can't fault somebody for not saying no."

Ira Tucker: "I think that Stevie has a very heavy sexy image. He really turns chicks on. Maybe it's because they know that it is a whole different trip with Stevie who is blind than with some cat who can see everything. He is so much more sensitive than the average man, his stroke is different, it's a sensory thing. You just ought to look at the girls when Steve wears his shirt open. They just love to see his chest, his broad neck. And Stevie also has a very expressive face."

Gypsie Jones looks at it from another point of view: "Steve is so many people. And that makes it so hard for him to be a one-woman man. Apart from the fact that women just spoil him. They fall at his feet and offer themselves to him. I often tease Steve about that.

"But seriously, for people like him it is difficult to love just one woman. While one of them may have a certain part in her character that fulfils his needs there is another woman who has something else to her character which matches his needs in another part of his character. And this is something that is very hard for a woman to understand and to cope with.

"But with Stevie, knowing that he is that way it would be a selfish thing for any woman to think that 'He's mine and I possess him and he is only my lover and he loves only me.' Instead I feel that everyone of Steve's women should be grateful for the time and love and attention that he gives to each and every one of them.

"It is hard not to love a man like him. Steve is a powerhouse full of energy. A person like him is rare. And any kind of moments that you spend with him are precious moments. And he knows a lot. You can talk with him about anything. Plus he is a genius that can relate his feelings into his music. And his messages which I think have spiritually been given to him. I mean there are a lot of people who can play nine different instruments and they don't play them like he plays them. He's a master. But then when you talk to him about it he is very modest."

Stevie is also very modest when interviewers ask him about his sex life. Opposed to what friends of his or people he works or worked with say, he does not necessarily admit to his obviously many lovers. He told one interviewer: "Sex, even though it is beautiful, is a man's weakness. All of mankind should be a little above that. It should be like one of the lesser things that he thinks about, because man has let that rule the world, control the world.

"Physical sex is not as important as communicating mentally. Mental intercourse is far more significant. It heightens everything. It makes what you do sexually so much better. To me, sex is a very intimate relationship that you share with the person that you're with, and that's it. That makes the two of you get it on. That makes you feel good."

This part of an article in *Soul* made people who know Stevie well burst out laughing. Especially after his new album, *Songs In The Key Of Life* had come out. In the booklet that goes with it Stevie admits to having "a polygamous" mind:

> My mind's heart must be polygamous and my spirit is married to many and my love belongs to all.
> Sweets Je t'aime
> Francine, Lois, Diane, Veronica, Angie, Syreeta, Yvonne, CoCo, Pam, Yolanda Z., YOLANDA and...............
> > (there's an empty space for you).

And when you ask Stevie's friends if they can think of any hobbies that he has, you usually get the answer: other than women and his daughter Aisha none that I can think of.

Lee Garrett is more direct: "Fucking and music – that's Steve's life."

The women in Stevie's life are generally all very beautiful. Ira Tucker: "You put him in a room with a bunch of women and he always picks the foxiest lady." Although Steve is not into anything visual at all, he does have a knack for choosing the most attractive girls around. Like CoCo, the lady who accompanied him a lot after his divorce from Syreeta. CoCo is a model and she has also started singing. Steve's relationship to CoCo was the usual on-and-off one. Today CoCo is married and has a little baby boy, but she and Steve are still good friends.

The same with Yvonne Wright, a scorpio lady Steve has co-written a number of songs with. Steve: "I met Yvonne a little after I met Syreeta. So like we broke up and then after my marriage we got back together again, broke up again, got back together again and I feel we have to get it together." Yvonne was on tour with Stevie when he came to England in 1974 and even though he chose another woman to be the mother of his child, Yvonne and Steve still see quite a lot of each other.

Session singer Gloria Barley is supposed to have played another big role in Steve's life. If you can trust the rumour, Steve wrote *You Are The Sunshine Of My Life* for her. Steve does not admit to it, but keeps it a secret who he dedicated this song to. On the other hand, Gloria sings the female part in it . . .

Trying to find a common denominator for Stevie's women, Doug Kee told me: "They are usually slim and I'd say bubbly. But not the empty-headed type. Not the old dumb-blonde syndrome. But they are fun people. And they all have extraverted personalities."

One of the things that allows Stevie to have more than one love without wanting to prove anything or hurt anybody is the fact that Stevie does not expect his women to be faithful to him. He says that he used to be jealous but then succeeded in overcoming this feeling: "This is one thing that I've tried to do, and I've done it successfully, that when you realize nothing really belongs to you, you begin to appreciate having an understanding of just where your head is at. That makes you feel so much better."

Anyway, apart from other things Syreeta did not seem prepared to cope with Stevie's way of life and asked for the divorce. Which everybody, Stevie as well as his and her friends, admired Syreeta for. It would have been so easy for her to put up with it and stick around for Steve's money and/or his fame. Gypsie:

"Everybody loved Syreeta for that. Most of all Steve. He even said that her leaving him proved that she cared. Believe me, a woman like Syreeta is one in a million."

The end of Stevie's and Syreeta's marriage was not the end of their musical partnership, though. Apart from singing backing vocals on Stevie's albums, Steve produced another Syreeta LP that, again, the two of them had co-written. This album is called *Stevie Wonder presents Syreeta* and it came out in 1974. Half of the tracks were written by Stevie, the other five by the two of them.

Cause We've Ended As Lovers is autobiographical. The melody that Steve composed for this song is melancholic, soft. The lyrics deal with all the memories that they share and in the chorus Syreeta sings:

> *Cause we've ended now as lovers*
> *Does that mean that we each other can't be friends?*

Stevie: "I always feel that Syreeta and I were closer before being married. It was better. And to stay close, before falling out of love, we decided to split. So that we could love each other forever."

In *Just A Little Piece Of You* (Wonder/Wright) Syreeta seems to draw a clear line between her and other people in connection with Steve:

> *They want to hold you, touch you*
> *They all want to be near to you*
> *But I'm satisfied with*
> *Just a little piece of you . . .*

But then the song ends with the words:

That's all you give me . . .

The next two tracks are both very short and seem to come right out of a musical: *Waitin' For The Postman* (1.52) and *When Your Daddy's Not Around* (1.11). As mere album tracks they don't seem to make much sense and sound more like a gimmick.

I Wanna Be On Your Side (Wonder) is a duet with Syreeta and G. C. Cameron and the last track on the second album side is a song Syreeta put the lyrics to. "It is basically about my outlook on life and God. Sometimes I feel so good inside and I wonder who in the world is feeling like I am, and I just want to groove with them. So I think that He just deserves a thankyou every now and then." For example in the form of Syreeta's song *Universal Sound Of The World*:

Sometimes it's hard for me to see
What you've got planned to make for me
But I will stop you here and now
And tell you I'm glad you're my friend
Thanking you for the sun in the sky
Thanking you for the moon and moonlight . . .

The first cut on the first album side is another song with a religious influence *I'm Goin' Left ('Til You Lead Me To The Right)* by Stevie and Syreeta.

The next song is a quick waltz which is beautifully built up to a melody that is *Spinnin' And Spinnin'* faster and faster. This song puts you in a kind of fun-fair mood and you feel like joining Syreeta on the merry-go-round.

Your Kiss Is Sweet is a reggae number and announced as:

This song goes out to all you fellas
Who think your kisses are as sweet as candy
But honey got you beat by a million miles . . .

The next cut is a Stevie Wonder song, a sexy soul number called *Come And Get This Stuff*. The tenth track finally, *Heavy*

Day (Wonder/Wright), is in the line of "the show must go on" songs:

> *She's feeling along just like yesterday*
> *Yeah, the show is going on her smile is in place*
> *She's feeling along with crowds everywhere*
> *'Cause the love she sings about*
> *Isn't here for her to share . . .*

Only in the last verse Syreeta, the singer, identifies herself with the entertainer she sings about.

This album was also arranged by Stevie apart from the strings (Paul Riser). Again the musicians came from Stevie's band Wonderlove: drums: Ollie Brown, bass: Reggie McBride, guitar: Marlo Henderson, Mike Sembello, trumpet: Steven Madaio and tenor sax: Dennis Morouse. The backing vocals were also sung by one-time Wonderlove members: Deniece Williams, Lani Groves, Shirley Brewer, Anita Sherman and also Minnie Riperton "who did two friends a favour" as Syreeta puts it.

This second album did not help Syreeta to get the break she had hoped for. So Syreeta decided to give her solo career a break and first of all try and find herself. She spent some time with Transcendental Meditation as she had done before. She also travelled to the heart of the bushland in Ethopia for what she considered to be "a period of self-intro-spection". Syreeta had done a pilgrimage to Africa before and this time while she was over there she trained TCM and was also a teacher of the technique for children and adults.

When Syreeta came back to Los Angeles, where she lives now, she got married and is also continually working in community projects for black children from the age of six to ten in what she calls "sessions concerning the way they relate to life. We ask them a lot of questions."

While Syreeta was pregnant with her first child she took up writing songs again and also worked as a session singer for artists like Billy Preston and Jermaine Jackson. At the end of 1976 Syreeta's baby boy was born and she went back into the studio to do her third album – the first one that was not produced by Stevie.

One To One Syreeta calls "a project of spirit – a one to one harmour love – a refreshening touch of joy humbly dedicated to YOU and the birth of my manchild, Jamal (which is kindness) Hekima (which is wisdom, understanding and intelligence)."

Syreeta's *One To One* album was produced by Leon Ware (who did Quincy Jones' *Body Heat* and Marvin Gaye's *I Want You* album) and co-produced by Syreeta and Curtis Robertson jr. Out of the seven tracks five were co-written by either Syreeta and Leon Ware, Syreeta and Curtis Robertson jr. or all three of them. One song was written by Ware/Robertson and another one by Stevie.

Harmour Love is the only Stevie Wonder song on Syreeta's new album. It was also produced by Steve, but had been released as a single before (June 1975). Only this song and the musicians remind of old times: Ray Parker, Michael Sembello, Eddie "Bongo" Brown and Gregory Phillinganes are amongst them. And also Stevie's recording engineers for *Songs In The Key Of Life*, Gary Olazabal and John Fischbach, engineered *One To One*.

Jim Gilstrap, who did backing vocals on this album, told me: "It was good for Syreeta that she could do her own thing. You could really watch her grow more and more secure of herself with every recording session. And as much as I admire Stevie's work – I definitely feel that it is better for her to work with other people."

Syreeta herself is pleased with the album: "The vocals are much better, because of my own development. I've studied harder, and I know that I'm a better vocalist, because I've improved my technique."

Overall, the album has a much more mellow or laid-back feel to it than Syreeta's first two LPs. It is a more mature album, the girl has grown into a woman. Syreeta: "Now, more than ever, my career and music are very important for me."

Syreeta's being a mother does not stand in conflict with her artistic determination: "I believe that it makes everybody in my family much happier to find a satisfied woman than some-one who would desperately try to lead a homelife only. I have Jamal with me most of the time and it's fine. I respect him as a little man and he has everything he needs. But he will also have to learn to respect me and my needs. I have far too much to do in life than to just want to sit at home and be a housewife and a mother only. And I find it easy to combine everything."

Syreeta lives about a ten-minute drive from the Regency Residential Hotel where Stevie lives in Los Angeles. They still meet when he is in town and they are both glad that things have worked out the way they did. Is there any sadness left that the two of them could not make it as lovers? "No," Syreeta answers. "We've had a beautiful time together and for a while it was almost like heaven. But one time you just have to come down and that's no reason to be sad. I would say I am happy about having had this time instead of crying over it. I feel the same way that Steve does: we both haven't lost anything but gained a friend for a lifetime."

Today Steve also thinks back with a smile. And if he was sad that their marriage had come to an end, it only lasted for a little while. Because Stevie had so much to do that there was not much room left for worries.

By the middle of 1972 *Music Of My Mind* was on its way to becoming a gold album and Stevie was already working on his next project: *Talking Book*. Also he was busy getting his new band together. Stevie got ready to go on a 50-day tour through Canada and the United States.

He had been booked as the support act for "The Greatest Rock'n Roll Band In The World" – the Rolling Stones.

CHAPTER EIGHT

Love Having You Around

On 3 June 1972 the Rolling Stones were to start their 50-date tour from Vancouver, Canada to New York. So Stevie, who supported them, had to do a lot of preparation.

In the beginning of 1972 Stevie had toured England with his own band, Wonderlove, which he had formed in 1971. The original formation did not stay together long as Steve was constantly trying to find musicians who were even better.

At the same time Steve was getting his staff together. Now he decided who would be his various managers. In the late sixties Tom Sherman, a disc jockey from Detroit, had been his road manager. Doug Kee: "Then he fired Tom and my father took over. Although his actual job was to be Stevie's band director, he didn't mind working as a road manager. By this time Steve was already working with musicians sensitive enough to know what Stevie wanted – so he did not need a musical director any more.

"After my father a guy named Charlie Collins took over. Charlie is really bad. He did not take no orders but from Steve and the Lord above. And he's got such a wide chest that nobody dared to go past him unless he had permission to. Charlie also has a detective agency in Detroit and used to be a Federal Narc in New York. He really stayed with Steve for a long time. We were working together when in 1972 I was hired to take care of Steve's equipment."

Originally Doug had been offered a job as Steve's valet. Dress him, drive him, make sure that everything was all right and get Stevie to wherever he had to go in time. "But when I was supposed to start working with Steve, he had changed his mind. His brother Milton had come out of the Air Force the same time as I did and Steve employed him as well as his brother Calvin. They both took care of Stevie's personal things and were also his companions. His brother Larry only worked with Steve for a little while. Nobody knows what he really does now. The word goes that he wants to be a musician, too, and that he's playing guitar somewhere."

Today Calvin is Stevie's valet and Milton more or less runs Steve's office in New York. Another relative of Steve's, his cousin John Harris, acts as his driver.

Also in 1972 Stevie made Ira Tucker jr., son of Ira Tucker sr. who is a founder member of the Dixie Hummingbirds, his publicist. Stevie and Ira jr. had met through Ira's sisters Sandray and Linda Tucker, original back-up vocalists in Wonderlove. Ira was originally hired to do the choreography for Steve's live shows, but then Steve offered him the job as his publicist. Ira: "I told him that I didn't know anything about this kind of work. But Stevie said I should just try. So I did, and surprisingly enough it worked out fine."

Stevie's personal manager now is Chris Jones and his road manager today is Reggie Wiggins who formerly worked with the Jackson Five and the Supremes for five years. Stevie also has working for him an average of four roadies to handle his equipment. But Stevie's turnover in roadies is incredibly high and before you get their names in print they have changed again. Doug: "Stevie keeps hiring and firing these cats. As a matter of fact I lasted with him longer than anybody – three years. But on the other hand it is easy for Stevie to find new staff, and also people who have worked with him usually don't have any difficulty in finding a new job."

When Stevie fires somebody it is over and done with within five minutes. He just tells you that it has been nice but that he thinks it is better to split. Depending on how long you have been with him Stevie pays you a salary for the next few months but at the same time asks you to leave at once. Doug:

"Stevie doesn't give any notice at all and it makes sense, too. There is no point in hanging around for another couple of months like Ford, when Carter was elected President. The vibe just isn't right because you know that you're going to go and everybody else knows that you've been sacked and work isn't fun any more. So Stevie prefers to pay you out. Because any way you look at it he's got to pay you for a certain amount of time anyway but everybody saves having the hassle of bad vibes."

"Bad vibes" is one thing that a creative person like Stevie definitely cannot afford. Especially not when he is on the road with his "whole entourage", as everybody calls his staff laughingly. With that many people working for him Stevie does not want to run the risk of anybody starting any kind of quarrel. And there is no way that Steve could reduce the number of his employees; he needs them all.

The road manager is responsible for the group on the road. He pays the bills for hotels and transport; he pays the band as well as keeping them together; and he is responsible for the equipment and its handling. The personal manager is employed to handle the bookings and approve the contracts when setting up tours, and he is responsible for everything that happens on the road.

The publicist has to take care of the press. He sets up interviews and also has to make sure that his act is written about even when nothing much happens. When Stevie stops touring to work on his latest album Ira has to see to it that Stevie is not forgotten despite the fact that he is not appearing in public. The valet has to handle personal things of Steve's like his clothing and make sure that he always looks all right.

These employees are quite stable with Stevie. The roadies and band members are not. Before Steve left to tour England in early 1972 he cleared out the whole band. The only musician he kept on salary was the bass player Scott Edwards. Within another month Stevie had a new band together. But even with the new Wonderlove there were frequent changes. People came and went and some of those who had left came back again after a while. Jim Gilstrap and Doug Kee who were on this tour to England and stayed with Stevie for quite a while cannot even remember exactly who was in the band when. Jim:

"Wonderlove is basically supposed to be a steady band. But a lot of the people who were first in the group are no longer there. And he had some really heavy musicians. Like he had a saxophone player called Dave Sanborne who has his own album out now. He had a guitar player Buzzy Feiton who at one time worked with Dylan and who also does his own thing now. He had a drummer by the name of Keith Copeland. There were some really bad cats.

"He had Deniece Williams singing with him. She's now a solo act on CBS. Lani Groves, who's singing with Roberta Flack now. He had Sandray and Linda Tucker. Linda is Linda Lawrence now and with the Supremes. He had Susaye Green who is also with the Supremes now. Shirley Brewer has been with Steve for a long time and it looks like she's gonna be there for another while. She's very faithful. And he had some chick called Jackson who was really odd. She couldn't really sing and got eliminated soon. And he had me."

Doug: "Yeah, Deniece left for the Stones tour. She had some trouble at home and Loris Harvin replaced her. She was with him for about a year and then Steve fired her and he hired her back some time in 1975. She stayed for a while and then she quit. And Buzzy Feiton – he was really a monster. He replaced two cats when he came – that's how bad a guitar player he was. But Buzzy quit about a year later. He had Ray Parker on guitar. He does a lot of sessions and you can hardly pick up an album without seeing his name on it. The same with Ollie Brown, the drummer who came into the band during the Stones tour. He had another guitar player Ralph Hammer. After Ray and Ralph left Steve got Michael Sembello who is still with him now and Marlo Henderson who is not. Reggie McBride replaced Scott Edwards on bass when he left. He really played his ass off that week when he came in. That was at the Whiskey or the Troubador in L.A. and somebody from Rare Earth saw him, made him an offer and he couldn't refuse. It took him about two weeks to make up his mind but he left us. Gloria Barley sang with him for a while and Terry Hendricks. And he had a bongo player, Daniel Ben Zebulon.

"When he got his band together they were practising in a

place called Baggies or something in New York City which is a loft. A dirty old dingy loft which was a rehearsal studio or whatever. And Steve rehearsed for a good while before he went on the road."

Other Wonderlove members at one time or the other were Steve Madaio (trumpet), Trevor Lawrence, Dennis Morouse (saxophone), Clarence Bell (organ) and Debra Wilson (backing vocals).

Musicians that were with Wonderlove when this book went in print are Raymond Pounds (drum), Nathan Watts (bass), Ben Bridges (rhythm guitar), Gregory Phillinganes (keyboards), Raymond Maldonado (trumpet), Hank Redd (alto saxophone) as well as Trevor Lawrence and Steve Madaio who seem to be the most faithful ones.

The reason for Steve's high turnover in musicians and backing vocalists is that most of them get to do their own thing after a while. Jim Gilstrap's reason for leaving was different: "I was doing my solo things anyway, even before I met Steve. The only trouble was that after a while people started telling me that I sounded just like Steve. That is when I quit." Laughingly Jim adds: "I'm not going to fight the establishment. And also, there are enough other singers already who sound just like Steve: George Benson and Danny Hathaway, for instance. I'd rather find my own style." Jim is right – when George had his hit *Nature Boy* in spring 1977 at first everybody thought it was a Steve Wonder single.

In early 1972 when Stevie was on his British tour he also did sessions in London studios. Ron Wood dropped in on one and Steve played drums on a few tracks for Eric Clapton (which have never been released so far). It was at the same time that Stevie bumped into Jeff Beck and they did some work together. Jeff plays guitar on Stevie's *I Believe (When I Fall In Love It Will Be Forever)*, which is a track on *Talking Book*. And Stevie plays clavinet on Beck's version of Stevie's *Superstition*, another song from *Talking Book*. This song caused arguments between Stevie and Jeff Beck and it almost meant the end of their friendship. While Jeff Beck insists that Stevie had given Beck, Bogart & Appice *Superstition* to play, Stevie gets himself mixed up in various versions of what happened back in 1972. Here are three of them:

"I had done a concert with Jeff in Detroit and we became sort of friends. I said that I was gonna write a tune for him one day. So when I met him again I had written a song called *Thelonius* for him. When it came to doing the album (*Talking Book*) he heard some of the numbers and wanted to play on *Maybe Your Baby* (Steve used Ray Parker jr. instead). Then he heard *Superstition* and he really wanted to do that one. But I couldn't see a guitar on that. It needed the horn section to make it drive. Anyway I said I'd think about it. Meanwhile Jeff said he wanted to record *Superstition* himself, before I did. Look, I told him, there was no way. Apart from wanting it myself I knew that Motown would go crazy if I gave a song like that away. Anyway, Jeff's cut it himself now and it's really a bit of a rip-off because he's just copied my version – I guess he thinks it's more commercially acceptable or something. I think that's kinda crazy. He's a good guitarist and I don't understand people who have their own artistry not using it."

In his version number 2 Steve says: "Jeff told me he'd like to record something funky, so I said I'd write a song for him. I said I'd cut it, too, and maybe include it on my album. Jeff said he didn't want my track to sound like his and I assured him it wouldn't. I played clavinet on his session, then finished off my own version and put it on the album, but his didn't come out. Then Motown told me they wanted to lift my version from the album, as a single. They insisted, as I hadn't put out a single to coincide with the last album. I understand that Jeff got upset about it, but it wasn't my fault and his disc hadn't been released, anyway. I tried to call him in Los Angeles, but he wouldn't take the call. I'll write another song for him, I'll do that."

The third version finally goes like this: "Well, I'd written a thing for Beck, Bogart & Appice – they wanted *Maybe Your Baby*, and I said no, do this, this is even better. I put a drum track down, a clavinet, and the basic melody, and then I put the Moog bass on. I didn't have no words yet and that turned out to be *Superstition*. Jeff wanted the track which I couldn't

179

give him, because of Motown so I said 'I'll give you a seven (a $7\frac{1}{2}$ ips tape) and you all work on it and I'll play on the session.' And I wrote another thing for them which was even more like Jeff Beck, a thing called *Thelonius*, but I told him that I was using *Superstition* for my album. The tune I wanted to release as a single was *You Are The Sunshine Of My Life* which was my favourite. But Motown did not want that and another tune I would have liked to be the single was *Big Brother* but that was done too late to come out as a single. Motown decided they wanted to release *Superstition*. I said Jeff wanted it, and they told me I needed a strong single in order for the album to be successful. My understanding was that Jeff would be releasing *Superstition* long before I was going to finish my album; I was late giving them *Talking Book*. Jeff recorded *Superstition* in July, so I thought it would be out. But I *did* promise him the song, and I'm sorry it happened and that he came out with some of the arrogant statements that he came out with. I will get another tune to him that I think is exciting, and if he wants to do it, cool."

For a little while Jeff did not speak to Steve, but he put *Superstition* on the album *Beck, Bogart & Appice* (1973). In 1975 the quarrel was completely forgotten and Jeff Beck used two Stevie Wonder tracks for his gold album *Blow By Blow*: *Thelonius* and *'Cause We've Ended As Lovers*.

The reason Stevie sometimes tells different stories about the same event is a simple one. Lee Garrett: "Steve is so much into his music that he forgets everything else around him. So if you ask him something he will just answer the question from the top of his head and a few days later you get a different story – again from the top of his head. See, he never bothers too much about all the shit that the press wants to know about. So I don't think he even remembers how it actually was.

"Like, Stevie often makes promises and then does not keep them. But he doesn't do it on purpose – he just forgets. I remember a time when he rang me up in L.A. and asked me to come to New York for a session with him. I said, 'Yeah, man, I'd like to. But I'm down to my last penny. I can just about afford the airfare.' So Steve said that was nothing to worry about. He told me to get on the plane, check into the hotel and he'd come and pay me the money back as well as all other expenses.

"Anyway, I get there and Steve is gone. I'm broke. So I ring up his New York office and tell them that I have arrived. I wait for him one day, two days, three days and all of a sudden it's a fortnight. All I did was sit in the bloody hotel and wait for him. I couldn't even get a plane back. Finally I got through to Steve. What had happened was that he had completely forgotten about me, gone some place God knows where and played his music. His office had never considered my phone calls important enough to pass the messages on to him. So it wasn't Steve but the people around him and once he became aware of what was happening everything was fine. But it is really hard to keep Stevie's mind on something. That is why you get all this confusing stuff in the papers."

But 1972 held more rows for Stevie. When he was on tour with the Rolling Stones, the press kept writing about arguments between Stevie and members of the Stones. What had happened were two things. For one, Stevie was taking the Stones' huge white audiences by storm. Although he played second billing, the Stones Fans raved about him as much a they did about "The Greatest Rock'n Roll Band In The World". The other reason was, that in the middle of the tour Keith Copeland, the drummer, had a nervous breakdown and quit. Doug Kee:

"We tried to get a new drummer in a hurry. But within less than a day it is just impossible, not only because you have to find one who is good and free and he has to be flown in, but also because he has to know Steve's music to some degree. You can't collect someone from the airport at night and put him straight in a concert. That's no good. And without a drummer you also cannot do a gig. That was the trouble we had. But the next day we got Ollie Brown."

According to the daily papers the Stones were so upset about Stevie cancelling this one gig, that they claimed that Steve was partying instead of working. Keith Richard is also quoted as having called Stevie a "cunt". This again was supposed to have annoyed Stevie and he was quoted as having said: "If Keith did say that, he's just childish, because I love people too much to just want to fuck up and miss a show. And it's crazy, the things he said, if they were said – and if he did not say them, he should clarify them, because I will always hold this against him; I can't really face him, I'd feel funny in his presence."

Stevie was also said to have given the impression of never having liked Keith Richard too much from the start: "I had mixed emotions about where he was coming from, so I wouldn't be surprised if he said it, but I'm really not too surprised about anybody saying anything about anything. What really bugged me was that our drummer was in a very bad situation, mentally and spiritually. That's why he left. What climaxed the whole thing was, we got into an argument. I told Keith that he was rushing the temp – this was in Fort Worth, Texas (24 June) – and he said, 'I tell you what: You know how to play harmonica, you take the mike, you sing, and play drums and all that shit at the same time, 'cause I quit,' and he split.

"I called up the Stones and said, 'Look, man, our drummer left, and we might not be able to make the gig, so we'll try to make the second one but we won't be able to do the first show.' And they said 'Okay, that'll be cool.' The next thing, I saw the Stones and they heard the new drummer and said, 'Oh, out of sight!' Then the next thing was I read all this shit."

Fact is, despite all that has been written about the row between Stevie and the Stones, it was not as bad as it seemed. Doug Kee: "Nobody hated anybody, because we all did a lot of hanging out together. Like all the Stones and Stevie and his crew.

"The only argument that came up was the one about us not doing that one gig. But you've got to understand that. The Stones were kind of lost because of that, too. All of a sudden they didn't have a supporting act. And I can see them being dragged by the fact that we more or less let them down. Even if it wasn't Steve's fault.

"But I tell you what: if your best friend is mad at you and he calls you an asshole in the heat of the moment – and the

Stones were under a lot of stress, too – that's really nothing. Because you know he doesn't mean it and the next day it's forgotten. What happened wasn't all that serious. The papers blew it up out of proportion."

As successful as the tour was for Stevie, it put a lot of strain on everybody who was on it. Touring is not much fun anyway. Jim Gilstrap: "Mostly it is only one concert in one city. That means getting up early to catch a plane or bus and going to be late because the concerts do not finish until the middle of the night. And then you are so awake and turned on by the gig that you can't just crash and sleep. Usually you have a few drinks before you get into your hotel room and all of a sudden you realize it's four o'clock in the morning."

In addition to the usual stress that touring brings with it, the Stones tour caused a number of riots and put even more strain on everybody involved. At the opening concert at Pacific Coliseum, Vancouver, thirty policemen were injured when 2000 disappointed fans, who could not get any tickets, tried to gatecrash the sold-out gig.

On 13 June at the International Sports Arena, San Diego, California, sixty people got arrested and fifteen were injured. A day later, at Civic Arena, Tucson, Arizona, police used tear gas to disperse 200 to 300 youths who tried to gatecrash the concert. The following day brought more trouble: a forged ticket scare at University of New Mexico, Albuquerque, made people faint when others rushed for their seats.

On 17 July a bomb went off under a Stones' equipment truck in Montreal. The concert at the Forum started 45 minutes late, because new equipment had to be flown in from Los Angeles. The same day a riot started when people discovered that 3000 forged tickets had been sold. Two days later Mick Jagger and Keith Richard got arrested in Warwick, Rhode Island, after a scuffle at the airport with a photographer. Boston's mayor, Mr. Kevin White, went to jail and bailed them out so that they could make the concert at Boston Garden, Boston, Massachusetts.

There were also nice events, like on 4 July (Independence Day) at Robert F. Kennedy Stadium, Washington: Stevie and the Stones met their oldest fan, Mr. Lee Hurley from Baltimore. The 72-year-old who hobbled into the stadium with a walking stick told an amazed reporter: "I wanted to have a new experience."

The end of the tour fell on Mick Jagger's birthday. He was 28 on 26 July 1972 when they played at Madison Square Garden, New York. He was presented with a cake and a giant panda on stage and he threw rose petals and custard pies into the audience. After the final concert he was given a birthday party at the St. Regis Hotel where Count Basie performed.

Still, most of the tour was one big stress, not only for the musicians but also for the road crews. Touring means packing, unpacking, loading and unloading the bus. It is setting up equipment and a few hours later taking it off stage again. Touring is hard work. Doug Kee:

"Working for Stevie is a tough job but it is also a lot of fun. When I first met him – that was at the Apollo in New York about nine years ago – it blew my mind for a minute. And, to be honest, I never really got off the clouds when I was working with him. He has such a great personality and he's a hell of a musician. The best, as far as I am concerned. And he is always listening to music, music that's in his head. And that's what his whole trip is about: music and creativity.

"And he always has to have some kind of keyboards set up somewhere. Even when he's travelling. So the first thing I had to do was to get the equipment from whichever airport it was and on the way to the gig stop at his hotel. Then I would carry some keyboards up to his room so that he could do his thing. The same after the gig. I could not crash out before Stevie had his piano or something. Only very seldom would he say that he didn't want anything."

Doug also tells stories about planes he missed because Stevie often was not ready when Doug wanted to collect the instruments: "We were going to fly to Paris and then go to Cannes. That was in 1974 for the Midem Festival. So on my way to the airport I had to stop at Steve's place to put all his instruments in the truck that was already loaded with the rest of the equipment. Knowing Stevie, I got to his place early and there he was playing all kinds of instruments. So I just sat there for about an hour waiting for him to finish so that I could pack up and split. Steve kept playing. He was so much into it. Finally I just got up and said 'Hey, man, I'm sorry but if you want the equipment to make the plane I've got to pack up now.' So he said 'okay', I packed it all up and split.

"The equipment made the plane fine – only I had to get on it as well. So I left the truck at the airport for the fortnight – it was only something like a dollar and a quarter a day – and rushed to the terminal. All I could see was the plane as it took off. The only problem was that I had to collect the equipment at the other end. At this time I was 75 per cent of the road crew. Unfortunately there was no other flight to Paris that day and I had to take an early plane the next morning.

"That plane I got – but then I was pretty lost getting to Cannes. Eventually I managed to sign language my way on to a train to Cannes. But what I did not know was that it was a local. So it took me twelve hours to get there. So when I got in I called Stevie and told him what had happened. And he told me that he was half paranoid by that time because he didn't have an instrument.

"The equipment was still at the airport. It had not even been through customs yet. It took me ages to get it all cleared and still I had to carry some stuff to Steve's hotel before we did the gig. That's the way it is – Stevie just has to have his keyboards round him all the time."

Although working for Stevie requires much more energy and efficiency than other musicians ask for, he does not pay better salaries. Doug: "When I started out with him I was getting 90 dollars a week. That's after taxes, and it's very little. When I left in 1974 I came home with 160 dollars I think. Plus I was getting ten dollars per day on the road. But in the kind of hotels that we stayed in you can eat up ten dollars per day easily. Like the George V in Paris and all those posh places. The first time I was on the road with Steve and stayed in an hotel I thought they'd given me Stevie's room. It was that luxurious."

While Stevie supported the Rolling Stones the band members

were paid around 550 dollars a week. "That was only for a period of time, though. After that it got down because the tour wasn't making all that much money. But the good thing with Stevie is, that he paid everybody in the band the same amount of money. At least as long as I was there. And 550 dollars per week is not too bad, considered he had twelve musicians."

The fact that the tour with the Stones did not bring much money was something that Stevie admitted openly and that he had known beforehand. "It was not even meant to be a money-making thing. What I needed was exposure. I wanted to reach people. I feel there is so much through music that can be said. And I felt that the Stones' audiences were the kind of people that we could get to so I thought we should do it. My biggest aim was to introduce the new Stevie Wonder.

"Because all they really knew were songs like *Uptight* and *I Was Made To Love Her*. A lot of people asked for *Fingertips*, and that is exactly the thing I wanted to get away from. I don't want people to think 'Ah, this is Stevie Wonder who was a child star and for the rest of his life he'll be singing *Fingertips*.' I wanted to tell people that I had grown. Not only in years but within my music, too. It is the same with the Stones, Mick Jagger can't be singing *Satisfaction* for ever and ever. People have to realize that."

Stevie succeeded in telling the audience that he had matured. His show stole some of the Stones' limelight and the fans wondered why there was not at least one number in the concert that featured Stevie and his band together with the Stones. Critics called Stevie "too important to be a mere opening act".

Also during the Stones tour a live album was recorded. It featured the Stones and Stevie with Wonderlove. Originally this album was supposed to be in the shops by Christmas 1972 but then it was not issued. Steve: "The problem with being an artist and having managers is that, whenever money is involved, people want to get their share. So contractual hassles mean the album is probably doomed to stay in the can. It's a shame but that's the way it has to be."

On his tour with the Stones, Stevie introduced the songs of

his coming album *Talking Book*. Like *You Are The Sunshine Of My Life*, which could have been on *Music Of My Mind*, "but I thought it would get lost. I wanted to see what happened with the new Stevie Wonder first." Today this song has recorded by dozens of singers, including Liza Minelli and Frank Sinatra. This magical love song includes lines like:

> *I feel like this is the beginning,*
> *Though I've loved you for a million years,*
> *And if I thought our love was ending,*
> *I'd find myself drowning in my own tears . . .*

Steve says about this song today: "That song is very special. It's special in that it's a very true song. And it's a song that when I hear it I can't believe that I wrote it. You know, you write songs certain times and you feel good about them. I always feel good about them. And then sometimes I go 'Wow, did I write that?' Especially when I hear other people sing it. It's incredible to know that you were given the ability to write and that it came from within your heart and your mind. And that definitely happened with *You Are The Sunshine Of My Life*.'

Maybe Your Baby, the song that Jeff Beck is said to have wanted to record, is a number dominated by the Moog, and kind of scary. It contains pictures like

> *Heart's blazing like a five alarm fire,*
> *And I don't even give a dare . . .*

The next track is a melancholy love song. Although its title *You And I (We Can Conquer The World)* is optimistic, it has the sadness of farewell in it:

> *I am glad at least in my life I found someone*
> *That may not be here forever to see me through*
> *But I found strength in you.*

The next song is also about parting. Malcolm Cecil says about the album: "It is a talking book about Stevie's life." He wrote most of the songs when his and Syreeta's marriage was falling to pieces. *Tuesday Heartbreak* is a track in which

Stevie sings about his girl having found another man. But he does not really want to accept it . . .

I wanna be with you when the nightime comes,
I wanna be with you when the daytime comes,
I wanna stay, oh baby, lemme, baby with you . . .

The last cut on the first album side is a song where Stevie put music to lyrics that his on-and-off lover Yvonne Wright wrote. Her lyrics come very close to reality, too, in *You've Got It Bad Girl:*

Yes, you know the plans I am making,
Are intended to capture you.
So you practice false reactions,
To delay the things I do.

The song that drove Stevie's audiences wild and which caused problems with Jeff Beck was to be Steve's biggest hit so far. When it was released as a single it went platinum almost immediately: *Superstition.* Stevie: "I don't know why but I've seen a lot of people – especially black folks – who let superstition rule their lives. This is crazy. And the worst thing is, the more you believe in it the more bad things really happen to you. You're so afraid that something terrible is going to come up, that you are much more vulnerable. And also – you can always find something that fits into your superstitious belief. It's mad."

Thirteen months old baby, broke the lookin' glass,
Seven years of bad luck, the good things in your past.
When you believe in things that you don't understand,
Then you suffer.
Superstition ain't the way . . .

The next track is a song which Stevie got inspired to write after he had read *1984* by George Orwell:

Your name is big brother
You say that you're watching me on the tele . . .

But the song *Big Brother* is also about politicians:

You say that you're tired of me protesting,
Children dying everyday,
My name is nobody
But I can't wait to see your face inside my door . . .

Stevie: "The most interesting (in history lessons at school) to me was about civilizations before ours, how advanced people really were, how high they had brought themselves only to bring themselves down again. And it relates to today and what could possibly happen here, very soon. That's basically what *Big Brother* is all about.

"I speak of the history, the heritage of violence, or the negativeness of being able to see what's going on with minority people. Seemingly it's going to continue to be this way. Sometimes unfortunately violence is a way of getting things accomplished. *Big Brother* was something to make people aware of the fact that after all is said and done, that I don't have to do nothing to you, meaning the people are not power players. We don't have to do anything to them because they are gonna cause their own country to fall.

My name is Secluded;
We live in a house of the size of a matchbox . . .

A person who lives there, really, his name *is* Secluded, and you never even know the person, and they can have so many things to say to help make it better, but it's like the voice that speaks is forever silenced."

The other three songs on *Talking Book* are love songs again. *I Believe (When I Fall In Love It Will Be Forever)* was later a hit for Art Garfunkel. The lyrics were written by Yvonne Wright. Stevie shows a strange kind of honesty letting two women who both mean very much to him – especially at this time – write lyrics for his album, and reflect their mood or feelings toward him. While Yvonne is very direct in telling her love, Syreeta's lyrics deal with the end of their marriage. *Blame It On The Sun* includes lines like:

Where has my love gone?
How can I go on?
It seems dear love has gone away . . .

In *Lookin' For Another Pure Love* Syreeta wrote:

> *Things you cherish most in your life,*
> *Can be taken if they're left neglected . . .*

Talking Book was to come out in November 1972. The biblical cover showed Stevie, the Prophet of Soul, in a caftan. This photograph, he says, was taken on Tableau Mountain in Los Angeles.

The American sleeve held a braille message from Stevie:

> "Here is my music.
> It is all I have to tell
> you how I feel.
> Know that your love
> keeps my love strong."

In Britain, just a few *Talking Book* sleeves contained this message in braille and when Steve was given one of them, he was a little disappointed: the album title was wrong. Instead of *Talking Book* Motown U.K. had made a *Picture Book* out of it. But on the other hand the company had shown good-will, so Steve did not do anything about the wrong print.

While on *Music Of My Mind* Steve had only used two musicians (Buzzy Feiton and Art Baron on one track each), on *Talking Book* he featured some of the musicians that were in Wonderlove. And this time Stevie also credited the background vocalists.

On *You Are The Sunshine Of My Life* Scott Edwards played bass, Daniel Ben Zebulon congas and the backing vocals were sung by Gloria Barley, Lani Groves and Jim Gilstrap. On *Maybe Your Baby* Ray Parker was on guitar. *You And I* was played by Stevie alone and on *Tuesday Heartbreak* Steve played all instruments apart from an alto solo by Dave Sanborne and for the background vocals he credits Shirley Brewer and Deniece Williams. *You've Got It Bad Girl* includes Daniel Ben Zebulon on congas and Lani Groves and Jim Gilstrap doing backing vocals.

On *Superstition* Steve used Trevor Lawrence on saxophone and Steve Madaio on trumpet. *Blame It On The Sun* is played by only Stevie but again Lani Groves and Jim Gilstrap support him with background vocals. *Big Brother* and *I Believe (When I Fall In Love It Will Be Forever)* are two tracks that Stevie did solely on his own while Jeff Beck and Buzzy Feiton play guitar on *Lookin' For Another Pure Love*. On this song Loris Harvin, Shirley Brewer and Debra Wilson sing the backing vocals.

Some of these musicians played with Stevie on the Stones tour. The rapport that Stevie had with the Stones' audience – as well as any other audience – was incredible. People just could not hear enough of him. Doug: "I've been with Steve for more than three years and he did a lot of tours in that time. But I've never seen him do exactly the same show twice."

For quite a while Stevie would open his concerts with a band tune called *Dirty Old Man* or some other instrumental. Then Steve would join Wonderlove at the keyboards, then go over to the drums and play them, then back to the keyboards and Steve would often also play the harmonica. From the opening tune he would go right into the first song which could be any of his hits. The closing tune used to be *Keep On Running*, then, when *Superstition* had come out Stevie would close his show with this song. Doug:

"In the middle it could vary. He'd usually do a medley of his biggest hits – but even that was not necessarily in the same order or the same way, because Stevie is a master at feeling the vibe of the crowd and feeling what they want to hear. So he could gather from that what would be the best song to do next, to either bring them up to a particular point where he wanted the audience or to bring them down, when he felt they'd had enough. And then he would just keep them down long enough until they were ready to be taken back up again. The great thing about live performances is, that you can get loose. If you want to stretch out a chorus you can do it and if you want to shorten it you might as well."

The Rolling Stones tour was the only tour on which Stevie went on and off stage on time. Ira Tucker told me: "That is really funny with Steve. First of all he sits in his dressing room with some keyboards set up and he is creating, or showing someone in the band a new riff, or something like that. So you almost have to beat him out of the dressing room to get him off the piano and on to the stage.

"And then you almost have to beat him off stage because then he is happy there with his music. A lot of promoters got really wired up behind the fact that Stevie would stay on stage for two hours and not get tired. And the amazing thing is that people don't get tired of hearing him either. Because he knows how to play the audience and how to play to their emotions. 'Cause you're really dealing on an emotional level. The only time we did short shows was during the Stones tour because we had to cut it short."

Later the same year Stevie played one week at the Whiskey in Los Angeles. Gypsie Jones: "He was too much. Stevie is so great. You would see the same people in there every night for a week. They loved his shows so much. They even cut a live album there, but for some reason it never came out."

One of the reasons for Stevie's shows being so fantastic is that he has an excellent understanding with the members of his band. As long as they are there Steve and any single one in the group are the best of friends. If anything should come between them – they also have to leave without notice. Steve knows how important it is to be on good terms with his musicians: if they did not like him they could let him down and ruin the whole show. Just one of them has to rush in tempo or to play too slow or pretend not to understand what Stevie wants to do next, and it would be a disaster.

But Stevie does not make friends with his band because he has to rely on them, but because he has to like the people he works with to start with. Jim Gilstrap: "When I was with him it was like a family. Not like the sickening type of sticking together. It was more like everybody went their own ways but at the same time we were together. We partied together or we didn't when we did not feel like it. It was a very easy, informal thing and I don't think that it has changed."

After the gigs Stevie usually stays with his band. Apart from his family they are more or less the only friends he has. Gypsie: "It's hard to have friends in a position that Steve is in. He is not

evie Wonder is hailed as a musical genius at only thirteen years of age. SYNDICATION

top Fifteen years old — seven stone — five feet tall. POPPERPHOTO

inset Clarence Paul who was Stevie's mentor. TAMLA MOTOWN

TAMLA MOTOWN

ter his near fatal car crash, Stevie arrives in London with his girlfriend Yvonne Wright. SYNDICATION

n Stevie announces his engagement to Syreeta Wright. SYNDICATION

top With fellow superstar David Bowie. TAMLA MOTOWN

bottom On stage with Mick Jagger during the Stones tour of the USA in 1972. TAMLA MOTOWN

evie Wonder and Grover of Sesame Street. TAMLA MOTOWN

n With Suzanne de Passe, vice-president of Motown's creative department. He has almost finished
GS IN THE KEY OF LIFE. TAMLA MOTOWN

Drums were Stevie's first instrument. TAMLA MOTOWN

MOTOWN

TAMLA MOTOWN

exposed to that many people apart from family or band members."

Also up to 1974 Stevie was on the road for about eight or nine months every year. Sandray Tucker: "Steve demands a lot of his musicians musically but he also really cares for them. Like he wants to know when something is wrong – not because he is nosy but because he wants to help. Also he has very good reason to want to know if anything's wrong because it might make you perform below standard.

"And he has to have the highest standard. That is why he is doing the best he can and that is also why he is hiring the best musicians. And, as I said, he really cares. He has a very soft touch. If there's anything that worries you and he can help he does it. No matter if it is financially or spiritually, Stevie gives it to you."

Unlike a lot of other superstars Stevie is not into a powertrip or startrip at all. When the band is touring he travels with them. Doug: "The Stones had their plane, we didn't. We travelled commercial. We'd all fly the same way and there is no such thing as Stevie being the one to go first class and the rest of us economy. He doesn't believe in that. A couple of tours we all went on a bus and Stevie would go with us. The only time he did not travel on the bus was when he had commitments like interviews or doing a television. Then he would take the Mercedes. But generally Stevie is careful not to make any difference between him and the band, or even the road crew, by using more comfortable transport."

Stevie is also very generous. Neither he nor his publicist talk about it, because Stevie does not believe in getting publicity out of things that for him seem the normal thing to do. But Doug Kee told me: "As long as I was with him he did at least one benefit show a month. That means that the money he was supposed to get for the gig went to whatever charity he did the concert for. Also Stevie paid all his expenses.

"He does a lot of benefit shows for black organizations. And for people that are blind or have any other handicap. When Stevie says that he is really not all that interested in making lots and lots of money for himself, then you can really believe it. With Stevie it is true – he's not after making a fortune. Although he *is* making one.

"But he mainly needs the money for his family to be secure and to help underprivileged people. Stevie himself is not into a luxury trip at all. Because most of it is all visual, man. Stevie isn't interested in visual things. All he needs is his bed and a chair and a table and his instruments."

The residential hotel that Stevie lives in on Hollywood Boulevard in Los Angeles really cannot be called luxurious. It has three rooms and it was already furnished when he moved in. The furniture is average, no expensive fancy stuff. But instead his apartment is crammed with equipment: synthesizers, clavinet, pianos, amplifiers, speakers. That is all Stevie needs.

But even if he were into luxury it would not cost him anything. Jim Gilstrap: "You just would not believe what people offer him. He could stay at hotels for nothing, because everybody thinks if Steve stays at their place it's good publicity and so they invite him. He does not make use of it though. And whatever else he would want: people just throw things at him. It's ridiculous.

"The same when you play with Steve. The girls I could have had in that time, just because I was one of Wonderlove, was incredible. Women were chasing me. And to be really honest with you, it made me kind of sad. Because I thought that has not happened before, why does it happen now? And it really freaked me out.

"I'm sure it also freaks Stevie. I am certain that he knows that a lot of people who keep sticking around are only there because he is the big Stevie Wonder. Superstar. If he lost his voice or his talent from one day to the other – which God forbid – there would be less people hangin' 'round. Showbusiness is a lonely business."

Gypsie Jones even talked to Stevie about this subject one time: "We were in the studio, working on *Songs In The Key Of Life* and all of a sudden this question popped up in my head. I saw all those people around Steve and they are always there and he actually is never alone. At least he doesn't have to be.

"So I told Steve what I had just been thinking and I asked him, 'Do you ever get lonely?'

"And he just kept playing his instruments and there were a whole lot of things going on and he did not answer my question. Then, about 40 minutes later Steve left the studio. And just before he went out the door he turned to me and he said:

" 'Yes. Yes I do. But I don't let it bother me.' And he left."

The thing that Stevie's friends are worried about most is that so many people try to take advantage of Stevie. Most of the people around him *overprotect* him and often he is the last to know about things that happen around him. This overprotection starts with some of the staff that he has hired and continues through people working in all kinds of Motown departments even to music magazine publishers, and is the result of variety of causes. Doug Kee:

"The main problem in this business is fighting egos. And with Motown, it seems worse than in any other recording company. Just look at the high turnover they have in staff (within three weeks three girls left the International Department at Motown last summer and this is nothing unusual). It's ridiculous. And it starts at the top executives and goes down to the secretaries. If you take Stevie, they all want to shield him from things that they think aren't cool or may not be cool. So there are many things that Stevie doesn't even know about because nobody tells him."

Lee Garrett: "He seldom gets messages you leave on his telephone answering machine. Because most of the time he doesn't listen to the tapes himself but someone else does. And *they* think it's not important and live out their ego trip."

While I was doing research on this book, Elaine Jesmer suggested that I should contact *Soul* magazine and check with their files on Stevie on a few facts. Elaine thought it would be no problem for her publisher friend Regina Jones to co-operate with me. But: whenever I rang up or called around the office personally, the lady was either busy or not there.

Finally her boy Friday asked me to write her a letter. I did. When I called back she had not even read it. Back in London, my publisher wrote to Regina Jones. This time she answered, telling him that their files were for their "own research purpose only" but

"I will discuss your request with Mr. Wonder's office and if he wishes us to assist you we will."

Soul publisher Regina Jones thought it even necessary to send a copy of her answer to Steve's publicist.

Gypsie Jones: "There are so many people – even some who have nothing to do with Stevie really – who think of themselves as super important. This overprotection could sometimes make you laugh if it weren't so sad. There are some people that I feel take a lot for granted. Because they've jumped on to Stevie's bandwagon and everybody is living with his glory and there's lot of money to be made.

"A lot of Stevie's employers have gotten behind that stage but there are still some of them who are starstruck and being selfish instead of thinking about Steve. And I think that some of them should think about him more often. Because if it wasn't for Stevie there wouldn't be their job. I say this, because I admire Stevie and it hurts me to see people take advantage of him or incapacitate him in a way that they make decisions for him without even telling Steve what's up."

Stevie's name works wonders. As soon as you mention that you work for Steve people just lay everything on you. Gypsie: "It's unbelievable. One day when we were touring we stayed in a hotel that had beautiful handpainted plates. I really fell for them and I asked the owner if I could have one. No way, he said, would he give me one of those plates. He would not even let me pay for it.

"A few minutes later Ira (Tucker) came downstairs for breakfast and I told him how much I would have liked to have one of those plates but that it was impossible. So Ira just called the owner again and said he wanted one for Stevie. You should have seen the guy: he offered us hundreds. 'Sure you only want one?' he kept asking and we said, 'Yeah, positive.' Now all of a sudden he felt like we were neglecting his beautiful plates. Anyway, I got the one that I wanted and later I told Steve about it. He just laughed."

It was in Texas that Stevie stopped a show right in the middle for a very unusual reason. Gypsie: "It was on some summer festival in 1974 in either Houston or Dallas. Somebody had come up to Stevie and told him that there was a lady from out of town and that her purse had been stolen. She was not so much worried about the money, although she had had quite a lot on her but more about her car keys and identity card and all that stuff.

"So Stevie stopped his show to say that there was a lady whose wallet had been misplaced. He didn't say stolen, I don't think. And he asked if the person who took it would either return it or never come to hear him again. Then the music started playing again and Steve continued the show. A few minutes later the guy who had told Stevie about the whole thing came on stage. He had the wallet with everything in it and he thanked the person whoever had had it for giving it back.

"The next day the papers carried big lines like 'Stevie Wonder convinces thief to give back purse'. See, this is something that shows you what kind of influence Stevie has on people. I mean how many thieves give back things? I don't think this one would have returned the purse if Stevie hadn't asked. And events like this really make you wonder. There is something to the wonder boy . . ."

As strange as it may seem there are many things to Stevie that you cannot explain. He does give out some kind of vibration that cannot be ignored by people. Stevie does not just play fantastic music, he also puts his audiences under his spell. Nobody I have met has ever left a Stevie Wonder concert disappointed. Critics credit Stevie with creating "a sound of relevance that is as universally appealing to middle-aged housewives as it is to Black Panther Party members".

Also other musicians of fame don't hide their admiration for their colleague Stevie Wonder. Elton John: "I guess I thought I was the only one totally immersed in music until I met Stevie." Roberta Flack: "Stevie's music is the most sensitive of our decade, and that means it has tapped the pulse of the people." Eric Clapton calls Stevie "the best drummer in the world" and Henry Mancini rushed up to hug Steve saying, "God, you've got rhythm!"

There is also hardly any contemporary musician who has not been influenced by Stevie. I have done many interviews with musicians while working as a music journalist, and most of them mentioned Stevie Wonder when asked what kind of music they listen to or who influenced them most.

One thing that Stevie can be very proud of, is that many of those musicians whom he listened to in his teens now name him as one of their favourite artists: Pete Townshend from the Who, all of the ex-Beatles, Keith Emerson and Jim Capaldi ex-Traffic.

Young groups that have come up mention Stevie as a big influence: The Doobie Brothers, the Eagles, Sailor and Rufus to name but a few.

Other singer/songwriters name Stevie as a musician they have always listened to: Bruce Springsteen, Gino Vanelli, Harry Nilsson and Peter Frampton for example.

Also young musicians who are just on their way up credit Stevie to having influenced them a lot. Like Chris de Burgh, an Irish singer/songwriter who is now produced by Paul Samwell-Smith (who worked with Cat Stevens, Paul Simon, Carly Simon) and had just released his new album *At The End of A Perfect Day* when this book went in print. Chris, who is said to be one of the up-coming stars within the next couple of years told me:

"As a singer and as a songwriter Stevie makes me feel like an amateur as he must make most other musicians feel. For not only can he sing a ballad with true feeling and Rock'n Roll songs with real balls but he also has the talent of going to the very nucleus of the emotions of a song making it very hard for the rest of us, as mere mortals, to consider venturing into his particular flower garden, or . . . while we just look over the fence in envy. God must love him a lot – and so do I."

To Motown's big surprise Stevie, since he had broken away from their musical control completely, had turned out to be an album artist. By the end of 1972 *Music Of My Mind* had turned gold and Stevie thinks it could have even done better had it had a "real fantastic" single on it: "I've been trying to see why it didn't do very good in the States. I think maybe because *Music Of My Mind* didn't have a really fantastic single on it. It was more of an album than something you could take a single off. I didn't feel with *Music Of My Mind* that here was a good chance to give out with some craziness. I just felt that the doors were open for me to play."

They certainly were. *Talking Book* became platinum as did his single *Superstition* which topped the American "Pop 100" and R & B charts (in Britain the single went to position 11). But also his singles from *Music Of My Mind* had been successful. After all *Superwoman/I Love Every Little Thing About You* was a gold disc and had come to position 33 in the "Pop 100" and 13 in the R & B charts. *Keep On Running/Evil* reached the "Pop 100" at number 90 and *Billboard*'s R & B charts at position 33.

But apart from Stevie's success and a Grammy for the Temptations most of 1972 had looked rather sad for Motown: They had lost the Four Tops, Jimmy Ruffin and Smokey Robinson had left the Miracles to pursue a solo career.

Within the next few months they would lose the Isley Brothers, Martha and the Vandellas would break up and the songwriting team Ashford & Simpson would sign with Warner Brothers. Gladys Knight and the Pips, who had scored two big hits for Motown in 1972 (*Help Me Make It Through The Night* and *Neither One Of Us*) would also be leaving soon.

The only Motown acts doing really well were the Jackson Five and the Temptations who had had a huge hit with *Papa Was A Rolling Stone*. Then there was Marvin Gaye who was going strong again and Diana Ross was back in the limelight as the late Billie Holiday in *Lady Sings The Blues*. But the price for Diana's success was that the Supremes had lost their magic since she had left the group. Generally, for Motown the all-chart-topping days were over.

For Stevie the really big time had just begun.

CHAPTER NINE

Higher Ground

In late February 1973 Motown released *You Are The Sunshine Of My Life/Tuesday Heartbreak* from Stevie's *Talking Book* album as a single. Soon the record went up to number 3 in *Billboard*'s R & B charts, topped the "Pop 100" and in England it went to position seven in *Music Week*. But while the single as well as the album were getting more and more airplay (*You Are The Sunshine Of My Life* became a gold disc) Stevie had almost forgotten about *Talking Book*:

"It always seemed that the things I wanted to do musically were somewhat ahead of the things that were being released at the time. And I think that's good because you are always looking forward to do something and progressing. I think that after you sing a song or whatever, after you've done it, it's done; the most important thing is to look forward to doing something that is another time, another place."

So Stevie was heavily involved in working on his new album. He would spend hours and hours in the studio and hardly get any sleep. And while Steve simply says "My rhythms go by my moods" his friends call him a "studio junkie". Doug Kee: "Stevie is someone who goes into the studio at seven o'clock at night and comes out at ten o'clock the next morning. Time doesn't mean anything to him while he's creating. He just goes on and on and on.

"He would stay in the studio even longer if the people who worked with him could keep up with it. Only when we say 'Hey, Steve, it's nine o'clock in the morning' then he'd say 'Okay, let me just get these two more tracks down' or something like that. To see Stevie in the studio was a real education for me. Just to sit there watching the ease with which he works there. It is fascinating, exciting. I've never seen anybody else who works that well in the studio. He works with so much professionalism. The way he gets the sound right and everything."

Deniece Williams: "Steve's got this incredible energy. He can stay in the studio for 48 hours and not get tired while any other person would just crash out. I have been in the studio at 3 o'clock in the morning and I said I don't believe I'm doing this. But I did. Steve's energy is kind of infectious – it makes you feel so good that you also can do much more than you think."

Malcolm Cecil: "I remember one day at the Air Studio in London. Eric Clapton came over for a bit and Stevie was just playing song after song after song. We'd done a string session and after that everybody was completely worn out – not so Stevie. He went on to record 17 new songs that night. Seventeen! And they had to come and throw us out the next morning because George Martin was booked in at nine o'clock. If Stevie hadn't had to leave the studio he'd probably still be there . . ."

Jim Gilstrap: "Steve stays up almost 20 hours a day. When he leaves the studio he'll still be working at home. I've never known anybody to need as little sleep as Stevie does. Even when you think he's gotta be tired-out he composes the most beautiful songs. And I've never seen anybody who is that creative. I tell you what: a lot of the stuff that he has tucked away on some shelves somewhere is even better than the tunes that have been released. I'm almost afraid what's gonna happen when people hear the songs that are *really* good. Stuff that he has buried away. Tracks that are pure *magic*.

"I don't understand why he chooses those other songs for his albums. They are great, yeah, but compared to what the public hasn't heard yet they are really nothing. Like he did a duet with Syreeta that would blow your mind. And so would dozens of songs that I know because I did some backing vocals on them. Maybe he doesn't realize the treasures that he's got. And he's got hundreds and hundreds of songs just tucked away.

Most of them are completely finished and some of them need some mixing. But there are hundreds of tunes. Hundreds."

An estimated figure of finished but unreleased Stevie Wonder songs has been given by *Soul* magazine as 600 "which represents 20,000 hours of studio time within two years". *Penthouse* and *Newsweek* wrote about 200 songs. Stevie sometimes denies it. "No. We don't have 200 songs. We do have a lot of material but a lot of it isn't finished. I have some things from a while back and a lot of tunes I've never really finished because they're still not presentable compared to what I've done since."

On other occasions he says they have not been released because "I don't want to be too big too fast." Stevie mostly understates the songs that he has canned away, but musicians who have worked with him or known him for a long time all say that they guess Stevie's already produced but not released anything from 400 to a thousand songs.

Robert Margouleff: "On those four albums we did over two years' time (*Music Of My Mind, Talking Book, Innervisions, Fulfillingness' First Finale*) you only find a very small percentage of the songs that were actually created. We did several hundreds of songs, the tunes would just flow right out of Steve."

Malcolm Cecil: "And in all those hundreds of tunes I've never heard a bad one. You can learn to hate them when you live with them that long, and Robert and I both had one tune that we could not stand – but compared to all the songs Stevie created that's really nothing."

Lee Garrett: "Steve must have close to a thousand songs by now. I was there for 300 of them and he had a whole case full then."

Billy Griffin: "Of all the songs I've heard when the Miracles came into the studio that Steve was in he has only put out a very small percentage. And that's just from what I've heard."

Gypsie Jones: "Just the songs that we did when we worked on his last albums go into the hundreds. If Stevie would never write or record a song again in his whole lifetime he could still put out at least one album per year."

Of songs that were started but not finished Malcolm Cecil and Robert Margouleff used to carry the "Blue Book", with all the song titles in alphabetic order. Then, when they did a recording session, the two of them and Stevie would go through the book, pick out a song to complete and – Stevie would create five new tunes while finishing the one off. Stevie explains what makes it so difficult for him to finish at a later time a song that he has started a while ago:

"It is hard to keep the same feeling that existed when I started a song. I have learned to not do the songs again until I am in the mood I was in when it began. Which means I have to be in a similar mood to when I started writing that particular song. Sometimes it contains an emotion that I cannot recapture – because often emotions are new and unique. And you get through a lot of changes all the time – so it is really hard to put yourself back into a certain kind of mood again sometimes."

Some of the songs that Stevie has lying around for ages do sometimes find the master's approval in the end. A good example is *Heaven Is Ten Zillion Light Years Away*. This track was actually meant to be on *Talking Book* but did not get released until almost two years later when it went on *Fulfillingness' First Finale*. According to Stevie it took him that long to get the song exactly as he wanted it.

To get all the studio time Stevie needs is no problem for him. Doug Kee: "As long as I've been around I've never seen Steve having any trouble to get studio time at all. Whenever he gets the urge to record as soon as he snaps his fingers he's got a studio. The best."

Stevie's favourite studios are the Electric Lady, Media Sound and the Hit Factory in New York as well as the Record Plant and Chrystal Industries in Los Angeles. Ron White, from the Miracles, says what it is like when Stevie has the "urge" to record: "We use the Chrystal Studio a lot ourselves. Sometimes it can happen that we've booked some time but when we get there, Stevie has occupied it. What can you do? We've worked it out in a way now, that we do Stevie the favour of letting him stay and some other day he understands when we record longer hours than we were actually supposed to. It's cool with us – and I think most musicians think the same and act the same."

The Chrystal Studio reminds Doug Kee very much of Stevie's apartment: "It's neither posh nor sterile but somewhere in between. And of course, it has an outstanding sound."

The Record Plant is the studio that people who work with Stevie like most. Doug: "This place is too much. They've got pinball machines and stuff like that. So the good thing about it is that you can get away from the studio but still be there when you are needed. It's got a very relaxing atmosphere." The thing that Steve loves about the Record Plant are "the jacuzzi baths and saunas and stuff" he says. Apart from the sound, of course . . .

Another thing that creates a friendly atmosphere is that Stevie's mother and his friends take good care of him while he is working. They cook for him and his musicians and staff and bring the food down to the studio. Barbara, Ira Tucker's lady, specializes in cookies and Gypsie Jones tells the following story: "I remember one day when Steve rang me up and asked what I was cooking for dinner. I told him I was preparing greens and cornbread and all this kind of *soul food* stuff. He said 'That sounds good' and I said 'I bet it is' and later that night I went down to the studio to bring him some of that. I had also made Stevie a huge blackberry cobbler – because I know that he's got such a sweet tooth.

"Anyway, I get down to the studio and five minutes later in walks Lula with a peach cobbler as big as the blackberry cobbler. And macaroni and cheese and baked chicken for Josette [Josette Valentino, Steve's secretary but also credited as his recording co-ordinator] and broccoli and pizza and God knows what. Another two minutes later this guy walks in – it's a shame I've forgotten his name – and he brings the health-food trip. So the whole thing is like a feast. There was food and plates all cross the studio and we all sat there and ate."

As much as Stevie can eat, he does not put on any weight. Leading the hard-working life that he does, food is just pure energy for him. Lately Steve has turned vegetarian. Not because of any religious beliefs but "because it is supposed to be healthier" he says.

Very often when you come into a studio Stevie is working in, the session looks more like a party than recording. But despite all the fun and joking around Stevie is a professional as few artists are. He does not care how long it takes to get a track down as he wants it. He also calls himself "my own worst critic", which does not come as a surprise. Results Stevie is not totally satisfied with he erases without even considering the idea of keeping some of it that may be good.

He plays the Moog – that with all its knobs looks more like the command module of a spaceship than an instrument – with such dexterity that it is as if he could see them all. Also his ears can pinpoint where people in the studio are positioned so accurately that it freaks someone who experiences Stevie in the studio for the first time. His musicians and engineers have got used to it, though. None of them consider Steve blind – he often knows more of what is going on than sighted people do. Gypsie:

"He is very psychic because his senses are extremely high. You can sit there and even though he can't visually see you he feels you. And he can know if the expression on your face is grim or if you're smiling. You don't even have to say anything. It's like many times he'd asked me 'What's wrong with you?' even though I did not tell him that I felt miserable or had a problem. You can even force a smile on your face and be in control of your voice – he still knows."

Elaine Jesmer: "When I first met him that really bothered me. It freaked me out how Stevie knows the mood you're in without you saying anything. But that is exactly what he is doing. And I simply cannot understand how he does it. It is probably because he never saw – he's developed his other senses a lot more than other people. But even with other blind guys you very rarely get that kind of sensitivity to what's happening around them."

Stevie himself admits to being psychic. He had a premonition that Benny Benjamin would die. And Wes Montgomery. "I wrote *Bye Bye World* on my Eivets Rednow album *Alfie* for Wes. I told him about the song and then not long after there was his tragic death."

He very often feels things that are going to happen. Ira Tucker: "I remember really sunny days in California when Stevie said it would start raining soon. Everybody laughed at him because that was the least thing we all expected. And then – an hour later – sure enough rain came just pouring down. None of us had seen the slightest sign of it beforehand, but Stevie just senses changes."

Most of the time, though, Stevie does not tell anybody about what he feels is going to come up. Stevie is a sensation enough as it is – he does not want people to start wondering about him even more. Only when he uses whatever he kind of foresees in his songs he gives another hint on this special sense of his. But again, Stevie does not write about it consciously – it is just something that occupies his mind and that wants out. Because Stevie mainly writes about his own experiences and feelings.

And just a few months before Stevie was to face death himself in a terrible car crash, he talked about dying. *Rolling Stone* wrote: ". . . He sees the earth zigging towards a destructive end; he can see himself dying soon and he hopes, by his music, to be able to leave something for the rest of us – even if we ain't that far behind him." At the same time Stevie also talked about the death of other musicians:

" . . . a lot of people that I thought would be major people have died. Otis, Jimi Hendrix . . . Michael Jeffery was just killed recently, goin' from Spain to London. Two planes collided, one exploded, the other landed safely. I heard there were some bitter things that went down, that Hendrix was ripped off fantastically by Jeffery, but I don't know how true those stories are . . .

"It's heavy, and I guess you could say if he did the things that I heard he did, then that's his kharma, but again, what about the other people on the plane? That's the question I always ask."

And some of the songs that Stevie wrote at that time dealt with death. Like *Jesus Children Of America*. In this song Steve talks about Jesus who died on the cross for us, and he asks if we know how much pain he went through and why.

Mother Mary feels so much pain
Looking at him.
So you better tell
Tell your story
Your story fast . . .

Also Heaven Is Ten Zillion Light Years Away, written in 1972, shows a much deeper, more "religious" Stevie Wonder:

They say that heaven is ten zillion light years away
But if there is a God we need Him now . . .
But if you open your heart you can feel it yeah yeah
Feel his spirit . . .

These songs were actually written for an album that Stevie wanted to call *Last Days Of Easter*. This album, which was later to become *Innervisions*, was scheduled for March 1973. Stevie: "It was about the last day of beauty. All the horror and hypocrisy in the world today. People neglecting other people's problems. And what needs doing socially, spiritually and domestically. I can only do it through my songs and I try to be positive about it."

Stevie had also worked out an idea for the album cover for *Last Days Of Easter*: "It should have been an old man, a very old man, who's been through it all and can now sit and look on at the confusion. He would have wisdom and contentment." But then Steve scrapped the whole album idea "because people would relate it to Easter and not to other things".

Higher Ground was written just under three months before Stevie was to face death so closely. "I wrote it on 11 May 1973. The song just came to me, the words, the music, it all happened within a few hours and I recorded it at once. I didn't know what it was all about, but it was almost as if I had to get it done. As if something was going to happen, some change would come up." In *Higher Ground* Stevie's being psychic let him write a chorus that would be so true soon:

I'm so darn glad he let me try again
'Cause my last time on earth I lived a whole world of sin
I'm so glad that I know more than I knew then
Gonna keep on tryin'
Till I reach the highest ground.

With "living a world of sin" Steve refers to taking too many things for granted, and also leading a hectic life which does not leave any time to realize how beautiful small things in life can be.

Stevie without any doubt is and has always been religious. Today he is not a disciple of any organized religion, although he very much respects Islam. Steve: "I appreciate the fact that you have to respect yourself before anybody else will. And you should not try to be like anyone but yourself."

Self-respect, though, has nothing to do with being conceited. "I am quite aware of the fact that I am only one of the zillions of people that have existed. I know it and I accept it. When you think like that you hardly have any time to be conceited. How could I even dare to think of being conceited with the universe as large as it is?

"But I keep thinking how can I do better than what I did before? How hard can I work to perfect what is not there yet? And that's the feeling that I still have; you have never reached the plateau until it is time for you to die. I have a long way to go, accepting that and realizing that.

"You do your best to express as much as you possibly can about things that have happened to you in your life, and to show love and appreciation to those who have all made it possible. There is no time to get big-headed. But you need self-respect to be able to express yourself."

Another thing that makes self-respect so important in Steve's opinion is the fact that "Love is respect and this again comes from respecting yourself. When you learn to respect and love yourself then you learn to love and respect others."

And "God", or our "Maker" in Stevie's mind is also different from what is taught at church or in school. "I guess a lot of people believe that God is in heaven, or somewhere. I don't believe that shit. I guess I used to when I was younger, but I didn't understand even then how you can *go* to heaven – like, just *how* did you do it? They told me Jesus left the earth with his hands up and he just flew away. So when I sing about 'God' in my music, I am really expressing a beautiful spirit deep down inside me."

The first half of 1973 Stevie spent mostly in either recording or television studios. He came over to England in the beginning of the year to do a promotion – but not a concert – tour and a Burt Bacharach TV special. One of the songs he recorded for this show was *Alfie*. In the middle of February he appeared at Carnegie Hall, New York, where Ewart Abner, who by this time was President of Motown, ruined the concert; about one and a half hours through the show – the audience was just getting relaxed and enjoying Steve's music – Abner walked on stage with no less than three stooges. He went into a rap and presented Stevie with gold and platinum records for *Superstition* and a gold album for *Talking Book*. As much as the audience was happy about Stevie's commercial success, they were disappointed about the interruption.

Stevie, who was then promoted as the Prophet of Soul, looked like an Egyptian prince on stage: he wore a sleek three-piece caftan and a carved necklace.

In April Stevie appeared on the American TV program *Sesame Street*. For this occasion on the 12th of the month Steve had composed original music for his appearance, using the words "Sesame Street" as the only lyrics. In addition to his *Sesame Street* Stevie sang *Superstition*. Within the show he also talked with the muppet Grover – making the insecure Grover proud of himself as they ad-libbed with each other to get across the concepts of opposites such as long and short, loud and soft, here and there.

Stevie also played at the Berkley Jazz & Blues Festival on 14 July. The Oakland Stadium, which holds 70,000 people during a baseball game, was only opened in half its size. The concert was sold-out: 35,000 people had come to watch Stevie, Rahsaan Roland Kirk, Esther Phillips and the Staple Singers.

Apart from some benefit concerts Stevie did a few other shows and in late summer/early autumn 1973 he was supposed to go on a tour through America and Europe.

At the end of July Motown released the single *Higher Ground/Too High* and on 3 August Stevie's album *Innervisions*. As on *Talking Book* Steve played most of the instruments himself. *Living For The City, Higher Ground, Jesus Children Of America* and *Too High* are played by Stevie only but credit Lani Groves, Tasha Thomas and Jim Gilstrap for backing vocals on the latter.

On *Visions* Malcolm Cecil is on bass, Dean Parks on acoustic and David "T" Walker on electric guitar. On *Golden Lady* Stevie used Clarence Bell, another blind musician, on organ; Ralph Hammer on acoustic guitar; and Larry "Nastyee" Latimer on congas. *All In Love Is Fair* has Scott Edwards on bass; on *Don't You Worry 'Bout A Thing* Yusuf Roahman plays shaker and Sheila Wilkerson bongos and Latin ground; while *He's Misstra Know-It-All* features Willie Weeks on bass.

All other instruments are played by Stevie. The reason he does not use too many other musicians on his recordings is simple. Steve: "Quite a lot of people think I do it because I am on an ego-trip. But that's not the case. The reason I play most of the instruments myself is that doing it this way I don't have to explain how I want things done. See, I can *hear* the finished recording playing in my head – I know exactly what I want each instrument to sound like. It is more or less a matter of *feeling* the sound. And there aren't too many people around who feel about my songs the way I do. See, somehow it is all music of my mind ..."

Innervisions is the only Stevie Wonder album so far on which Stevie wrote every track himself. The concepts which he had for it were twofold: (1) he wanted to speak of himself in relation to the world; and (2) Stevie wanted to speak to himself in relation to his closeness to music and his involvement with it. "People shouldn't expect a set thing from me – I love to grow."

Although *Innervisions* is said to be Steve's real vision of his own innervision which he had become aware of within the past year, most people who worked on it – as well as many of his friends and fans – think of *Talking Book* as an album which reveals more of Stevie's personality.

Bob Margouleff: "I think *Talking Book* should have been an album to get a Grammy. For engineering, for contents, for music, for everything. I think it is really the cream of the four albums that Stevie and we did together. The whole essence of it – it had a concept to it and it really was a talking book about Stevie's life.

"*Talking Book* was also the album with the most teamwork feeling. It had the highest effort to it. It had the most feeling of belonging together to it. It was really the height of the flow. The vibrations that we had going at that time really were the high points of my career."

Malcolm Cecil: "I like *Talking Book* best, too. Somehow it went through smoothest. And also the relationship with Stevie at that time was at its best. We had already broken the ice with *Music Of My Mind* and then came *Talking Book*. Which really was in my opinion from the cover on down with everything about it exactly the way Bob and I and Stevie felt at that time.

"I also think it was the breakthrough for Steve. It broke him through all the barriers. His genius is always there, I'm not saying that the album made him or anything, the album *is* him. His genius is the album. His genius is always there. But I think that *Talking Book* was the combination of a lot of things and I think he liked it the way it was. The way that it flowed and everything. I must say that *Talking Book* is my favourite – with *Innervisions* as the very hot second."

Innervisions is an album that does not include as many love songs as Stevie's former LPs but deals with the America of today and life in general. Steve: "Everyone has good times and bad times. But you cannot really appreciate those good times if you have not had bad times. You look upon those times and say 'Wow, life surely brings a lot of changes.' The circles of life go up and down so if you expect it to be just one way you are cheating yourself out of that spice that is life – variety."

Too High and *Innervisions* is a song about a girl who does not want to go through all the ups and downs in life and escapes into drugs and the isolation of a superficial paradise. Steve: "For some people this seems to be the solution. For me it is the beginning of the end." The way Steve pictures the scene is excellent:

> *She's a girl in a dream*
> *She sees a four-eyed cartoon monster*
> *On the TV screen.*
> *She takes another puff and says*
> *"It's a crazy scene."*

The next cuts, *Visions* and *All In Love Is Fair*, are two songs that Steve describes as "typical ballads of America" with which he hoped to get away from the soul image for good. Steve: "After writing those songs I think it's wrong to speak of me as a soul artist. I am a black man but music is music. I want to inspire people, but I think it really is about time that they stopped categorizing me."

Visions is a song that critics have called "sardonic and bittersweet, a lament for the kind of world which might have been but never will be". Stevie, though, does not give up on the hope for a better tomorrow and he calls *Visions* a song about how life *could* be. Apart from *Higher Ground* it is also Steve's favourite track on the album: "If there's anything to be remembered from *Innervisions* I'd like it to be that song."

> *People hand in hand*
> *Have I lived to see the milk and honey land?*
> *Where hate's a dream and love forever stands*
> *Or is this a vision in my mind?*

In the other ballad *All In Love Is Fair* Steve's attitude towards love is given in the title. It is a song about the crazy game of love, two people promising each other to stay in love forever but

> *The future none can see*
> *The road you leave behind*
> *Ahead lies mystery . . .*

Steve: "Love, for me, is the most important thing in life. Love in its various forms. Like the love you feel for friends, the love you have for your family, a love towards life and for the people in this world.

"But there's also a passionate kind of love. The one you have for your lover. The intimate love between two people who at one point decide that they are going to try and make it through life together. Sometimes you think that this is the strongest love you feel and at the same time it is the most fragile kind of love. Because passion can get mistaken for love and passion does not last forever. It is nothing you can build love upon. And when one day you find that passion has gone, then you have to accept it. It doesn't mean that you have never felt love for the other person but it wasn't fundamental enough to last.

"People should realize that 'all in love is fair' and learn to live with the changes and try to make the best out of it. You cannot demand love. I for myself am very glad to know that my woman loves me today and when I feel that there is a chance that she might still love me tomorrow. But to expect any more than that is crazy. It only means that you are more possessive than in love. Love is something you have to be grateful for and which you have to treat tenderly. Very, very tenderly. But it is nothing that you can take for granted."

Another track on *Innervisions* is *Living For The City*, a song that caused a lot of controversy when it came out as a single (in October 1973). Billy Griffin: "There are very few people who can put out a heavy song like *Living For The City* and not only get away with it but get awarded a gold single for it.

"Stevie is a master at telling story songs. Not just the love from me to you theme but lyrics that talk about everyday life and human behaviour. He worked this song out beautifully. The story about a guy coming from the South Eastern part of the United States and moving to the big apple, New York. It is amazing how Stevie told the things that this guy goes through seeing the new city."

Stevie: "Being Steveland Morris and becoming Stevie Wonder I had to ask myself 'Who is Stevie Wonder?' And now I know that I'm only a vehicle – in being Stevie Wonder – that allows me to express experiences I've had in my life and people I know directly or indirectly have gone through. Some people say I am writing a lot about the negative things in life. But I do it to bring the better part that there could be to realization."

> *His patience's long but soon he won't have any*
> *To find a job is like a haystack needle*
> *'Cause where he lives they don't use coloured people*
> *Living just enough, just enough for the city . . .*

Stevie also says: "People must realize that both the middle class black and the middle class white people have basically the same struggle."

Some critics made the point that this kind of life Stevie talks about in this song is hardly his. Then again they seem to have forgotten that this kind of life would have been Stevie's had he not been gifted with his enormous musical talent. Stevie, though, is well aware of that. And if he does write songs like this it is not that he just sings about grievances, he also does a lot to fight them. Malcolm Cecil:

"Stevie has the power to be a very important figure, not only musically. His songs do more than sell millions and millions of copies. For one, they reach other people and also quite a lot of money the records make Stevie uses to help underprivileged groups of people. So all of a sudden you find money going from white people to black people, even if it's only for their bloody music . . ."

Talking to Stevie's friends you will find that they all tell you that Stevie really *is* concerned about what is happening around him. He donates high sums of money to black organizations and only a small proportion of these donations are written about in the press. Steve does not believe in helping people for the sake of his own image but he feels very deeply towards everybody who needs help.

"It's good to do something for sickle cell anemia or for the Black Panther Party if they want to give clothes to kids or food to the community, if it's really a sincere move on one's behalf to do something for people and I can contribute my services, I will do so."

But it is not only money that Stevie contributes to help. That would be making it too easy on himself. Steve's sincerity in his concern shows when he comes up with ideas that provide a start in educating young children so that they do not just take over their parents' attitudes but learn to think for themselves. Steve told *Penthouse* about an idea of his that he discussed with Detroit's first black mayor, Coleman Young:

"Last year (1975) I did a benefit for the mayor's programme for bussing children into different communities to visit places they wouldn't ordinarily be able to go – different art exhibits and films. I have a lot of respect for Coleman Young and I told him that he should encourage a special screening of a film I'd seen that can explain the situation in the ghettos to a lot of people.

"That film is *The Education Of Sunny Carson* – I loved seeing it. It touched me. The 'blacksploitation' films, on the other hand, have basically only two approaches – either 'Yeah, boy! You're so ba-ad you can beat the law, just go out and do it,' or the 'If you go out and do it, you'll get what's coming to you.' Both invite crime. The white movie companies portray very unprogressive images of black people – it's not good for young kids. The same with radio and television.

"I remember in Boston seeing a news item on television, 'Twelve black kids jumped on one little white boy today . . .' What happened, I later found out, was that a black kid got beat up by a gang of white kids first. But if I were a Middle-American and I'd seen that on TV I'd be angry as hell and I'd want to go kill every nigger that ever existed. Things like that pull people apart and make conditions ripe for mass violence."

Although Stevie is heavily engaged in social politics, he does not give himself to any political party to raise votes with his name at election time. Stevie: "I don't think that is the right thing to do. I don't want people to vote whatever I may vote just because they happen to like me. I don't want anybody to follow anything or anyone blindly but rather I want to help people to think for themselves."

This attitude is one that Janis Ian, who in 1966 at the age of only 15 caused a lot of discussion with her song *Society's Child*, also has. In 1975 the American singer/songwriter topped the charts with *At Seventeen,* which includes lines like:

> *I learned the truth at seventeen*
> *That love was meant for beauty queens*
> *And high school girls with clear-skinned smiles*
> *Who married young, and then retired . . .*

When I interviewed Janis Ian we were discussing if and how much performers have political influence on their audiences. I learned that Janis and Stevie think very much alike about what they want to do and what can be done with songs. Janis:

"I think performers have an influence sociologically. A young girl who learns from a song like *At Seventeen* that they don't have to believe all that nonsense that's told them by ads and things will be less inclined to vote for somebody who's lying to them.

"But I don't think that it is good for any singer to get up and say 'Ban the bomb' for instance. I don't think that that makes any impression any more. At least in the States. I mean we've never been attacked on our soil. In the States none of us have any idea what it's like to be bombed. Some of us have some idea what it's like to be at war. The guys who went to Vietnam for example. But even then none of us have any idea in Steve's and my generation what it is to fight to survive. It's very difficult then to create any kind of concern for that. Because there's nothing to relate it to. And if you say 'Ban the bomb' or whatever they just become slogans.

"But if you can change the way people feel about themselves – and that it what Stevie is aiming at and what I am also trying to do – if you can strip away the defences, open them up to *feeling,* they are less likely then to agree to bomb someone. To hurt someone. They are less likely to believe that anyone from China is out to destroy the United States. Or that black people are lesser people than the white ones just because of their colour. They are less likely to swallow that.

"And in that sense you have a political influence. Because you can constantly be educating them to like themselves. And then to like everyone else. But beyond that I don't think you can do anything. If I were to go up and say don't vote for such and such they would probably tell me to go fuck myself. And the same they would say to any other performer if their fans have any sense. You've got to educate people to think for themselves."

He's Misstra Know-It-All from the *Innervisions* album is another song that should make people think. For one, it is about the "coolest guy with the biggest mouth" and, Steve says, "it could be anybody. Someone you know in your circles or people like politicians. Or – even me. Really, when I played that song back after I'd recorded it I thought 'Wait a minute, am I writing about myself?'"

Golden Lady is another love song on the album. But this time, opposed to *All In Love Is Fair* the lyrics are purely optimistic:

> *A touch of rain and sunshine made the flower grow*
> *Into a lovely smile that's blooming*
> *And it's so clear to me that you're a dream come true*
> *There's no way that I'll be losing . . .*

The next three tracks are *Higher Ground, Jesus Children of America* and *All In Love Is Fair*. The second last song on the album (before *He's Misstra Know-It-All*) is called *Don't Worry 'Bout A Thing* and, as Steve says, "Sergio Mendes inspired". It reflects the easygoing mood of the Brazilian way of life: don't worry too much, especially not about things that other people tell you you should have. Check things out for yourself and find a way for your own happiness. This time Stevie handles the message he wants to put across with ease and the light melody turns it into a happy singalong song.

Three days after *Innervisions* had been released, on 6 August 1973, Stevie was in a car on his way to perform a benefit concert in Durham, South Carolina. He was in the front passenger seat fast asleep. His cousin John Harris was driving the car.

In the late afternoon the car was on Highway 85 from Greenville to Raleigh, following a truck loaded with logs. Reports of what happened next vary. Either Harris attempted to pass the truck, or the truck came to an abrupt stop – or perhaps both. The two vehicles collided and a log from the truck smashed through the windshield and broke Stevie's skull. Stevie did not wake up – and for a while it looked as if he never would.

Stevie was rushed to the Rowan Memorial Hospital in Salisbury, North Carolina, the nearest hospital, in a coma.

On the same day Stevie was transferred to the North Carolina Baptist Hospital in Winston-Salem, North Carolina. A press release from this hospital on 7 August, 10.30 a.m. said: "Stevie Wonder was listed in satisfactory condition at North Carolina Baptist Hospital.

"He was hospitalized in the intensive care unit of Baptist Hospital soon after arriving at the hospital at 8.55 p.m. on 6 August. He remains in the intensive care unit today.

"He is being attended by a team of physicians. He was described by one of his attending physicians as having a brain contusion, which is a bruise on the brain. He is making satisfactory progress and is slowly regaining consciousness, the doctor added.

"Stevie Wonder was transferred here from Rowan Memorial Hospital in Salisbury, North Carolina, where he was first taken after being in an auto accident near Salisbury. The transfer was desirable because of the presence of a Department of Neurosurgery at Baptist Hospital. No surgery, however, is indicated or contemplated."

This telex was taken over by Motown and send out to all radio stations and the press. At the same time Motown vice-president Michael Roshkind asked the company's employees not to call the hospital or send cards or flowers at this time. The inter-office memo also said that everybody will be kept informed as further progress reports are received.

The hospital's press release was supposed to calm down wild speculations on Stevie's state of health. The first unofficial reports had been very vague. Rumours had started that Stevie had fallen into a heavy coma and was not expected to survive. More than one paper pronounced Stevie Wonder dead.

On the other hand Stevie's situation was not quite as optimistic as it sounded in the telex. Stevie, who had been pulled from the car wreck bloody and unconscious, remained in the coma for several days. Ira Tucker says that it was "about a week" while articles give a time between four and ten days. The only positive statement that Stevie's doctors could make was that "there was no possibility whatsoever of permanent brain damage".

Ira: "Still we all freaked. When I first got to the hospital in Winston-Salem I could hardly recognize Steve. His head was all swollen up to about five times its usual size. And nobody was allowed to visit him."

Stevie does not remember anything about the car crash: "I can't recall what I thought when I was semi-conscious after the accident. I was asleep before it happened, and I never did wake up, so I was not aware of pain or anything, which is a very beautiful thing that Allah, or God, the Supreme Being, did for me.

"It was very peaceful. I had no conception of time or space or sound or anything. It was a very peaceful thing, but I can't remember how long it went on for."

His friends, though, were desperately trying to get through to Stevie. Just see him breathe, maybe hear him say just one word. One word was all they prayed for to let them know he was *alive*.

Ira: "After I had a long talk with the doctor I was allowed to visit him. I had told the doctor that Stevie lives and breathes music and that this might be a way of getting him back to consciousness. The first day the doctor was sceptical, but I explained to him that Stevie always listens to music very loud and that I wanted to try to at least speak to him in a louder voice than the staff at the hospital had done so far. Finally the doctor gave me the go ahead.

"When I tried I first didn't get any response from Stevie. But the next day I went back and very loudly I sang *Higher Ground* directly into his ear while I had taken his hand:

Till I reach my highest ground
No one's gonna bring me down . . .
Gonna keep on tryin' . . .

After a while Stevie's fingers started going in time with the song. Then I knew it, that he was going to make it!"

But slowly gaining consciousness again tore Stevie out of his peace and he was beginning to feel pain. "I was aware of people around and they had to give me blood and everything. I was still semi-conscious but then I felt pain – because I'm scared of needles."

About this semi-conscious state Stevie remembers another thing: "There was a girl there with me and I kept saying, 'C'mon, get into bed – let's go to sleep!' And she would say, 'Where do you think you are?' and I said, 'Well, we're in New York, aren't we?' and she said, 'You're in a hospital in Winston-Salem, North Carolina and you had an accident.' It was really heavy."

After a two-week stay in Winston-Salem Stevie got transferred again, this time to a hospital in Los Angeles, where, according to Motown, he was "closer to home". Stevie: "I think a lot of people from the Motown office in L.A. were very concerned after the accident and wanted me to be close to them. They made a mistake by saying 'close to home'. That's not my home."

Still, Motown had at least shown good intentions. Because Stevie is blind, the doctors had assumed that the total impact of the accident had been increased threefold and they wanted him to stay in familiar surroundings to feel as much at home and comfortable as possible. Stevie, on his side, had fortunately dedicated himself totally to making a quick recovery. Steve: "My brother Calvin I think had to keep pushing me back into bed so that I wouldn't get up before I should in hospital. You know it was close – it was very very close, closer than people let me know at the time, but I did find out how close it was."

With this accident Stevie had lost some of his sense of smell and taste. He took it easy. "Listen", he said, "it's either you lose your sense of smell or your life! Which would you choose? When you get a contusion in the head it can affect a lot of things, and I can't smell things that I used to be able to."

But there was one thing that Stevie was afraid might have been affected by the contusion: "I was frightened that I might not be able to play again. To create again. But then I just tried playing a few tunes on the clavinet – and I knew that it would be all right again."

Ira Tucker remembers: "You should have seen Stevie's face when we brought the clavinet to hospital. For a while, he just looked at it and you could tell that he was afraid to touch it. He didn't know if he had lost his musical gift. And then he finally started playing. And you could actually see the relief and the happiness all over his face. I will always remember that."

Motown had also been afraid of Stevie having lost his creativity and his skill to play. Malcolm Cecil: "Everybody was whispering, talking, asking 'Is he the same?' when Steve was back in the studio. At the first few sessions everyone watched him anxiously. People were looking, staring at him: did the accident affect his music? Has he still got the ability to play? Fortunately Stevie's creative and technical abilities had remained the same." Questioned if the accident had changed his music, Stevie answered:

"I would like to feel that all the time, even in the past, my music has changed somewhat with each album or each song or whatever."

Steveland Morris, the person behind Stevie Wonder, had also changed. Although he said that he had been prepared for a major change in his life. "I knew that something was going to happen. Something that was very, very significant. And it did – the accident happened."

About how significant this event was Stevie says: "I guess God just said, 'Steve, you need a rest,' and I didn't rest, so he said 'You need to rest,' and I still didn't rest. So I guess he said, 'You need to rest – I'll give you the *big* rest.'" And a lot of time to think: "I was unconscious, and I was definitely, for a few days, in a much better spiritual place that made me aware of a lot of things that concern my life." Something the accident made Stevie realize is:

"There are a lot of things I took for granted. And it's made me check out myself and the people around me. It's made me more sensitive toward people. I have also realized how precious time is. To waste the time of someone else's life is an insult, I believe.

"You realize how important time is. How it's necessary to do as much as you can with the time and space that you are allowed in life. You learn to value life and time much more. But you also learn to take time out and relax. Like go fishin' or lay on the grass for an hour or so."

Stevie did slow down, but only a little and only for a short while. In 1973 Ira Tucker told *Esquire*: "The accident has changed Stevie more than anything. It's really cooled him out. He never used to sleep. He'd call me at four in the morning and say, 'Hey, we gotta go to the studio, right now.' But I think he's over the hump now; he's got an idea of what it's all about. He called me the other morning and he said, 'Tuck, when I was in hospital, out cold, did I do a lot of heavy breathing?' I said, 'Yeah, man, you sure did.' And he just said, 'I thought so', and hung up."

Bird of Beauty, from Stevie's *Fulfillingness' First Finale* album, is a song that Stevie said he wrote about slowing down:

> *There is so much in life for you to feel*
> *Unfound in white, red or yellow pills*
> *A mind excursion can be such a thrill*
> *You please satisfy – take the chance and ride*
> *The bird of beauty of the sky . . .*

Steve: "This tune is God telling me that I should do other things to help me. I've never gone hiking, really, and there are so many things I know are beautiful and though I've never gone or done these things I know I've experienced them in my writing. And I'm also going to live them out."

But although the accident has made Stevie realize even more how much he enjoys living and according to him made him find himself he has gone back to staying up almost 20 hours a day and calling his friends or business associates at four or five in the morning. Gypsie Jones: "Soon after the accident Steve was a very introvert person. He was too introverted. I prefer the now-Steve. He has loosened up again."

Doug Kee: "I agree with what Gypsie says. Although there

222

is no doubt that he became more spiritual after the car crash. The probability of Stevie dying through the accident was so great, he was so close to it, that when he came out it made him deeper. Deeper within himself and also in his relationships with other people. I'm sure that in time Steve would have gotten that deep anyway. The accident just sort of hurried it up."

While Stevie was in hospital his single *Higher Ground* had reached the top of *Billboard*'s R & B charts and gotten to number four in the "Pop 100". (In England the single went up to number 29 in October.) On 7 September, not even four weeks after release, *Innervisions* had top sales of one million dollars in U.S.A.

Four days later Stevie gave a press conference at the Fifth Avenue Hotel in Greenwich Village, New York, the city he called his home. He had arrived one week earlier to visit his mother, left again for another day, and come back. Within the week he had turned up backstage at Buddy Miles' show at the Schaefer Festival. "It was the first time I had been anywhere in public [since the accident], except to see *Detroit 9000* [a movie] and *Gordon's War* – which, I think, is the best black movie in a long time," he told the journalists.

Questions regarding his state of health Stevie answered with: "I feel okay. But I'll have to be on medication for at least another six months. The loss of my sense of taste and smell may be permanent. It goes, then comes back, goes again, comes back. The doctor said I would sometimes get tired, maybe late at night, but I can do it."

The only thing that physically reminds Stevie of the accident today are two nasty scars over his right eye which the crash has left him with. But the scars, still favourite subject for some photographers who take pictures of Stevie, do not bother him. He does not even mind his face being photographed from the scarred side. "It doesn't make any difference to me," he says, "but I suppose that the photographers make better money with these kind of pictures."

During the press conference Stevie also thanked his friends and fans who gave him moral support when he was in hospital. "I was able to feel the spirit, and the vibes of love from many,

many people who were hoping that everything was cool. I would like to say that for all the concern and love I got that helped me pull through, I was very happy. I'd like to thank you for showing your love. I hope you will hear this love on my next album. Together, we can conquer the world."

Stevie also said that his dreams were no crazier than before, that he was thinking of going to Africa for a vacation and that his first performance after the accident would be in New York. When journalists mentioned his nomination for Grammy awards he said:

"I definitely feel that Marvin Gaye should have received a Grammy. And Al Green should have gotten an award. If they say Stevie's music is *black music*, it's up to us black people to create a situation that others will not have to go through this, because this is supposed to be the Land of the Free.

"I hope that the person I'm about to mention will receive a Grammy because he has given so much to the music industry. I hope he receives it before he dies. Hope it's not like Mahalia Jackson or Louis Armstrong. That person is Ray Charles."

Steve also said that he might like to score movies and when someone asked if he felt that he'd been ripped-off by Motown he answered: "As long as I'm satisfied I don't feel I'm being ripped-off. I contractually have a deal with Motown where my songs are given to them through my production company which is Taurus Productions, and Taurus gives the material to Motown.

"We give 50 per cent of the publishing to Jobete Music, but Black Bull is my company. There are people now who are working on placing my material with different artists, producers, and A & R people at various companies, because we'd like that to happen faster than it's been happening. I am satisfied with this arrangement, and I know that it's a special one.

"Of course, if there were ever a time when I wasn't satisfied with it, I would contractually make sure that it were changed."

Rumours that Stevie was *not* completely satisfied with the deal he had made with Motown in 1971 had already started coming through. It would not take much time for them to become stronger. Still, Stevie said he did not think of forming his own label: "Too much money. Even before my business what I enjoy doing is performing, singing and writing, producing, mixing, and after that I don't think you have too much time for controlling a label or running a company. I have business consultants and attorneys and they handle the business aspect of it and I will basically tell them how I feel about particular things. But my thing is creating."

After the press conference there was a party and journalists as well as Stevie's musicians and staff gathered to celebrate his return. But apart from joking around with everybody, Stevie already started to work on songs again. He had not seen his band for six weeks and the next day Steve and Wonderlove started rehearsals for his next album at the Upsurge Studios on West Nineteenth Street. Stevie was also working on producing an album with just Wonderlove – but that he has done since the band started and nothing has come out of this project so far.

For *Fulfillingness' First Finale* Stevie had already played most of the instruments on quite a lot of tracks. But now he wanted the band to learn the tunes for their live shows. Stevie and Wonderlove were back in their element and the rehearsal worked out great.

Three days later Stevie and his entourage went to the Yankee Stadium for the annual benefit football game between Grambling College and Morgan State. The stadium was crowded with 60,000 to 70,000 people as this game is the sporting and social event of autumn in Harlem. As soon as some people had recognized Stevie, the news spread in no time and Steve found himself surrounded by thousands of fans of his who asked him for autographs and also wanted to know how he was. Ira Tucker took care of the situation by telling the crowd that Stevie was all right but still a little too weak to sign his name. So he handed out photographs instead.

By the time Stevie had finished with that the first half of the game had been played. Then a woman stepped to a microphone, giving out a long blues shout. The audience went wild and Stevie immediately recognized the voice: Aretha Franklin, the Queen of Soul. After the second half of the football game, it took Stevie almost an hour to get through to his car. Everybody who saw him just wanted to talk to him for a little while. Many of his fans told him that they had prayed for him while he was in hospital.

On 25 September 1973, Stevie went to New York. He had been invited by Elton John's promotion people to join Elton at a concert at Boston Garden. Steve's attendance was planned as a surprise for Elton, so they hid Stevie and his people in one of the back bedrooms of Elton's Boeing 707 *Starship I*. The plane, painted gold and maroon, had the letters *Elton John 1973* on the fuselage and Ira could hardly stop looking at the big bird that was glowing in the sun. Ira:

"At this moment I would have really liked to talk Stevie into buying a plane. Elton's *Starship I* is just out of sight! It is so extravagant that you can't imagine it unless you've seen it. The interior is done in thick maroon plush and it has a shiny reflecting ceiling above. You just sink into the seats and there is a long, brass-topped bar with a built-in electric organ. In the back bedrooms and – what am I telling you? – one is ruined for touring on a bus forever. It even has a real fireplace. Ohhoo, it's all too much!"

When the plane was airborne Steve sneaked out of his hiding and began playing the organ. Elton was then persuaded to meet the "cocktail organist". Ira: "You should have seen Elton's face when he recognized Stevie. And Stevie, enjoying himself like a little kid, kept on playing *Crocodile Rock*. After he finished the number the two of them rapped a little and then Elton went back to his seat. He wanted to relax a little before the gig."

Stevie: "The thing that amused me even more than the whole trip was when Elton showed me his famous light-up eyeglasses which spell out *Elton*. I think that's hilarious!"

Elton was on stage for almost two hours, then, after he had given a rousing encore, Elton introduced Stevie to the audience: "A friend of mine is here. He was badly hurt in an accident some time ago . . ." But before Elton could finish the sentence the 20,000 Elton John fans started to scream with joy. Ira: "They had to wait for almost fifteen minutes until they could start playing. That is how excited the audience was. Then, when it had become a little quieter, Elton and Stevie would jam into *Honky Tonk Woman* and Steve took off on a side-shot at *Superstition*. You should have heard those 20,000 people breaking into applause and screams. They clapped their hands, stomped their feet and they just couldn't get enough of it."

Now everybody knew that Stevie had really come back. Still, the doctors had not allowed Stevie to do concerts of his own until the end of the year. So he kept working on *Fulfillingness' First Finale* and Motown released another single from *Innervisions*. *Living For The City/Visions* came out in October and a month later topped the R & B charts. In December it went up to number 8 in the "Pop 100" and in England it hit the charts at position 15 the beginning of the following year.

In November 1973 Stevie was presented with the Netherlands Edison Award for *Talking Book*, which was also Steve's first album to turn platinum (two million dollars in sales). The Edison Award is presented annually to members of the recording industry for "excellence in recording and production", after a polling of independent jurors that include record critics, radio and television producers, disc jockeys and record retail experts.

In the same month *Cashbox* magazine named Stevie Wonder as the top selling album artist. Results of the survey are based on chart positions and length of time in the charts. Stevie reached the number 1 position through his two million-selling albums *Talking Book* and *Innervisions*, both of which topped the charts. Second in the album section was Elton John. In 1973 Elton's *Don't Shoot Me, I'm Only The Piano Player* and *Goodbye Yellow Brick Road* had been released after *Honky Chateau* in 1972.

In the single section it was just the other way around: Elton came first with his *Honky Cat, Crocodile Rock* (1972), *Daniel, Saturday Night's All Right For Fighting* and *Goodbye Yellow Brick Road* (1973). Then came Stevie with *Superstition, You Are The Sunshine Of My Life, Higher Ground* and *Living For The City*.

At the end of 1973 Stevie could look back on three chart-topping hits which at the same time were gold discs (*You Are*

The Sunshine Of My Life, Higher Ground and *Living For The City*)
and another million selling album which was to become platinum: *Innervisions*.

Talking about the changes that had happened regarding
his career and his private life, Stevie said that he would do it
all over again the same way if he was given a chance to:
"It was a learning experience and that's what the journey of
life is: to learn, experience, and remember." Steve did not
even quarrel with the fate that brought him the accident:
"See, you can never change anything that's already happened
anyway. So why should I worry about it? Everything is the
way it is supposed to be. For me it is, and I accept it." Steve
also said: "Life is a chance. Walking out there, going downstairs, getting in the car is a chance you take. Every time you
open your mouth you're taking a chance, so what?"

But 1973 had also held something else for Stevie, that would
change his life again. At the end of the year he had met
Yolanda Simmons, the lady who would fulfil a long-felt yearn-
ing in Stevie.

For Stevie wanted to be a father.

CHAPTER TEN

Isn't She Lovely

Stevie met Yolanda on the telephone. "She was applying for a job as a secretary with my publishing company Black Bull in New York. Fortunately I was around when she rang up and so I talked to her. I liked the way the lady's voice sounded, so I asked her to come into the office. I was right about my first impression: Yolanda is one of the warmest people I've ever met. We soon became friends and eventually lovers."

Yolanda, who is the same age as Stevie, was lucky to get to talk to Steve himself. Black Bull's telephone number was then in the phone book. Today it is ex-directory, not only because fans would ring up all the time and ask for Steve, but also so many people were taking advantage of Steve. Lee Garrett: "Everybody who rang up said that he was a friend of Steve's and made collect calls to his office. You can imagine the amount of money that Steve had to pay on his phone bill every month with hundreds of people transferring the charges, not only from all over the States but also from other continents. That is why he finally decided to keep the number secret and just give it to very good friends or business associates."

When you ring Steve's New York office, you very seldom find his secretary Lynn answering the telephone, but you hear Stevie's voice from an answering machine. He changes the messages every now and then, because he just loves playing with tapes, but generally he says something like:

"Hi, this is Stevie Wonder. And this is an answering machine, and now you guess that I'm not in and you've just wasted a nickel. You're right. But you can make up to this loss if you leave your name and telephone number on the tape. Then I'm probably gonna call you back." Sometimes he plays music from his tape machine and tells you to have a nice day, even though you have just missed him.

But even if Stevie is near the telephone in either his office or his homes in New York or Los Angeles, even friends of his have a hard time getting through to him. Gypsie Jones: "Like when we did all those long sessions on his new album [*Songs In The Key Of Life*] and I would leave the studio at some odd hour in the night, Stevie always asked me to call back when I'm home to let him know that I've arrived safely.

"And when I do, there's someone on the phone who says Stevie is not taking any calls or that no one can talk to him or that he's busy or some bullshit. And the next day Steve wants to know why you didn't ring back. It's ridiculous. Sometimes some idiot even tells you that Stevie's not in town and you know that he is because you've just seen him an hour ago. It's crazy."

Elaine Jesmer: "I remember trying to call Stevie a few years back. Clarence Paul, who is a mutual friend of ours, was going through some really heavy, really bad things. He was down and out, he was drinking heavily and he desperately needed help. But as Clarence had too much pride to call Steve – Clarence would never ask anyone for any favours – I tried to get through to Stevie. Of course there was no way to get hold of him through Motown.

"I finally got Steve's number from a friend of his, but even then he didn't answer his own phone at home. It was someone doing the really heavy number like 'Who are you and what do you want and what are your credentials?' So I said, 'Listen. Just tell Steve that if he cares about Clarence Paul he'll talk to me.' In two seconds Stevie was on the phone. So I told him 'Clarence needs your help but he is too proud to call you. He's waiting for you to call him.' Steve did at once. He had had no idea that Clarence was having problems. Had he known he would have gotten there a lot faster.

"He is such a genuine person and he never lets a friend down. He is so genuine, that I don't even want to say he's genuine because everybody uses or misuses the word."

The problem of getting to Stevie is one that bothers most of his friends. Steve is surrounded by so many people who want to make every decision for him that they don't even tell Steve what is happening. Malcolm Cecil: "He has to deal with so many levels of reality through the eyes and mainly the trust of other people. If it hadn't been for Stevie I wouldn't have put up with the things that his organization put me through at times. But then I kept telling myself that it is not Stevie who is to blame for it but all those people around him."

When you hear all this the natural question to ask is why Steve does not get rid of people who want to run his private life. Lee Garrett: "See, somehow Stevie wants to believe the people who surround him. If he would not it would be very frustrating for him to live with them. And you know yourself how long it takes 'til you can really trust someone.

"Stevie I think sometimes guesses that a lot of bullshitting is going on around him. But then he just does not want to be bothered with it because it would take him away from his music. One day we had a row even – Steve didn't talk to me for almost a year. Just because someone in his organization had told him some shit about me which wasn't true at all. I won't go into what it was – but Stevie believed him. And it took a long time until we met again and sorted it all out."

Gypsie Jones: "Steve knows what's wrong with his organization. But on the other hand he is well protected and if he sacks some people today there will be others tomorrow who are the same. I guess he just puts up with it as we all have to. It's only lucky that Yolanda got hold of him . . ."

Although Yolanda and Steve met in late 1973, they did not spend too much time together in the first few months of their friendship. Stevie was busy travelling around with other ladies accompanying him. In early 1974 he started giving concerts again – only just over five months after he had survived the car crash.

Stevie's first official concert after his unwilling break was in January at the "Midem" Convention in Cannes, France. He opened the first gala on 20 January with the Pointer Sisters. From Cannes Stevie flew to London where he gave two concerts at London's Rainbow Theatre. Both dates were sold out within a few hours and the ticket prices on the black market were around £50 each.

Quite a number of tickets were sold to Steve's fellow musicians. Linda and Paul McCartney had especially flown in from the North of England. Ringo Starr, who says "I wish I could sing like Stevie" was there; and also Pete Townshend, Charlie Watts, Denny Laine, Jimmy McCulloch, Kiki Dee, Steve Clarke, Rod Stewart and Eric Clapton who declared Stevie after he had played a drum solo "the best drummer in the world". David Bowie is said to have asked for tickets for a block of 20 seats but was told "not to be silly". Even for stars it was hard to get tickets for their friends.

Both concerts were recorded live by Radio Luxemburg and Ken Evans, then head of the radio station in London, told me that a double album was scheduled for release some time in 1977. In the beginning of February Stevie did two extra concerts at the Rainbow which were also sold out in no time. But before that Steve flew to Bremen, West Germany, where he did a one-hour-special for Mike Leckebusch's TV show *Musikladen*.

Strangely enough Germany is one country where Stevie has not given a live concert to date (1977). Jochen Kraus, Motown manager Cologne: "When Stevie was in his teens black music was something that did not go at all in Germany. Even now black acts find it very difficult to break in Germany. Another problem with Steve was that there seemed to be not only a language barrier but also a lack of understanding of the messages that Stevie puts across. Many of the problems that Steve talks about in his songs do not occur in Germany. People don't know what it means to have ghetto or colour problems to that extent. They cannot relate to it. Also, the music scene in Germany is very different from what it is in the rest of the world and apart from teeny-bopper music it takes much longer for a new kind of music to get through to people."

Germany is the one country where David Essex did not come to fame. While his concerts in America and England were crowded with raving fans he only sold 78 tickets for a concert in Munich. A press conference Helen Reddy gave before a TV show was only attended by three journalists. Helen, whose *Angie Baby* was in all other charts got so mad about being neglected that she left the reception as soon as she had walked in. She cancelled her television appearance and got on the next plane from Hamburg back home to Australia. Rod Stewart also feels misplaced in Germany and Bruce Springsteen never even went there. And Frank Sinatra left Germany right in the middle of a tour because he did not get a warm enough welcome. It is only lately that Stevie seems to be getting recognition in Germany. In April 1977 Steve was awarded with the Preis du Deutschen Phonogesellschaft in Bonn in the category of black music, and also the Record of the Year for *Songs In The Key Of Life*.

When Stevie came back from Europe he gave a concert at New York's Madison Square Garden. It is almost superfluous to mention that this concert was sold out in a matter of a few hours and became The Date and The Concert of the year. On this March day 21,000 people had gathered to see Stevie's first scheduled public appearance in the United States since his accident.

Stevie started the concert with an instrumental jazz number, introducing every musician in his band. *Contusion* was the instrumental that he had composed just after he had left hospital. (Still Steve did not put this tune on his next album but used it on his double album *Songs In The Key Of Life* which was released in autumn 1976.) From *Contusion*, still low-keyed, Steve went into *Superwoman* slowly to build the show up. When he played *Keep On Running* nearly one hour after the concert had started, Stevie had gotten the audience where he wanted them. He then did songs from his last album and towards the end played hits like *Living In The City* and *You Are The Sunshine Of My Life*.

When he closed with *Superstition* his fans were in for a special treat: Roberta Flack, Sly Stone and Eddie Kendricks were joining in the song. Steve was especially happy to have Roberta with him on stage. She is one of his favourite female vocalists. "The great singers are the ones who can take a song and make it mean a lot to many people. Roberta is one of them." The

233

audience got on their feet, dancing, clapping their hands and singing along. Stevie had again succeeded in uniting the audience with the musicians on stage. The band played *Superstition* in the longest version ever and whenever the audience seemed to be getting a little quieter, because they wanted to hear what Stevie was doing, he asked them to keep singing along, "so that maybe our Father, our Maker can hear us!"

For Stevie, performing live and getting the audience on to his vibes is "a challenge to make the audience aware of everything that's within me". He stays on stage for at least two hours per show and sometimes, even after a long concert like this, he gives an encore. Doug Kee: "Encores were a very rare thing, though. Because Stevie feels that once he's played that amount of time non-stop he's really given everything he can possibly give and even more so, that the audience has heard enough. He knows that if it were up to them he could go on playing for another two hours without them getting tired. But there is a line that you have to draw when you're in the music business. It is better to stop a show when people still want more than to tire them out until they feel that they want to go home."

Another reason for not giving encores often is an experience that Steve made on his extra dates at the Rainbow Theatre in London in February 1974 and which was written up in the *Melody Maker*: ". . . when he heard the reception his first concerts drew he stayed an extra week to play more shows. The extra ones proved almost too taxing (Stevie still tired quickly). He couldn't get into his groove, the shows spluttered and faltered but still his audience called him back for two encores.

"The second one he could not play and knew he did not really deserve. He edged towards the front of the stage and took off his dark glasses – 'This is the only pair I have with me,' he said – and he threw them to the audience. By that gesture he was saying 'I've given you everything. These glasses are about the only things I have left.' Without them his unseeing eyes were naked for the whole hall to see. I felt like crying."

Stevie is one of the very few artists who can even touch the heart of pop journalists who generally are not that easily moved by anything that goes on on stage. Unless he is a very young journalist who is still enchanted with the music scene, a critic will tend to react rather bluntly to what he sees and hears in concerts or gets told in interviews. Not so with Steve. There is hardly any review or interview concerning Stevie where the writer can distance himself. What Burr Snider wrote in his article "Hey, Stevie Wonder, How's Your Bad Self?" for *Esquire* is typical of the feelings that most journalists get when dealing with Stevie:

"I've just met Steve a little while ago here in the bar, but it is already clear that we are not to relate solely as writer and subject. Whatever objectivity I've brought into this is crumbling fast. My God, I'm thinking, I don't want to write a press release on the guy, but I love him already."

It is true. When talking to Stevie you are not doing an interview any more but you have a conversation with him. When you speak to Steve it is no longer for the sake of an article you have to write but because *you* want to find out what makes this man tick. Stevie has so much to say and so much to give that you can only learn from him. Sometimes he is joking around so much that he is laughingly called "the black version of Jerry Lee Lewis". He is discussing attitudes and life, singing new tunes to you, he is humorous, genuine, sincere and he radiates such a warmth that you cannot help but love and adore this man.

There are very few people in the music business that make you feel like you really want to *talk* to them. Once you have spoken to a few it does not take much to figure out what the others are going to tell you. There are, of course, exceptions; like Paul Simon, Jackson Browne, Pete Townshend, Chris de Burgh, Harry Nilsson and John Denver. There are Paul Anka, Peter Allen, Janis Ian, Peter Sarstedt and Joni Mitchell who can make your heart smile with their songs or make you very lonely at times. Or very strong and who can make you think. They, too, have something to say not only with their music. But if you added them all up, the singer/songwriters of our time

235

who put out albums where every song means a lot to you, you probably would not count more than 50 really important artists. And still none of them are as extraordinary as Stevie, because of the circumstances under which he has grown into the artist that he is today.

With Stevie it never ceases to amaze what blindness, being black, religion, facing death, the blues and the ghetto have produced. Ron Miller once said: "Stevie's artistic achievement does not surprise me in the least bit. The success of it surprises me. Because you don't really expect someone who is capable of evolving that high to actually evolve that high. With many other gifted people personal things screw their career up somewhere along the way. And even if they do evolve that high you don't expect that all the world really realizes and rewards it."

Fortunately for Stevie people did. In March 1974, he was nominated for seven Grammies, and awarded five of them: for *Innervisions* as the album of the year and the best engineered recording (non-classical); for the best pop-vocal-performance-male with *You Are The Sunshine Of My Life*; for the best R & B vocal-performance-male with *Superstition*; and the songwriter award for the same single as the best R & B song. (The Grammy is the music business's Oscar.)

Doug Kee: "When Steve won all these Grammies it was as much of a trip for everybody working with Steve as it was for him. Everyone was there, the whole band, the lot. The whole thing was televised from the Hollywood Palladium in Los Angeles and Stevie had insisted on inviting each and every one of us and he paid for it. Like he flew in people from New York and all over the place and he paid every cent of it – even down to the renting of the taxis for everybody. Because Stevie felt that everybody of his crew had contributed something to the fact that he got all these awards.

"And we really felt like we'd all won. Every time they said his name our table went crazy. It was so bizarre – although we all knew what was happening – I don't know why we were so sure before – it was like a dream when we really walked away with five Grammies. It was really weird. There was some vibe going on between everybody which made us know what would happen, but when it finally did it blew our mind. And Stevie, that is really typical for the good people that he is, took a page in *Billboard* to say thanks to everybody. And he had all the names down of anybody who had anything to do whatsoever with anything. That really felt good. Stevie is really one of the most fantastic people that I've ever met."

When Stevie was awarded with the Grammies he said "I would like to thank you all for making this night the sunshine of my life." Then Stevie passed his Grammy for the best engineered recording for *Innervisions* on to his recording engineers. He felt that Robert and Malcolm deserved it.

Also in March Motown released another single from Stevie's *Innervisions* album: *Don't You Worry 'Bout A Thing/Blame It On The Sun*. In April this single – which also became a gold disc – got to number 2 in the American R & B charts. In *Billboard*'s "Pop 100" it got to position 16 in May. In England, where *He's Misstra Know-It-All/You Can't Judge A Book By Its Cover* had come out instead this A-side made number 10 in the *Music Week* charts. (*Don't You Worry 'Bout A Thing* was put out as a single in the U.K. in July but never entered the charts.)

At the beginning of 1974 Stevie was also doing some production work for others as he had done before with the Supremes (the single *Bad Weather*) and Main Ingredient (LP *Afrodisiac*) to name but two. This time Steve produced the *Stevie Wonder Presents Syreeta* album and also an LP with Rufus, then a relatively unknown group. *Tell Me Something Good*, a track from this, the band's second album (*Rags To Rufus*), topped the American charts in summer the same year. Around the same time Stevie also produced and wrote three songs for the Jackson Five: *You Won't Give Up Your Buttercup, Keep Your Love For Me* and *No News Is Good News*. The latter was a song that Stevie had done at the Rainbow Theatre in London. Originally he had thought of recording it himself. "But," he says, "there was a party for me after the Grammy awards and when I played this song the Jackson Five asked me if they could have it." The Osmonds, the white counterpart to the Jackson Five (Alan, Wayne, Merrill, Jay, Donny, Jimmy and

Marie Osmond – the youngest being born in April 1963, the oldest in June 1949) wanted the song, too. Steve: "The decision which group to give it to wasn't easy. But in the end I went for the Jackson Five." They thanked him for it by singing the backing vocals on one of the tracks of Stevie's next album. Stevie also did a few things with the Temptations, "one of them being their version of *Golden Lady*. The way it came out I even prefer their recording of the song to the one that I did. I wish I had thought of that earlier." Steve was also a session guest on B. J. Thomas' version of *Happier Than The Morning Sun* and in the beginning of the year he was responsible for Aretha Franklin having a number 3 hit in the American charts: *Until You Come Back (That's What I'm Gonna Do)* was a song that Stevie had co-written almost 13 years earlier. Aretha's producer had found it, she recorded it and another one of Stevie's tucked-away songs had come to fame.

As well as working with other artists and doing a few gigs here and there Stevie was busy writing and recording tracks for his new album *Fulfillingness' First Finale*. From all that people could see and also from what Stevie had said in interviews, it seemed that he was even heavier into his work than ever before – if that was possible.

So it came to an enormous shock to everybody when at the end of March 1974 the music papers carried the headline that Stevie Wonder had decided to quit. The *New Musical Express* ran a story in which Stevie announced that for the next two years he intended to tour extensively throughout North America to raise money for charity. He also said that at the end of 1975 (January 1976 the latest) he would go on a Farewell World Tour, then quit the music business completely and go to Africa. There in Ghana he would work with handicapped, blind and underprivileged children.

Why Africa? Stevie explained: "People ask me why am I going to Africa when there's so much to be done here. Well, America doesn't make a lot of people aware of what's happening in other parts of the world. I hope to bring back an alternative way from Africa.

"Also I want to do something for blind people over there.

Like 40 per cent of the blindness in Ethiopia, for example, is caused by a fly that carries a fungus to the cornea. We have to *do* something about this disease which is called 'sleeping sickness' and causes blindness. I want to try to set up a foundation to combat this illness."

Up to that point Stevie had only talked about going to Africa on vacation and mainly because of the music: "I want to go to as many countries in Africa as possible and it will have a great significance on my next album. There will be no recording in Africa but if we write any songs (in Swahili) we will bring a translator and musicians back.

"The reason that I'm going first of all is to just become aware of what it's all about. To meet people and to meet not just the dignitaries but the common folks because that's when you get down to the real nitty-gritty.

"In Africa there'll be a lot of things musically which I will experience and I can incorporate into my music. But I will make the people aware of where I got it from. Because when you go into a culture or a different country and you hear a certain kind of music that you enjoy you can really show your appreciation of the music and of that country or culture by letting them know on a record or whatever that you have a lot of love for it."

Now Stevie did not seem to be as interested in Africa's music any more but only commented: "Maybe I'll take a tape recorder over there and just sit out and write some stuff. But my main reason for going to Africa is that I want to help other people."

When Stevie came out with these statements Motown's executives tried to play it cool. By now Berry Gordy jr. had moved the company to Los Angeles (in 1972), made himself chairman of his conglomerate and gotten involved with movies while he had made Ewart Abner president of Tamla Motown.

Abner had started his career in the music business in 1950 on the staff of Chance records in Chicago, and later became president of Vee Jay records. When this company folded in 1966 he joined Motown as a producer. Although officially he is said to have become Motown's president in 1973, he held a special position within the company in 1971 already. He was the one who Stevie had told that he wanted out instead of re-negotiating his contract. Abner left Motown at the end of 1975 and Barney Ales became his successor.

A Motown employee: "Not even we know who runs the company really. It's quite chaotic. There are lots of vice-presidents and Barney Ales had an important position with Motown before Abner was made president. We heard rumours that Ales did not want to work with Abner, so he left Motown or did not move with them to Los Angeles respectively. He did his own thing in Detroit and all of a sudden we get told that Abner's gone and Barney Ales is back."

According to Elaine Jesmer, Ewart Abner left because he was "too nice". Elaine: "The rumour that came up when Ewart Abner left was that he really had had good intentions. Like also seeing the artist's and not only the company's point of view. I heard he was a pretty nice guy. But nice people don't seem to stick around Motown in top positions for long. Hustling and hard necks make it there, so the word goes . . ."

What Elaine told me is a rumour that many other people told me: Abner was too friendly. Barney Ales, on the other hand, carries a reputation of being "slightly vulgar but taking a kind of pride in it".

However, when Stevie publicized his intention to quit the music business for good, it was Ewart Abner who had to try and convince Stevie otherwise. Having been in the business for almost 25 years he did not panic but his comment on Stevie's plans was: "We shall try to point out to Stevie that he can do more good for the cause by raising money in concert than by going out there to work."

It was very obvious, though, that the last thing that Motown could afford was to let Stevie Wonder go. When he was 21 they had to make him stay. Even if Motown had not had a clue how big an artist Stevie would turn out to be they had to keep him for the sake of their reputation. After all, Motown had raised him. They wanted to be looked upon as a family – and it looks bad when children leave their parents the day they come of age.

This time it was even more important for Motown to make Stevie stay. They had already lost Johnny Bristol, the Four Tops, Gladys Knight and the Pips, Martha Reeves, Ashford & Simpson, the Spinners and four of the Jackson Five to name but a few hot acts. The company was signing more artists releasing more product and getting fewer hits. Jim Gilstrap: "Like the Four Seasons who were signed to launch the Mowest label when Motown moved to L.A. and started it. They never made it there. But as soon as Franki Valli left for Private Stock he was back on top again."

The following table is based on entries to the British Market Research Bureau/BBC Top 20 and shows how rapidly Motown lost chart positions:

September 1972 to August 1973:

   12 hits out of 46 releases = 26.1 per cent.

September 1973 to August 1974:

   6 hits out of 46 releases = 12.2 per cent.

September 1974 to August 1975:

   4 hits out of 62 releases = 6.5 per cent.

More and more artists were openly complaining about Motown's business politics, and only few acts still at the top at Motown are too close to leave: Marvin Gaye, who is an ex-brother-in-law (he is now divorced from Anna Gordy); Diana Ross is a special protégé; Smokey Robinson is one of the many vice-presidents and Jermaine Jackson was married to Berry Gordy jr.'s daughter Hazel.

Shortly after Stevie had caused such a stir by wanting to leave the music business, the subject was dropped. Some Motown employees like the company's then London press officer Michael McDonagh are even said to have denied the whole story by answering journalists' further questions with "I doubt if Stevie would have made that sort of statement." He sure had, but then Stevie is not the only one who declared his retirement and changed his mind again: David Bowie, Ian Anderson and Frank Sinatra for instance did the same. Stevie explained his decision to only go to Africa for holidays instead of living there by saying: "I wanted to go to Ghana but then I made up my mind not to. There are people here I would like to help. America makes me very angry at times. It's the closest to being right – but it could be out of sight."

Had Stevie emphasized before that "America doesn't make people aware of what's happening in other parts in the world" and that he hoped "to bring back an alternative way from Africa" he had now come to the conclusion that he might as well stay in America and take it from there. In many interviews Stevie told everybody what he thinks is wrong with our Western culture:

"People are too much into materialism. Their values are that they need the finest and baddest of all." In regard to himself he said: "Luxury frightens me. It is something that fucks people's heads up. Like when I'm on the road all I need is a little sleeping bag. I don't need no luxurious buses or planes to rest my body." Stevie also talked about something else that freaks him and that he would like to see changed: the way that people treat other people depending on *what* you are instead of *who* you are. This subject had come up when *Penthouse* asked Stevie if he had ever thought what it would be like to be an average person rather than a celebrity. Stevie answered:

"It's funny – sometimes I pretend not to be a star to see what happens. I just say to somebody that I'm Steveland Morris. The person doesn't know who that is and they say 'Yeah, yeah' – very bold, very negative – 'Yeah, well what do you do?' And I say, 'Well, I'm an artist and I've done some things.' And they say 'Really? Your name is Steveland Morris?' Then I say I've done some tunes – have they heard *Sunshine Of My Life*? They say, 'Yeah, I heard Frank Sinatra do it on TV,' and I say, 'Yeah, well I wrote that.' *'Steveland Morris?'* 'Yeah,' I say, 'my professional name is Stevie Wonder.' 'You're Stevie Wonder? Son-of-a-bitch, man!' And all of a sudden they're really nice.

"One time I had to take my woman to a hospital, it was an emergency in Washington. It was dragging along until they recognized me and then it was immediate service. The doors were open – flowers, everything. It's really jive – every human being deserves the same respect just because they're a human being. I remember thinking at the time, 'Wow, what if my lady had been there just by herself?' "

But it was not only the Western culture that Stevie was fed up with. Rumours had come up again that Stevie felt the same way towards Motown and that he wanted to leave the company. What had started those rumours was the fact that in 1973 Stevie's lawyer started to re-negotiate Stevie's recording contract with Motown. By early 1974 nothing had come out of it. There were also talks about Stevie meeting executives from other record labels – but none of them were confirmed.

While all sorts of speculations were going on, Stevie was about to finish the work on his album. *Fulfillingness' First Finale* was released on 22 July 1974 and it shipped gold the same day, one of the industry's largest advance sales up to them. Within three weeks the album went to number 1 in the American charts. *Fulfillingness' First Finale*, the critics said when it came out, was even more versatile and mature than *Innervisions*. Stevie prefers to call it "an album made with and from love".

Nine out of the ten album tracks had been written by Stevie alone, *They Won't Go When I Go* was co-written by Yvonne Wright. Stevie had produced this album again in association with Robert Margouleff and Malcolm Cecil. The LP had been recorded at The Record Plant and Westlake Audio in Los Angeles and the Electric Lady and Media Sound in New York.

Apart from musicians in Wonderlove Stevie had also been supported by stars – and friends of his – like Minnie Riperton, Paul Anka, the Jackson Five and The Persuasions. Sergio Mendes is credited on the album sleeve "for translating the words of my *Bird Of Beauty* to Portuguese to enable me to speak to my people of Mozambique and the beautiful people of Brazil". Not only Africa, but South America as well had now found Stevie's love.

The first cut on *Fulfillingness' First Finale* is a song that Steve says "I wrote when I was in a very down mood. But then I felt that things were getting better." On *Smile Please* Stevie plays all instruments apart from guitar (Michael Sembello), bass (Reggie McBride), congas and bongos (Bobbey Hall). The backing vocalists are Jim Gilstrap and Deniece Williams. This song – as most tunes on this album – was written before Stevie's accident. The lyrics to *Smile Please* give more or less the old beauty recipe: laugh lines are prettier than wrinkles.

The next track is *Heaven Is Ten Zillion Light Years Away*. Stevie plays all instruments on this one. Paul Anka, Syreeta Wright, Shirley Brewer and Larry "Nastyee" Latimer sing the backing vocals.

The following song *Too Shy To Say* is dedicated to one of the many ladies in Stevie's life. Her first name is Ellen, her surname remains a secret. In the sleeve notes Stevie says: "ELLEN – I'm not too shy to say." The words of the song speak for themselves. Stevie tells Ellen who makes him smile and sing and feel so much in love:

> *I wanna flyaway with you*
> *Until there's nothing more for us to do*
> *I wanna be more than a friend . . .*

The next cut, *Boogie On Reggae Woman* is only on the album thanks to Bob and Malcolm. Bob: "We loved that song so much and Stevie wasn't too keen on it. It took us ages to persuade him to use the song for the album. Thank goodness we finally succeeded." *Boogie On Reggae Woman* has a sexy Latin beat (Rocky on congas, Steve on all other instruments) and the lyrics are very straight forward at times:

> *I'd like to make love to you*
> *So you can make me scream . . .*

whereas on the other hand Stevie can only hardly bring himself to say *naked*:

> *I'd like to see you na . . .*
> *Under the stars above . . .*

And this, *after* he has told the lady that he would like her to make him scream . . .

Stevie calls *Boogie On Reggae Woman* "a very nasty tune" and at the same time adds "but you can say things without being vulgar". Stevie gives such a shy impression when it comes to talking about sex, but actually he is quite the opposite. Only we will probably never hear him sing any dirty songs – Stevie sticks to making up vulgar songs only in the company of other musicians. Billy Griffin: "When the Miracles recorded *Love To Make Love* Steve was in the studio and we started joking around. Because there are thousands of ways that this song can go. Stevie was singing some things . . . But he wouldn't do that kind of stuff with ladies around or when his daughter is with him. But between men, Stevie's dirty lyrics are quite a lot of fun . . ."

Lee Garrett: "Steve and shy? Oh boy! You've gotta be jokin'! Ira's got some tapes tucked away that you wouldn't believe! With Stevie, Ira, myself and sometimes other musicians making up dirty songs. Really dirty – but funny. It's a pity you're a lady and you won't get to hear them. Those tapes are strictly for men . . . To be quite honest, they are rather filthy . . ." In making up "dirty songs" every now and then Steve is in good company. I have heard other musicians who would not dare to say "nasty" things on their records and who write the most gentle love songs – but catch them in a crazy mood and you'll be amazed. Backstage, waiting to start their gig or bored stiff in dressing rooms of television studios they sometimes make up the wildest songs you have ever heard or put new lyrics to some other songs. Guess what Gordon Lightfoot did to Andy Kim's hit *Rock Me Gently* (1974) or what almost every musician sang when *What A Diff'rence A Day Makes* was a hit for Esther Phillips in 1975 . . .?

The last track on the first album side *Fulfillingness' First Finale* is *Creepin'*. Steve plays all instruments and Minnie Riperton sings the backing vocals. It is a song about a common nightmare that probably everybody has experienced at one time or the other: a love affair has broken up and the one of the two who is still in love cannot get any sleep at night. Stevie recalls the days when the girl said she would stay beside him forever and re-lives all the moments of ecstasy. He wonders why the girl has to keep creepin' into his dreams and then he asks:

When you're a sleep at night babaa . . .
I wonder do I creep into your dreams
Or could it be I sleep alone in my fantasy . . .

The first cut on the second album side is the one that Motown chose as Stevie's next single. Like *Living For The City*, *You Haven't Done Nothin'* caused a lot of discussion. (Reggie McBride plays bass, Stevie is on all other instruments and the Jackson Five do the backing vocals singing nothing but *Doo doo wop* eighteen times . . .) *You Haven't Done Nothin'* is very evidently about politicians. He accuses them very straightforwardly of making promises but not keeping them, talking about changes they don't pull through. Steve sings:

We are amazed but not amused
By all the things you say that you'll do . . .
'Cause if you really want to hear our views
You haven't done nothin' . . .

Steve considers this song to be one of his most important tunes, and he picked just the right time to release it: When *You Haven't Done Nothin'* came out the Watergate Scandal was being talked about all over the world. The single, which was released one day after the album came out, went straight to the top of the American R & B charts and the "Pop 100" and became a gold disc. (In England the single only got to position 30 in the *Music Week* charts in late 1974.)

When interviewed about this song Stevie made it very clear that he did not get along with anybody's politics in the States at all: "*You Haven't Done Nothin'* says it all. Everybody promises you everything but in the end nothing comes out of it. I don't vote for anybody until after they have really done something that I know about. I want to see them *do* something first. The only trouble is that you always hear the President or people say that they are doing all they can. And they feed you with hopes for years and years. But that is probably typical of most people in very important positions who have a lot of power. But I'm sick and tired of listening to all their lies."

Stevie, who generally plays a lot of fund-raising shows even turned down one of them (in 1974) because the President of the United States was involved. Steve told *Penthouse*: "I turned down a UNESCO (United Nations Educational, Scientific and Cultural Organization) thing. They had a bunch of stars and I would have been the only black person there other than ambassadors from various African countries.

"A woman from UNESCO called me on behalf of President Ford to invite me, and I said, 'Oh no, miss!' And she said, 'But this is from the President of the United States!' 'I know, miss, I know who he is, I know exactly, and *that's why* you're getting this opposition.' " As heavy as *You Haven't Done Nothin'* is from the lyrical point of view, Stevie has put the words to a rhythmic dancing melody:

"The best way to get an important and heavy message across is to wrap it up nicely. With songs, I've found out, it's better to try and level out the weight of the lyrics by making the melody lighter. After all people want to be entertained which is all right with me. So if you have a catching melody instead of making the whole song sound like a lesson people are more likely to play the tune. They can dance to it and still listen to the lyrics and hopefully think about them. It's the same with movies, I guess. Like *All The President's Men*, the film about the Watergate Scandal was really entertaining to watch. But at the same time people get an idea of what it was all about."

It Ain't No Use is a song that Stevie wrote around the time when his marriage with Syreeta was about to fall to pieces. The lyrics show very well the frustration of one-time lovers who painfully realize that they cannot make it together:

> There ain't no reason trying to force a smile
> When pain is really in its place.
> 'Cause we know the truth!
> It ain't no use!
> Let's part before we lose love's trace . . .

On this track Stevie plays all instruments. The backing vocals are sung by Lani Groves, Minnie Riperton and Deniece Williams.

247

On the next track *They Won't Go When I Go* Steve plays classical piano as well as all other instruments. This song – co-written by Yvonne Wright – is the prophetic song on the album. In the middle part of it Stevie is talking about the innocent for whom there is a resting place. But the sinners' future he paints black:

> *They will never see the sun*
> *For they can never show their faces*
> *There ain't no room for the hopeless sinner . . .*

But Stevie, the singer, stands removed from this part's convictions. He says where he goes no one can keep him from his destiny and:

> *My soul will be free and they won't go when I go*
> *Since my soul conceived all that I believe*
> *The kingdom I will see 'cause they won't go when I go . . .*

The second last track on the album is *Bird Of Beauty*, a song with a Latin-American feel to it. Part of the lyrics Steve sings in Portuguese and he plays all instruments apart from Quica (Bobbey Hall). Steve: "The song starts off with Bobbey playing the Quica. It is an instrument that I believe originates from South America and it is used in many of the Brazilian songs. I like experimenting with all sorts of instruments. This way I don't restrict myself within my music." On *Bird of Beauty* Shirley Brewer, Lani Groves and Deniece Williams sing the backing vocals and if Steve did not sing the lead vocal the song would just sound as though it came off a Sergio Mendes album. It is a beautiful happy tune that makes you want to get up and dance.

Stevie closes *Fulfillingness' First Finale* with one more love song. As the title says, *Please Don't Go* deals with one lover wanting to leave the other. In wanting to hang on to love Steve promises to do everything the lady wants him to do – as long as she stays. The lyrics remind very much of Rod McKuen's *If You Go Away*. Only while McKuen specifies all the things that he is going to do if he or she stays, Stevie talks mainly about what happens to him if the girl leaves. He sings how sad and blue, his heart would grieve and:

I'll break down and cry a river of tears
With just the thought of you not here in my life . . .

On *Fulfillingness' First Finale* Stevie has not mentioned
Yolanda Simmons among the "special credits" on the album
sleeve that he gave to musicians and friends. Still, by the time
this LP was released Yolanda had become a very important
part of Stevie's life. She now was with him most of the time
and in late summer Stevie announced that "Londie", as he
lovingly calls Yolanda, had become his fiancée. For a little
while the couple even declared wedding plans, but then
denied them again. Steve, who had already experienced that
his relationship to a woman he loved had been better when
they were not married, said: "When your hearts are joined
together it's love with or without a ring. I just think that
marriage turns love into a commitment which can make you
feel trapped. Marriage can bring about chains and fences that
make you feel like you want to get out. It can turn into a very
heavy possessive thing. But love is supposed to be freedom.
Freedom to be with each other, happy and loving one another
and communicating with ideas. I think only as long as you are
not married you can be sure that you are with your love
because of your own free will – because you want to. And that
is for me what love is all about."

To Yolanda it does not make any difference whether Steve
and she are legally married or just living together: "As long
as we love and respect each other we will be together anyway.
If one day we should fall out of love, that piece of paper that
makes me Mrs. Morris could not prevent it. Marriage is no
guarantee of happiness."

Even when Yolanda positively knew that she was pregnant
with Steve's baby the lovers did not decide to get married for
the sake of the child. Steve: "Sure, this child is going to make
Londie's and my love for one another even more beautiful and
it is going to join us together even stronger. But this has
nothing to do with our attitudes toward marriage. On the
contrary: I do not one day want to make our innocent child
responsible for me feeling chained to a wife. And anyway:

249

Yolanda getting pregnant did not happen accidently. We *wanted* a child."

It has always been one of Stevie's dreams to be a father. Lee Garrett: "Even when Steve was only a teenager he talked about wanting to have children a lot. I remember him saying 'I want to be young with my kids. Children to me are real happiness. Boys or girls – it doesn't matter. Children are a part of *you*, they fulfil you. Children bring sunshine into your life. If I ever make enough money to raise them I would love to have two dozen kids!' "

As long as Stevie did not have a child of his own he lived out his love for children being godfather to a number of boys and girls. Nobody's sure just how many, but it has to be about a dozen or two. Steve is, for example, godfather to Lee Garrett's little daughter (5) and also to Gypsie's boys David (13) and Jamal (9). Lee: "I'm sure that if anything happened to me Steve would take care of my little girl. He really cares about her."

While Stevie stood godfather to Lee's child when she was born, he only became godfather to Gypsie's children a few years ago. Whereas in Europe standing godfather or godmother is rather an official ceremony that usually takes place when children are christened, those rules do not seem to apply in America. Gypsie: "When Steve and I met David and Jamal were already born. And after Steve and I had become friends, he said that he would like to be my children's godfather."

For Stevie this is not just a title: he is really interested in his godchildren. He does not have much time to devote to each and every one of them, but he tries to let them know that he loves them and that they mean something to him. Gypsie: "Sometimes my kids keep nagging me to ring Steve and ask him to come over, but often he is just too busy. And when I tell Steve that David and Jamal keep asking for him he sometimes rings them up to tell them that he really loves them and that they mustn't feel neglected because he's so much involved in his work." But then again, on special occasions like birthdays Steve tries to be with his godchildren. Gypsie: "Last August, when we were in the studio, I asked Stevie if he needed me for recording on Sunday, because it was David's twelfth birthday [22.8.76] and that we thought of doing whatever David wanted to do. So Steve said, 'Well, what are you going to get him for his birthday?' and I told him that David wants a camera and some tennis shoes and a cassette recorder that his grandmother wanted to get him and that he wanted to go swimming.

"So Steve said 'Don't worry about the camera, I'll get that for him.' And he laughed and said 'I've got some *cash*' like he was really proud of that because Stevie usually doesn't carry any on him 'cause there is no need to. And he asked me what kind of camera I was gonna get for David. So I said well, just one of those instamatics. Not anything too expensive for him to tear up and take apart. Anyway, come Sunday the children and I first went to get the tennis shoes, then we went swimming and after that visited a friend of mine.

"Later on I called Steve in the studio and he asked 'Did you get David a birthday cake?' I said no. He said 'NO? Why didn't you get him one. *All* children should have birthday cakes. I'm gonna call a bakery and order one.' I told Stevie not to worry about the cake because David isn't crazy on it. I said I'd asked him and he'd said he didn't want a cake or ice-cream or any of that sweet stuff. 'Well,' Steve said, 'why don't you all come down to the studio?' So we went down there and recordings were going on and all the usual routine.

"When Stevie heard us coming he stopped playing. He said 'Hey, David, come here for a minute.' And Steve gives him this beautifully wrapped-up parcel and says 'This is your birthday present. Happy birthday.' So David opens it up and as soon as he sees what it is he goes half crazy. 'A camera, a camera!' And Steve and David fell around each other's necks and hugged and kissed one another. It was really touching to see how much Stevie really loves my kid. You could almost *see* the vibes.

"And you know what? The camera that Stevie had gotten for David is one of those where you take a picture and a minute later you've already got the colour photograph in your hand, right? I thought that was much too fancy for David but he really takes care of it. Because his uncle Stevie gave it to him and the children just worship Steve. David took a lot of pictures that same night in the studio. With Stevie and the engineers and the musicians and just everybody who was around. It's a really nice bunch of pictures. And Stevie was so happy whenever he heard David scream with joy when another photograph had turned out right."

Gypsie was also one of the first people who Stevie told that he was going to become a father: "When Steve found out that Yolanda had conceived and that there would be a child that was made from love – just as the song *Isn't She Lovely* (from *Songs In The Key Of Life*) about his daughter tells it, he was very, very happy. And also very, very anxious about the whole thing. That everything with Yolanda and the baby would be all right."

As soon as Stevie knew that he was to have a family, he decided to settle down and find a house for them. Up to that day Stevie had more or less lived in residential hotels (in Los Angeles he still does). Steve was on the road most of the year anyway and never needed a *home* just for himself. Jim Gilstrap: "Steve is totally satisfied as long as he has a sleeping bag in which he can crawl up to get a few hours of sleep in a day. The rest of the time he lives in studios, concert halls or hotels anyway."

But now the situation was different and Stevie purchased a Civil-war-period brownstone house on East 18th Street, New York, for 175,000 dollars. But he also kept his apartment in the Regency Hotel on Hollywood Boulevard in Los Angeles. Steve explains why: "Los Angeles is the place where I do most of my work. In New York I want to live my private life. It's a really nice city, you know. I like the excitement of New York, the springtime, the winter. I like to see the seasons change – in Los Angeles it is summer almost straight through the year. I also find that people in New York are basically a lot warmer than people can see."

Steve also talked about the importance of stability of family life: "My career and my family life are both equally important to me, because one makes the other work. That is a great thing, it means that you are constantly inspired. Also I've always wanted to be a father. The only reason that I waited so long was that I knew I had to wait until I'd meet the right woman who would give my children all the love they need."

That Stevie chose Yolanda to be the mother of his children did not surprise his friends in the least. Jim Gilstrap: "At first it freaked me that Steve and Syreeta had broken up and that Steve would have a child with Yolanda. But then I realized that Stevie had his reason for it: Yolanda is very different from the other girlfriends that Stevie has. She is not the fashionable type of career woman like Syreeta, CoCo, Yvonne or other ladies that Stevie usually surrounds himself with. Yolanda is a very warm, but also a very average and normal person, I think. Nothing glamorous.

"I believe that with Yolanda Stevie feels that he can be sure of her to devote all her time and love to their children. She is the type of woman that you like to come home to. She doesn't give a man a hard time by wanting to do her own things so much. The kids and Steve are the most important things in her life. Yolanda is what I would call a good woman or a good wife – even though the two of them aren't married."

Doug Kee: "Yolanda is a very quiet person. She isn't into partying and all that stuff but a smooth home life is more what she prefers. She's not an extroverted person but very reserved. Yolanda is not overexuberant and she's kind of sedate."

Gypsie Jones: "There was a time when some journalists wrote that Stevie and Yolanda were married. Quite a lot of people asked me then if that was true, and if he was really gonna stay with Yolanda. I told them that I didn't know and that I didn't care about it. Because the only important thing is, that the two of them love each other *now*. Also they both knew what they were doing. As I've said before, Stevie isn't a one-woman-man, but Yolanda knows that. She knew it before they made up their minds to found a family.

"I don't think it is easy to live with Steve, because he is so many people. In some ways there must be a strain on Yolanda. But maybe she's the one who can cope with it. And apart from all the other loves or affairs or whatever you want to call it Yolanda knows that Stevie loves her dearly. There are many kinds of love. And the one he feels for her is certainly very strong. Just look at the booklet that goes with *Songs In The Key Of Life*. The part where Steve gives accreditation to the women of his life.

"Yolanda is the only one he mentions twice and he also gives her special thanks for being the mother of his daughter. He says: 'P.S. TO YOLANDA, IF LOVE WAS FOR WHAT I SOUGHT, THEN YOU HAVE GIVEN ME MORE THAN I EVER KNEW EXISTED!' I think those words speak for themselves . . ."

Today Stevie still lives in Los Angeles most of the time while Yolanda stays in their New York home. Steve flies up to see her every few weeks and sometimes she comes down to California to visit him. Steve: "We don't believe in clinging to each other all the time. We both have our things to do. With me it's music and Yolanda is interested in fashion design which she studies four nights a week." Contrary to some reports, Yolanda does not work as Stevie's secretary and bookkeeper. In fact she never really worked for him but pretty soon after they met had become Steve's companion.

When Yolanda accompanied Steve on parts of his tours, it was she who took care of Stevie. His brother Calvin was still his valet, but most of the time Yolanda dressed Stevie, washed his hair and put it in whatever fashion he wanted it. And she was the one to make sure that Stevie had his dark glasses ready before he went on stage.

At the beginning of 1975, Stevie as usual spent most of the time in the studios in Los Angeles while Yolanda stayed in New York. Just before their first baby was due, Stevie interrupted his recording sessions and flew to New York. When the labour started Stevie went with Yolanda to St. Luke's Hospital, New York. He was at her side during the birth of the child.

On Monday, 7 April 1975 at eight minutes past three in the afternoon, Steve's and Yolanda's baby daughter was born. She weighed eight pounds, ten ounces and Stevie and Yolanda named her "Aisha". Steve: "That is African for 'Strength and Intelligence' which I think are the most important essential qualities that men should have. And I wish for my daughter to have them."

With Aisha's birth, Steve says, "My life has changed for the better. She is the one thing that I needed in my life and in my music for a long time." Steve also says: "I always told people that I thought of children as something very special because they are part of you. With Aisha the feeling of belonging together is even stronger than I ever had imagined: I can sense Yolanda and me in her." In spring 1977 the magazine *Blues and Soul* reported that Stevie had a son. The child was born in New York on 16 April 1977 and was named Keita Sawandi.

All of Steve's friends agree that the children are his main interest in life now. At one time, when Stevie was asked if he could think of anything that could make him lose his temper very badly, he answered: "The only thing that could make me hit someone is if somebody was messin' around with my kid. But other than that I think to beat somebody is a very vulgar thing. When I get in a rage I usually find other ways to cool out my anger. Most of the time my voice is my best weapon. But if somebody did anything to my kid I couldn't guarantee anything . . ."

Whenever Stevie can make it possible, Aisha is around him. Billy Griffin: "You see those two together very often. Stevie takes his little daughter almost everywhere. Like she was with him when Steve went down to a discotheque called Nick's Fishmarket, which is just where Sunset turns from Hollywood into Beverly Hills. There he played a few tracks of his *Songs In The Key Of Life* that he had just cut in the studio. It was really beautiful to watch Stevie with Aisha. Whenever the music got a little loud he grabbed the little one and put his fingers in her ear. He is so concerned about Aisha and you can really see the vibes of love that he has toward her."

Gypsie: "Stevie also had Aisha with him when they previewed *Songs In The Key Of Life* on a ranch in Massachusetts. There were lots and lots of people. Friends of Stevie's, people from the business, journalists and God knows who. And amidst them was little Aisha, tripping away, with all the chickens and ducks and animals like that that were running around on the farm. And she was so funny. There was this one scene where this duck snapped a candy out of her hand. You should have seen the expression on her face. Aisha looked down to the duck like she wanted to say 'What do you think you're doing? I'd wanna kick your ass!' But at the same time she was not quite sure how the duck would react on that. It was so funny . . . And Stevie is the nicest father you can possibly imagine. He just adores his daughter."

Now that Stevie has children it seems that he does not feel like going on tour as much as he did before. He wants to be with Aisha as often as possible and his studio work keeps him away from his family more than enough. But when he did his last big tour Aisha was not born yet.

In September 1974 Stevie began an exhausting tour through Japan and the United States. "Stevie Wonder's Fall Festival Tour – Wonder Loves You" was his first long series of concerts since he had been on the road with the Rolling Stones two years previously. It began with a star-studded party thrown in Stevie's honour at Park Avenue's Delmonico Hotel Grand Ballroom in New York. Besides the Nassau Coliseum concert's promoters and Motown records the party's hosts included Robert Flack, engineer Don Cornelius from the TV show *Soul Train* and photographer Peter Beard. Among the 450 guests were Edgar Winter, Rick Derringer, David Johansen, Andy Warhol and Mick Jagger.

Stevie's Fall Festival Tour took him and his crew to 44 States of America. When he played at the Olympic Stadium in Detroit, mayor Coleman Young presented Stevie with the golden key to the city and also declared that day from then on the "Stevie Wonder Day". During this tour Stevie received 20 keys to various cities.

While Steve was on the road Motown put out *Boogie On Reggae Woman/Seems So Long* as a single. It topped the American charts at once and became another gold disc.

In autumn 1974 Stevie was given the "Golden Mike Award" by the National Association of Television and Radio Announcers as the best male vocalist. At the same time Marvin Gaye got this award for his LP *Let's Get It On* which was voted the album of the year by members of the organization. In the British music paper *Sounds'* music poll Steve was voted 1st Top

Musician and in six other categories (from Top Keyboard Player to Top Record Producer) he ranged within the Top Ten.

In December "Stevie Wonder's Fall Festival Tour – Wonder Loves You" ended triumphantly with a special sold-out Christmas concert at Madison Square Garden in New York. The takings from this show Stevie donated to various New York City area charities in the form of badly needed equipment for homes, hospitals and organizations of underprivileged children and the elderly.

At the end of the year Stevie could look back on another three gold singles (*You Haven't Done Nothin'*, *Don't You Worry 'Bout A Thing* and *Boogie On Reggae Woman*) and his third platinum album with *Fulfillingness' First Finale*. His plans for the coming year were to put out a sequel to his last album, called *Fulfillingness' (Second) Finale* and besides America tour Europe.

But none of this happened. The next year was full of surprises.

CHAPTER ELEVEN

Songs In The Key Of Life

In March 1975 Stevie was awarded with another five Grammies. One of them was for *Living In The City* from his 1973 album *Innervisions* for the best R & B song. The other four were for *Fulfillingness' First Finale* which was voted album of the year and won him the best R & B male vocal performance as well as the best production award. Stevie was also given Grammies for the best pop vocal performance (male) and the best R & B performance (male) for *Boogie On Reggae Woman*. The top award of the evening – for the record of the year – this time went to Olivia Newton-John for her version of Peter Allen's *I Honestly Love You*.

The ceremony was held at the Americana Hotel in New York and at the nearby Uris Theatre, from where it was broadcast live on television. Among the artists taking part were John Lennon, accompanied by Yoko Ono, who together with Paul Simon presented Olivia with the record-of-the-year Grammy. Art Garfunkel was there and Andy Williams, David Bowie, Ann Margret and Bette Midler to name but a few.

Another Grammy went indirectly to Stevie: Rufus had been presented a Grammy for the best R & B group for their *Tell Me Something Good*, which was a song Stevie had written and produced with Rufus. *Tell Me Something Good* was a number 1 hit in America and also a gold disc.

In Britain that year Stevie appeared four times in the *Melody Maker's* pop poll: male singer 8th, keyboards 9th, arranger 10th and his single *He's Misstra Know-It-All* 10th.

Then on 7 April 1975 Stevie's daughter Aisha was born and he called her his "biggest Grammy ever". Later in April

Stevie was named the special honoree of Washington D.C.'s Human Kindness Day. This is an annual event held on 10 May when the entire city turns out to celebrate the arts through community involvement. Steve was chosen the special honoree on the basis of his "humanitarian efforts and artistic brilliance". Stevie thanked for this honour by giving a free concert to over 50,000 fans on the Washington Monument grounds.

On 31 May Stevie and Minnie Riperton did a fund-raising benefit concert for black journalism students. 18,000 fans had gathered at Cow Palace in San Francisco. Minnie Riperton who opened the show sang most tunes from her latest album *Perfect Angel* including the title track which was written for her by Stevie.

In June Steve flew to New York to make a special guest appearance on Geraldo Rivera's annual *One To One* telethon for mentally retarded children. There Steve sang, answered pledged phones and donated 10,000 dollars. Four hours later Stevie flew to Shaw University in Raleigh, N.C., and donated money for an elaborate sound system and set up several scholarships.

The Shaw University of Raleigh is a very special project for Stevie. Ira Tucker: "One day when we were at Duke University for a gig, Shaw University was playing football against Duke. Stevie wanted to see the game so we went over to Raleigh, got some tickets and went in. Then Stevie heard some of the kids at the football game say that Shaw University was going to be closed down. Stevie immediately made up his mind to do something about it. So we went to see the University's officials and with them agreed to do a show. It brought 10,000 dollars. We also hooked them up with La Belle and other artists." For Shaw University Stevie has also set up a programme whereby he puts money in the bank and Shaw receives the interest. Apart from the things already mentioned Stevie is also thinking of financing a student exchange programme for Shaw with Jamaica and he has already set up a teacher's education programme. The President of Shaw University, J. Archie Hargraves, gave special thanks to Stevie for all that he has been and still is doing for Shaw when he announced

Stevie elected to the Board of Trustees of the University. With this for the first time in the history of Shaw a member of the entertainment industry had been elected to the board proper. In the past showbusiness people such as Isaac Hayes and Sammy Davis jr. had only been made honorary members.

In 1975 Stevie was also a presenter of the American Music Award and of the National Association of Record Merchandisers' Presidential Award, an organization which represents about 80 per cent of all record buyers in the United States. Stevie was the youngest-ever recipient.

The same year Stevie donated 40,000 dollars to the School for the Blind in Jamaica and in October ground was broken for the Stevie Wonder Home for Blind and Retarded Children which was completed in spring, 1976.

The year before Stevie had also donated 34,000 dollars to the Mink-Sink Town House for boys. Ira: "It's really incredible, all the things that Stevie does for other people. But for him it's the natural thing to do and he always gets very upset when he reads about his good deeds in the papers."

Apart from holding charity concerts, a few public appearances in Jamaica with Bob Marley and the Wailers and a performance on *The Dinah Shore Show* Stevie did not appear in public but worked on his new album and also did some songwriting with Gil Scott-Heron and James Taylor. Although for a while Stevie was expected to join Elton John and the Beach Boys for the Summer of 75 jamboree in Wembley Stadium he did not come over to Britain. Rumours were that Steve had cancelled his appearance because he would not get star billing over Elton John. Plans for him to headline a Crystal Palace Garden Party fell through for various reasons. Steve had also planned to release a double album *Fulfillingness' (Second) Finale* in the first half of 1975. But it never reached the shops.

Instead strong rumours came up that Stevie Wonder was about to leave Motown soon. Ewart Abner is supposed to have run into representatives of rival labels when he occasionally dropped into Stevie's recording sessions. Although these representatives from other recording companies had the power and the authority to out-bid all-comers should Stevie show himself interested, Abner kept calm. Asked whether Stevie wanted to leave Motown for even more artistic freedom and cash incentives, he said: "There are companies to whom the acquisition of an artist like Steveland is worth losing money on because of what he might do for them in terms of setting up a chain of events and lead them into another area. Thus, we made the decision early that we would pay Steveland what he could get or better than he could get anywhere else, but for different reasons than the other labels."

Later both Epic and Arista Records denied having been involved in any bidding war. Epic publicist Pat Siciliano: "That rumour probably started because we signed the Jackson Five." Arista's Stu Werbin: "It is possible that some of Arista's artists have approached Stevie to produce them, but the company has never made Wonder any kind of contractual offer."

On 5 August 1975 Stevie re-signed with Motown Records. The seven-year contract calls for guarantees to Stevie of more than 13 million dollars. With this Stevie Wonder signed the biggest recording contract in the history of the music business. Superstars like Elton John and Paul McCartney are supposed to have signed eight-million-dollar contracts with their recording companies and Elvis Presley was said to have a ten-million-dollar deal with RCA.

No matter how shaky things had looked for Motown in connection with Stevie for the last few months, when signing the contract the company and Stevie did everything to give the impression of a big, black, happy family. And both sides talked about the deal extremely philosophically.

"The future is very positive," said Stevie while the ink dried on his contract. "There are faults at Motown but they can be corrected. If you went somewhere else there'd be other problems – probably a lot worse ones. I feel comfortable here. I've known some of the people a very long time. They've let me get away with things that other companies may not have allowed."

Stevie also said, that of course, he was very happy about this enormous deal and then he added: " . . . but there is something perhaps even more important involved. I'm staying at Motown because it is the only viable surviving black-owned company in the record industry.

"Motown represents hope and opportunity for new as well as established black performers and producers. If it were not for Motown, many of us just wouldn't have had the shot we've had at success and fulfilment.

"In the record industry we've all seen many cases where the big companies eat up the little ones and I didn't want this to happen to Motown. I feel young black children should have something to look up to.

"It is vital that people in our business – particularly the black creative community including artists, writers, and producers – make sure that Motown stays emotionally stable, spiritually strong, and economically healthy."

Stevie's explanation sounds rather touching. However, it must be said that Motown, years ago, also ate up little companies to become bigger. Black companies.

Stevie has said in interviews that he "was trapped" at Motown "for many years" – before he was twenty-one – and that he never felt too much of a Motown artist as far as their pattern of music is concerned; that he well knew that he was one of the very few people at Motown who could do his own thing; and that he could even understand other artists leaving the label. He had told *Rolling Stone*:

"I do [understand other artists leaving Motown], when you become one of the others, it's difficult to be a sustaining power for a long period of time. It's like a person comes out with a beat, and you keep on doing it and doing it and driving it to the ground."

However, it seemed that suddenly Motown really was the nice black family of music that they wanted people to think they were. "With a few faults," as Stevie had said, but nothing grave.

There had been rumours that Stevie had changed his mind about leaving Motown after a late-night visit from a Motown executive. Bob Fisher, press officer Tamla Motown London:

"Yeah, lots of people talk about Stevie having been threatened into staying. But that is a lot of bullshit. Also you get this rumour with other artists and labels all the same. What about the one about —— and the X label. There people said they'd hung him out of the window every time he wanted to leave . . ." Elaine Jesmer: "There were some rumours of that kind. But on the other hand it is said that white companies threaten their stars by beating them up if they want to leave. Stories like this come up every now and then but you never know how much of what is written is really the truth . . ."

As important as the deal was for Stevie – moneywise – so it was even more so for Motown. In a *Rolling Stone* article, Judith Sims said: "One cynical industry observation is that Wonder's re-signing 'saved Motown's ass'." After naming all the acts that Motown had lost over the last years the articles continues: " . . . and since the label hasn't built any new names in the past few years, some observers wonder if Berry Gordy's interest in film production has hurt the record company. But almost everyone agrees that the retention of Wonder will keep Motown in the business."

Over three years ago, when Stevie's lawyer Johanen Vigoda had made Stevie's first contract with Motown since Steve had turned twenty-one Vigoda had said: ". . . in breaking tradition he opened the future for Motown. That's what they understood. They never had an *artist* in 13 years, they had singles records, they managed to create a name in certain areas, but they never came through with a major, major artist." Even if you take Marvin Gaye and Diana Ross – as big as they are they are not nearly as creative as Steve is. And it was very obvious that Motown again could not afford to lose Stevie. Talking about losses writer Sylvia Moy once explained how Motown feels about them. In an interview with BBC's Stuart Grundy Sylvia discussed why Motown did not put out *My Cherie Amour* until 1969 – and then only as a B-side: the disc jockeys turned the song that she, Hank Cosby and Stevie had written in 1966 into an A-side and a million-selling hit.

"The problem was that you could do something different but if you did you could not get it out. Motown's success with certain kinds of ingredients and patterns had made them afraid of newer things . . .

"You know when you really come from the street and you make it – you know you're gonna make it and you hope you're gonna make it and you bet you're gonna make it but you don't *really* think you're gonna make it – then when you *do,* you become very paranoid about protecting what you've made. So you don't really take the chance that you would if you had nothing to lose. And I think when Motown became a major force financially in the business, I think they got a little afraid. Make sure they kept what they had . . ."

Motown definitely seems to be paranoid in terms of their security. Any kind of security. The company has its own bodyguards who work in the security department. Elaine Jesmer: "Motown's had a security department for years. They started it back in Detroit. The only other record companies I know that are like that are the ones in Chicago. But that's another thing, 'cause the police were always going after the musicians and they wanted to see if they had any dope. Then that's cool – the musicians then are protected in a sense. With Motown the thing is that they are absolutely paranoid. They always think that somebody wants to do them in, one way or another."

There are even rumours that Berry Gordy has somebody to test his food before he eats it. Bob Fisher: "That's gotta be a story!"

And an ex-Motown employee from their Los Angeles office told me: "I had joined to work on the accounts. First of all it took me six hours of interviewing. I had to see the head of accounting, his assistant, Berry Gordy jr., the attorney, a lady whose name I've forgotten and I had to take all kinds of tests.

"Then I wondered what I was doing there. Motown actually seems to hire girls just to sit in an office and to file their nails. Because that's what they're doing most of the time – and sometimes they have to buzz people in and out doors, because all the doors at Motown are security locked.

"The most ridiculous thing is, that you have to work at Motown for six months before you get a key to the restroom.

264

If you want to go to the john you have to sign in and out. I worked up in the penthouse in their highrise office on Sunset. When I left the office there was a girl sitting at the door where you had to sign your name when you left for the toilet. Then you got the key and when you came back you had to sign in again. The time even. It's crazy.

"I worked there Monday, Tuesday, and on Wednesday I went downstairs to the coffee shop for lunch. And everybody was watching me and it was really insane. The whole atmosphere at Motown is just terrifying. Anyway, after this lunch I left and I never went back."

However, Stevie stayed at Motown and with the new contract Motown had definitely made sure that they kept what they had. Although Motown's President Ewart Abner, who left the company later that year, talked as philosophically as Stevie about the whole re-negotiation: "It is difficult to translate Stevie's special kind of creative genius as an artist, producer and writer to a dollar sign.

"When a performer gets to the plateau that Stevie owns, he stands alone and it is obvious he could command just about anything he wanted with any record company in the world.

"That is why we at Motown are especially gratified with Stevie's philosophy that he can best help his brothers and sisters by keeping Motown strong so there will be a market-place for their creative talents."

Abner also pointed out that "Stevie is the only artist ever to win ten Grammies over a two-year period, winning five in 1974 and five again in 1975." At this time Stevie had also been nominated for The First U.S. Rock Awards Presentation, and shortly after been named the best male vocalist. The First Annual U.S. Rock Award was a TV special on CBS and was co-hosted by Diana Ross and Elton John.

After mentioning Stevie's incomparable achievements, Abner continued: "We take a great deal of pride in saying it's the best deal ever made for any artist and that we're making it not because we're trying specially to top someone else, but because he deserves it. This deal is a statement about how

265

Motown feels about the artistry of Stevie Wonder. He's the premier artist, composer, performer of the day and he should have the best contract."

The first thing that Stevie had wanted for signing the new contract was, that Motown would not release its much publicized triple *Anthology* album, even though the LP had been pressed already. Stevie wanted 200,000 album copies destroyed. He felt that the multi-set album was too much like a *Greatest Hits* package than a history of his music. At the moment Clarence Paul is working on a new *Anthology* album. Clarence:

"In co-ordination with Stevie I'm gonna put an album together that will have two – yet unreleased – recordings per year since Stevie started with Motown. In between the *Anthology* is gonna have interviews with disc jockeys who broke Stevie's records and friends of his. Depending on how much stuff we're gonna use it's either gonna be a double or even a triple album. But one thing is for sure: it's gonna be a lot of fun to listen to it. And it's gonna surprise many people in terms of what stuff has been canned away and not been put out when it was fresh."

With the new contract Stevie also gained the right to pick which of his songs will be released as singles, and the right to produce artists on other labels "to a prescribed degree", as Motown Industries vice-chairman Mike Roshkind put it. But he did not say whether Stevie would also get credit for the outside productions. Roshkind: "I don't know, we haven't gotten down to that yet."

It looks as though Stevie has. When he produced Minnie Riperton's album *Perfect Angel* in 1974 he had used the pseudonym "El Toro Negro" and although the English translation of this is Black Bull and he had also composed music for this album Stevie had denied any involvement with the Epic LP, but today it is even listed in Motown's compilation of the records Stevie produced.

The most important thing that came with the new contract for Stevie was even more financial security. Within the seven-year-contract period Stevie is guaranteed the sum of over 13 million dollars. For this he has to deliver one album per year.

Although some reports wrote about a dozen albums Motown's Bob Fisher assured me that it is definitely only seven albums. For Stevie seven albums is really nothing. If he wanted to play it cool or if anything happened to him there would be no problem in finding enough tunes from those already canned to fill seven LPs, and for him or his family to get the guaranteed amount of money.

With Stevie's re-negotiation of the contract his royalty rate as an artist increased enormously. On exactly how much Stevie is getting now the reports vary. Some articles say it is 20 per cent. Referring to the *Songs In The Key Of Life* album the *New Musical Express* explained: "... that is approximately £1.40 on every single album retailing at £6.99." Other journalists wrote that the royalty rate for Stevie as an artist is now 50 per cent, whereby music critic Jack Slater claims to have been given the 50 per cent figure by Ira Tucker jr., Steve's publicist. Tucker is supposed to have told him: "With any less than that Stevie would not feel secure."

If you try to figure out yourself if 20 or 50 per cent could be the closest possibility you will get as frustrated as I did. First of all, superstars like Paul McCartney and Elton John can get a royalty rate of up to 21 per cent – which is incredibly high. But then, Stevie is the one who has the contract that is said to be "the musical equivalent of the French Revolution": Divide more than 13 million dollars by seven and you get just under two million dollars per album – or rather Stevie gets it. That means almost every penny up to a platinum album (two million dollars in sales) would go straight to Steve and only then Motown could start trying to get their costs back. After all they press and distribute Steve's records. If you think this calculation is rather silly, try it the other way. Let's take the British price example for *Songs In The Key Of Life* retailing at £6.99. First of all, take off six and a quarter per cent which goes straight to the publisher. This is roughly 44 pence. Then take off another 50 per cent as Steve's royalty rate as an artist which is approximately £3.50, and you have £2.95 left. With this money you would have to pay everything from the artwork for the cover and booklet, the printing of the two, the pressing of the records, the cellophane which keeps the package together, the packing, the distribution and whatever else is involved from making a record until it is in the shops. And don't forget the retailer, because he also wants to live. And the production, but even if Stevie paid for the recording himself, £2.95 is very little money to pay all the other costs with. And any way you look at it it seems that Motown is actually losing money. Which is unlikely.

The only conclusion I came to is that for a change Motown is making very little money on Stevie (even if you take the singles into consideration) and Stevie is lousy rich.

Lee Garrett: "He sure is, and today we are making a lot of jokes about it. After all we've known each other for more than ten years now, and in the old days the times were pretty rough." Lee even put Stevie's wealth in a song of his, *A Sad Story* on his album *Heat For The Feet*. Toward the end of the recorded version Lee sings:

> *I wanna ride around like James Brown*
> *I wanna be rich like Stevie Wonder,*
> *David Bowie, Zowie Bowie,*
> *They've got riches and lots of ha ha ha*
> *I wanna be rich, baby . . .*

The original ending of the song is a different one, though, but you can only hear it in live concerts – the recording company has censored the song. Lee: "Steve and I were joking about all the money that he has got and at one point he said 'Yeah, I'm a rich nigger. A rich, blind nigger. Would you believe that?' So I made up this tune using those words in the chorus. Like 'I wanna be rich, I wanna be a rich nigger, I wanna be a rich, blind nigger, I wanna be Stevie Wonder.' Steve thought that was funny – but Chrysalis didn't.

"See, although Stevie gives a lot of his earnings to charities or God knows what he still digs being rich. And why shouldn't he? After all you don't necessarily have to come out of a ghetto to enjoy the things money can do for you. You can travel, you can buy the finest sound system to listen to your records, you can buy presents for friends and be happy when they are happy.

And as much as Steve hates luxury in form of all the stuff he could put in his house or flat and stumble over he still appreciates the money that he makes.

"See, I'm not into anything visual myself – the most expensive Picasso wouldn't do me any good because I couldn't look at it. But that doesn't mean that blind people can't have other dreams that they can fulfil with cash. And believe me, it can be quite a comfortable feeling to be rich . . ."

However, when Steve had signed his multi-million-dollar contract he said: "It's not that I want to have a lot of money and go crazy about it. I want my family to be secure. Just in case something happens to me."

When Stevie speaks about his family he does not relate only to his children and Yolanda, but his mother, brothers and sister. While Milton works in Steve's New York office and Calvin is with Steve all the time (Calvin, as well as Ira Tucker, has an apartment in the Regency Hotel in Los Angeles) the rest of the family are also well taken care of. Stevie bought his mother a house in San Fernando Valley, California, where she and the other children live. Lee Garrett: "Stevie feels responsible for his family. He loves them very much and he also always thinks of all the things that Lula did for him to help him along."

On the other hand Stevie's providing his family with everything does lead to a complicated situation. Lee: "Larry wants to be Stevie. He thinks that he can also do it and he doesn't see much point in getting his life together as much as he would have to if Steve weren't there. With the other two, Timothy and Renee, one can't really tell yet. They still go to school. And it looks like they're gonna be able to stand on their own feet one day. Lula is trying hard to see to that. Although you must admit that it is rather tempting to just lay back because Steve would always be there to help them financially. He's got so much money that it really doesn't matter how much of it he gives to his family. After all he's come to a point where materially he has everything that he wants. Except for spending money on new instruments or equipment he really doesn't need much money. And for the young ones it is really hard to realize the value that money has.

"I've often told Steve that he cannot devote his life to them, that they have to live on their own. If you never learn to fight for your position in life you are quite likely to have a nothing personality. If you never have to work hard to achieve something you can't appreciate what you have. The more blood, sweat and tears you put into something the happier it makes you when you finally reach your aim. But for Stevie it is really difficult to decide what's best for his family – apart from Lula of course – because he knows that they need independence but at the same time he doesn't want to see them struggle. Because *he* knows how hard it is to make your way to the top. But again they can't learn from his experiences, everybody has to learn the lessons for life himself. After all this is what life is all about and what makes you become the person that you are.'

Jim Gilstrap: "It is probably quite natural that the rest of Steve's family would like to get involved with music, too. And Stevie helps them wherever he can. I'd say the most musical one of the family – apart from Steve – is probably Timothy, the young one. He plays drums. Timothy sometimes used to play with Stevie while I was with him, and he was only twelve, thirteen years old then. But he'd just come on stage and take over the drums. He's good and it was fun."

After Stevie had signed the legendary contract, Motown announced that his next album would be released on 1 September 1975. Opposed to what Stevie said earlier, this album would not be called *Fulfillingness' (Second) Finale* but *Let's See Life The Way It Is*, and it was planned to be a two-record set. Simultaneously Steve explained why he had gone off the idea of writing a second *Fulfillingness'* album:

"Aisha has changed my life so much, that I've gotten another outlook on life within the last few months. I've been writing a lot of new material. Like songs that get into the essence of knowing what it is to have a child say 'daddy', and what it is to know what it does to you as a parent when your baby cries. It is as if you felt the child's tears in your own eyes." Although it hurts Steve to see Aisha cry, he still prefers her to do silly things and find out herself that she better not do them again, than if Aisha would wait to be told everything. "Like me, she is very inquisitive about the way things work. She'll open a drawer, stick her head in and lean on it. Then she'll cry but soon feel around until she finds the handle. That's good. She's learning fast."

In regard to the album Stevie also said that there still would be songs on *Let's See Life The Way It Is* that had been written either before or just after *Fulfillingness' First Finale* and which he had wanted to put on the second *Fulfillingness'* concept album. Those tunes were *Saturn*, *If It's Magic* and *Ebony Eyes*. All of them were finally to be found on Stevie's next album. But that would not come out before another year had gone by.

With the proclaimed September release date, Stevie had already changed his original plans for the second time: the album following *Fulfillingness' First Finale* had originally been scheduled to come out in April 1975. The reason was that Stevie did not want to wait too long with the sequel to it.

Still, September came and went but there was no sign of Stevie's new album. The next thing that was heard about Stevie came from Danny O'Donovan, one of Britain's top concert promoters who also represents the Tamla Motown stable in the United Kingdom. In the middle of November O'Donovan announced that Stevie would be doing "multiple days in London" and that he would also play several provincial concerts during the visit. O'Donovan: "I would stress that contracts have not yet been signed, simply because we are awaiting a release date for his new double album *Songs In The Key Of Life*. But I am hoping that Stevie will be coming as early as January 1976." Again, neither Steve nor the album were heard or seen.

Instead rumours began to make their way from the United States to Europe. They said that Stevie was holding back the release of his new album on purpose. For one, the longer he let people wait the faster they would rush out and buy it when it was finally released. Which is a way of increasing and controlling both supply and demand. The rumours also spread that Stevie was not too sure about which of the hundreds of tracks

271

that he had recorded to put on the album. Supposedly he was trying to find out into which direction music would go. Should go. Should he choose nostalgic songs, soul, funk, reggae, MOR, blues or electronic music . . .

Stevie referred to these rumours as "nonsense" and said that he was not ready because he was still mixing and re-mixing the album. Apart from this, Steve also spent some time working with other artists like the Burrito Brothers.

The next news was that Motown would release *Songs In The Key Of Life* on 14 May. The stories that went with this release date were: 1. Stevie had held back the release date of the record until May because he wanted it to be released under the sign of Taurus. His astrologer had informed him that 1976 was a good year for Tauruses. If that is so, Motown could have put out the album earlier than May: the sign of Taurus begins on 21 April and ends on 21 May. Version number 2 said that Stevie wanted to play it extremely safe: He wanted the release date of the album to coincide with his birthday because his personal astrologer had advised him to do so.

For this scheduled release date Stevie's publicity office sent an invitation to America's music journalists:

"After nearly two years Stevie Wonder has created what we feel is his most exciting album to date. He is most anxious to share this achievement with you in a very special way.

"We would like to invite you to a preview of this important musical statement in a relaxed and tranquil atmosphere which, we feel, will heighten and enhance the event.

"The already-platinum two-record album is presently scheduled to be released by Motown on or just after 14 May.

"Steve, Black Bull Music and we would like to extend an invitation to you to join us early one weekday morning on a special 20-minute charter flight to Worchester, Mass. You will then be transported to nearby Longview Farm, a rambling recording studio/farm deep in the countryside near the peaceful village of North Brookfield.

"There, for a full spring day, amid green valleys, ponds, white fences, gentle barnyard animals and sweet smelling hay, you will be served a country style breakfast and lunch, hear the album played over Longview's elaborate sound system, and be able to participate in its many facilities. You will return to Manhattan by 5.30 that same day.

"We are interested in knowing if you will be able to join us, sharing in what we feel will be a relaxed day in the country, listening to the best music that life has to offer!"

The journalists were ready. The people at Longview Farm were ready. Motown was ready, their representatives all over the world rushed around their countries with their order books again. The promoters were ready, the fans were ready, in short: everybody was ready. But Stevie was not. The invitation was postponed.

Then came June. This time it seemed that Stevie was going to make it. It was announced that he was to play at Wembley Empire Pool on 5 June. Introducing his album. But before the posters for the gig had been put up it was cancelled again. It was understood that reports elsewhere that had led to the news, had been incorrect. Mid-July was the next date that a spokesman for promoter O'Donovan told the press: "It now seems, that if Wonder flies in to play just one concert, it could be at Wembley Stadium, but in July instead of June. Otherwise it's likely that he will play a smaller venue for a full week, or even longer. The venue will probably be London New Victoria Theatre."

July still did not show Stevie or the album, but Motown was sending out photographs that put the press and Stevie's fans in a hopeful mood again: On these pictures Stevie was wearing a T-shirt either saying "We're almost finished" or "It's nearly finished". Motown London sent out T-shirts to pop journalists which stated "Stevie's *Almost Ready*".

Another two months later Stevie was. In the middle of September 1976 Motown London had the first white pressing. On Tuesday, 21 September, the media got a preview of the album at EMI's studios on Abbey Road in London. There Motown's press officer Bob Fisher announced that the album would be released on Thursday, 30 September simultaneously with the rest of the world. Also simultaneously the disc jockeys from the radio stations all over Britain would get their promotional copy on Thursday, 30 September, at 12 o'clock, high noon. No radio station would be given the advantage of getting a copy earlier than the other, it would all be fair play. And if you think the dj's could have gone into a record shop at nine or ten o'clock that morning and bought the album, you're wrong. Because *Songs In The Key Of Life* wasn't actually in the shops until Friday, 1 October 1976. Anyway, Bob Fisher played the album plus the EP that goes with it once through and on special request repeated the most-asked-for tracks. Motown served a cold buffet and wine. The vibes were good, the mood was mellow, the sound system collapsed every once in a while – showing no awe of the long-awaited album, here at last. And while Motown London's employees saved the preview with friendly smiles, jokes and technical skill, Motown U.S. together with Wartoke Public Relations and Black Bull Music Inc. threw one of the most dazzling press parties ever held.

The chickens, ducks, and all the other animals on Longview Farm, Worchester, Massachusetts, saw one of the craziest days in their life: dozens of people had arrived and turned the peaceful place into a beehive. Most of them were carrying tape recorders, cameras, notebooks and pens and they all followed a man who was wearing a cowboy outfit and smiling all over his face:

Stevie Wonder had dressed up to fit the country mood and to personally introduce *Songs In The Key Of Life* to members of the media. Apart from letting press and radio people hear his often delayed new masterpiece, Stevie made himself available for a short rap with his guests. He patiently answered their questions – apart from the rather silly one when his follow-up album to *Songs* would come out – and posed for hundreds of photographs. Stevie with his family, Stevie with Ira Tucker, Stevie the lonseome cowboy, Stevie proudly holding the master tapes for the album, Stevie and members of Wonderlove, Stevie and whatever the photographers wished for. Everybody was served the long promised country breakfast and lunch, filled up with wine and music, and by the time the journalists had come back to their office desks, most of them were still that joyful, that they wrote long and raving articles about *Songs In The Key Of Life*.

In Britain the situation was a little different. Whereas in the States Stevie's presence and fresh, clean country air for the album preview had helped to make up for the many release dates that had turned out to be false alarms, in the U.K. the pound had dropped again. Consequently the first subject many pop critics picked upon was the price for Steve's album. Not only had he made his fans wait for it for almost two years but also the long-awaited album was one of the most expensive ever to be released.

Music Week wrote: "The view of one major chain's record buyer about the cost of the album was 'It's not a price, it's a telephone number' and this statement found other supporters." Many articles compared the price of Stevie's album of £6.99 (in the States it sells for $13.98) to other double albums that had come out around the same time and sold for less than twice the price of one single album like Elton John's *Blue Moves* (£5.99) and Led Zeppelin's *The Songs Remain The Same* (£5.49).

Motown, though, claimed that £6.99 was a "fairly tight costing constructure" considering that *Songs In The Key Of Life* consists of two full-length albums, an EP (which altogether add up to 21 tracks of just over a hundred minutes' playtime) and a 24-page booklet including the lyrics to the songs. Another cost factor, Julien Moore, Motown general manager at EMI London stated, was the shrink-wrapping which was necessary to keep the package's contents together. And regardless of the cost of other people's albums or double albums the price of two separate full-length albums by an artist of Stevie Wonder's format would still add up to more than £7.00. Moore also said that the EP is a *bonus* after all and that an extended play is selling for £1.00 nowadays, leave alone the booklet.

But with his statement Moore could not reconcile most journalists to the album price. Critic Roy Carr from the *New Musical Express* wrote: "Personally, I can't think of any artist worth 13 million dollars or a double album worth £6.99. But like the man said, there's a free EP. He did say free didn't

275

he!" Carr was also talking sharply about the many delays of the album:

"The way this particular game has been played gives the distinct impression that a boardroom stalemate between Wonder and Motown has been artfully manipulated by everyone concerned into a sort of ultimate Artistic Super Hype.

"Wonder's public have been left to cliff-hang for two years, while young Stevie has been busy getting his thing together – all 13 million of it. So has the theory been, make the punters wait and they'll pay anything? Let's get one thing straight: *Songs In The Key Of Life* was ready for release at the beginning of the year."

It was not. Although the album could have definitely been in the shops at least two weeks earlier: music journalists in Germany had gotten their promotional album copies at the beginning of September! – while America's Stevie Wonder fans had to wait for *Songs* for two weeks longer than the British. In the United States the album was released on 14 October 1976. There, two days later *Songs*, the already-platinum album, went straight to number one in *Billboard*'s album charts, where it stayed for twelve weeks. Then it fell back to position 2 and 3 and on 29 January 1977 went back up to number 1. The following week though, it dropped back down to position 3. (The single *I Wish/You And I We Can Conquer The World* was released in America on 18 November 1976 and one week later entered both, the "Pop 100" and the R & B charts. Strangely enough Stevie had decided making a track from his *Talking Book* the B-side.)

However, even if *Songs In The Key Of Life* could have been in the shops by early September 1976, before this date the album really was not finished. Not to Stevie's satisfaction, anyway. Although at the beginning of the year most of the 21 tracks had long been recorded, Stevie spent months and months mixing and re-mixing the album tracks until he had them exactly as he wanted them to sound. Ira Tucker: "And sometimes it happened that Stevie all of a sudden had a new idea for a song and then it had to be done this way. He would not be satisfied with any other than what he had heard in his

276

head." A good example for this is *Isn't She Lovely*, the song that Stevie wrote for Aisha.

It was one of those spur-of-the-moment things that Stevie decided he wanted the song to begin with the first cry of a new-born baby. So he sent Nelson Hayes (credited for "special effects") out to various hospitals to find a tape of the birth of a baby. Naturally Nelson had problems getting it. Because there were no such tapes. Finally he talked a doctor into letting him talk to his patients – maybe he was lucky enough to find a lady who would let Nelson record the birth of her baby. That again caused problems. Because most mothers did not want to be bothered. They were too busy having babies and in pain than to listen to what he had to say about making a tape.

Finally, and quite a few weeks had gone by by now, Nelson found an Indian lady who gave her consent. So he taped the birth of the baby. The only trouble was that when the baby was born it was ever so quiet. The child did not cry. Nobody believed it and least of all Nelson. The doctor said that the baby was perfectly all right and to calm its mother he smacked the baby's bottom to make the child cry. But all the baby did was that it went 'mmmmh'. Very quietly. So the tape was no good.

Nelson played the recording to Stevie and tried to convince him to give up on this crazy idea. You'll never get your album out if you insist on the birth of a baby he said. But there was no way that Steve, the Taurus, would give up on anything. "Once a Taurus wants something he sure tries everything to get it," says Steve. "We are very stubborn."

It was all very well for Stevie to be stubborn. Nelson was the one who had to come back with a good enough recording that Stevie could use for a record. Half desperately, half jokingly, Nelson asked the girl singers in the studio if one of them could not do him the favour and give birth to a baby – "but in a hurry". The singers could not, but Gypsie Jones rang up her gynaecologist – and Dr. Larry Scott prevented Nelson from losing the rest of his nerves.

"When Gypsie rang me up I just told her to send Stevie over to the New Los Angeles Hospital that evening. I had one lady in labour and one on the way. I told her I need a so and so tape recorder and that we would get it together." They did. That same night Stevie finally got his recording of the birth of a baby for his song *Isn't She Lovely*. Dr. Scott: "See, it was just a matter of telling the mother in labour the right thing. My patients are usually not worried about the birth of their babies. We've talked about it so much beforehand that they know what's going to happen and they are really relaxed. Well, and all the rest of it was very easy. You can bet that most people love Stevie Wonder – so why should they object to a recording? Also, the mother could hear it before Steve used the tape on the album. She had nothing to lose. On the contrary – the lady is quite proud of her baby having turned into a recording star the minute it was born . . ."

After Stevie had gotten this recording the album was still far from being finished. Billy Griffin: "Steve kept mixing and re-mixing the tracks until he thought they were right. But even then he wasn't quite satisfied. The thing is, when you hang around with a song for a long time you are so involved in it that after a while you can't really tell any more *what* you want. So what Steve did then, was to check up what he considered the final mix with an audience."

The place Steve chose to play his songs in public for the first time was Nick's Fishmarket. René Rott, who has been managing Nick's Fishmarket since it opened in early 1975: "Quite a lot of artists bring their tapes over here to test the audience's reaction on the mix. Like the Average White Band or Sammy Davis jr. I think the reason for people to come here is that we've got an extraordinarily good sound system and also the people who come in here for our disco are pretty well mixed." In the early evening Nick's Fishmarket presents itself as an exclusive seafood restaurant. René: "We are quite expensive – a dinner for two doesn't cost less than 40 to 50 dollars. That's excluding drinks. So our dining room guests are really very high class. We get all the biggies like Sammy Davis, Jack Haley, Liza Minelli, Clint Eastwood and so on. They all come here for dinner at least once a week. But that is only for dinner, and we wanted to make something more out of this place.

First we decided to put a piano into the dining room and get a pianist. But somehow that didn't work. Then we changed it into a disco. That means that from ten o'clock, ten thirty, you can't move in here. The dining room takes about 96 people at a time, the disco from 100 to 120. The disco guests reach from average, normal people to starlets and rock stars like Rod Stewart, Elton John, David Crosby, Stephen Stills, Graham Nash, Neil Young and so on. So it's really a fun place."

Billy Griffin laughs: "Yeah, man, Nick's Fishmarket is a place where you see all the fine ladies and where you hopefully get picked up by one. Well, it's a hip place and it has great music. So that one night that my brother Donald, who has just joined the Miracles, and I were there, Stevie played a few tracks from his album. *I Wish* we thought was a really funky tune and the audience just *loved* it. Then *Black Man* started playing and I said 'Oh no, man.' Nick's Fishmarket is a place with mostly white people there. I thought: how does this song get over? But people really accepted it. I said to my brother 'Don, if that was anybody else but Steve they would take the song off. Or they wouldn't dance to it. If it had been James Brown they would probably have thrown him out.' It was Stevie Wonder so they held it. Only Stevie's got that much power. He can make any social comment and people don't question it."

Black Man is a social-political song, although its title might easily mislead you. It is Stevie's statement which he has already made in *Heaven Is Ten Zillion Light Years Away*: this world is meant for all men. In *Black Man* Steve says that all races have contributed to the advancement of America. The song is divided into two parts. In the first half, Steve sings:

> Heat surgery
> Was first done successfully
> By a black man   (Dr. Daniel Hale Williams)
> Friendly man who died
> But helped the pilgrims to survive
> Was a red man   (Squanto)
> Farm workers rights

> *Were lifted to new heights*
> *By a brown man*   *(Caesar Chavez)*
> *Incandescent light*
> *Was invented to give sight*
> *By a white man*   *(Thomas Edison)* . . .

The second part of the song is a teachers' and students' question-and-answer session played by the Al Fann Theatrical Ensemble, Harlem, New York.

> *Hear me out*
> *Who was the first man to set foot on the North Pole?*
> *Matthew Henson – a black man*
> *Who was the first American heroine who aided*
> *the Lewis and Clark expedition?*
> *Sacajawea – a redwoman* . . .

According to Billy Griffin Stevie did the audience reaction test on *I Wish* and *Black Man* some time in August 1976. Stevie was in no hurry to release his album. Again, his friends say that he wanted to wait until his stars were in their luckiest zodiac position and also take plenty of time to produce this album as perfectly as possible. Some people even say that Stevie is beginning to get a little insecure. Elaine Jesmer: "Nowadays you can read quotes on Stevie where he says things like 'Well, and if people don't like the album there is nothing I can do. I've done my best.' Until *Songs In The Key Of Life* came out Steve has never even worried about people not liking his music. That's sad – he really wouldn't have to even *think* about anything like that, like he never did before."

Lee Garrett: "See, the problem that Stevie has now is that since *Talking Book*, and that is almost five years now, all his albums went platinum in no time. Including *Songs* we're talking about four albums, and *Music Of My Mind* didn't do badly either, after all this one went gold. So for a good five years Steve's been in a top position constantly. And all of a sudden he seems to realize that the only way he can go from there is down. Or stay at the top. But once you really sit down and think about your life and your career and you find that you've been at the top for such a long time – and I'm not even counting the first ten years of his career – then you're bound to all of a sudden get a little frightened. And you start asking yourself how much longer you can stay at the top. And for how many more years your good luck is gonna stick with you. And in order to keep his position Stevie wants to do things with perfect perfection, if you know what I mean. And that makes him do things over and over again and to a certain degree chose tracks for his albums that he thinks might be more commercial than others."

Other friends of Steve's or people who have worked or work with him say more or less the same. The reason for Stevie's albums shipping platinum in no time is always the quality of his last album. If it should happen that Stevie's fans do not like *Songs In The Key Of Life* as much as they did his previous albums, his *next* LP will have to suffer for it. Then the advance sales would not be as high and people would want to listen to it first before they go out and buy it. And as much as people like all of Steve's albums so far most of them still think of *Talking Book* as their favourite. Malcolm Cecil: "This album had more spontaneity than all the rest of them."

However, as cautious as Stevie has become when it gets down to perfectionism, there was one time last summer where Stevie did not care about it. In July 1976 Stevie played a rough mix to someone he did not even know: The Kaiser Hospital in Los Angeles had an 18-year-old patient who loved music more than anything else in the world. Marvin Braiden had a cassette recorder at his bedside and lots and lots of tapes, which he had bought himself. The money to be able to afford them he had earned doing a part-time job after school. But as much as Marvin liked the music that he had, he kept talking about one tape "which I don't think I will get a chance to hear – *Songs In The Key Of Life*". Marvin had cancer – and he knew it. First of all the doctors had wanted to amputate Marvin's leg where the metastasis had started. But when they did not Marvin knew that the cancer had already spread too far and that he would not have much longer to live. And he was hoping so much that Steve would hurry up with his new album so that he could hear it before he died.

Stevie heard about the young boy in hospital some time in May and the same day he sent him a present. Marvin's mother remembers how excited her son was: "Guess what," he said "Guess what – I got this great big basket of fruit. It's got everything in it. Coconuts and pineapples and oranges and pears and all kinds of nuts and candy. And guess who I got it from – *Stevie Wonder*! It has a card that goes with it and it says 'Hang on in there, see you soon. Love, Stevie'." At first his parents didn't believe Marvin, but then they saw for themselves when they visited him. And he was so excited about it that he would not even leave the hospital for a few hours in fear that Stevie could turn up just then and that he would miss him. Because by that time the cancer had gone so far that Marvin, although a patient of the hospital, was allowed anything that he wanted to do. The doctors wanted him to spend the last days of his life as happily as he could.

By the beginning of July Marvin's situation had become really bad. His life was going toward its end rapidly. And Marvin had not had any other sign from Stevie. Everybody in the hospital, his friends and his parents told Marvin to forget about Stevie, and that a superstar like Stevie Wonder would never take the time to visit someone he does not even know. "But he sent me that great big basket of fruit," Marvin insisted, "and he wrote me a card, telling me that he was coming over to see me."

"Well, maybe he wanted to," Marvin's friends said. "But by now he surely has forgotten all about it. Don't put your hopes too high." But despite all the things that people told him, Marvin still believed that Stevie would keep his promise. And even when the pains that the young boy had had gotten stronger and stronger he pleaded with the doctors not to put him under morphine – he would rather bear his pains than be drugged when Stevie would finally find his way to the hospital. But the doctors, who had given Marvin plenty of drugs already, assumed that he was hallucinating and kept on giving their patient morphine to kill the pain.

On 10 July Stevie came to the hospital. He had not forgotten about the young boy and he had brought with him his own tape recorder and two tapes that he had recorded for Marvin: one of them contained all the music of *Songs In The Key Of Life* and on the other tape Stevie was talking to Marvin, explaining all the songs to him. But by the time Stevie got to the hospital, Marvin was unconscious. Morphine had put him into a deep sleep . . .

Steve stayed at Marvin's bedside for a couple of hours, then he had to split. But he left him his tape recorder and the tapes and he had also fixed headphones to the recorder and put them to Marvin's ears. Just before Stevie left Marvin he had put on the tape with the music and then he pushed the button "play" . . .

Still, Marvin did not hear the music. He never woke up again. By nine o'clock that night the doctors informed his parents that their son had died. A few hours later Marvin's mother had the recorder and the tape of *Songs In The Key Of Life* delivered to Ira Tucker. The tape of Stevie talking to Marvin she kept. She still has it, but she does not play it to anyone without Steve's permission. And as Ira said before, Steve does not want to get publicity out of things that he does for others. When Steve heard that Marvin had died the same night that he was at the hospital he was very upset. He had really wanted to fulfil Marvin's last wish – but he had come too late. To show Marvin's parents how sorry he was he gave them his platinum album for *Fulfillingness' First Finale*: he explained to them that it was really touching for him to have someone wanting to hear his music so much. And that this platinum album was just a token of thanks to Marvin for telling Stevie that he had really meant something to him. Marvin's mother was so overwhelmed by this gesture that she could not thank Stevie. Later she wanted to write him a letter but she says: "Every time I sit down and think about it, I just can't find the words to say."

This story is one of the examples of how kind Stevie really *is*, and how many things he does, small things, big things, that one usually does not read about. *But* it also shows how warm-hearted and how dreadfully inconsiderate Steve can be – both at the same time. It has happened more than once that Steve has had good intentions but by the time he actually got down to put them into reality he had missed the point where he was needed so badly.

However, as long as it had taken Steve to finish *Songs In The Key Of Life*, when the album finally came out sarcastic critics wrote that even though Steve had left his public to cliff-hang for two years, his latest masterpiece had now been released just in time for the Grammy close. And promptly Steve was nominated for eight of them for *Songs*. This time Stevie got four Grammies: *Songs In The Key Of Life* was voted the best album of the year and in addition to the best album award Stevie received three Grammies for the best male pop vocal, the best producer and the best male R & B vocal of the year.

It was the third time for Stevie to win the best album award, presented each year by the National Academy of Recording Arts and Sciences in America. The only other artist to have won this Grammy three times is Frank Sinatra. Stevie's fourteen Grammies altogether make him second only to Henry Mancini, who holds the Grammy record with twenty of them. The only other artists to have 10 or more Grammies are Vladimir Horowitz (12), Roger Miller (11) and Ray Charles, Aretha Franklin, Leontyine Price and Paul Simon (10 each).

In 1977 Stevie was not present at the Hollywood Palladium in Los Angeles, where the Grammy festivities were held. At the moment the Grammies were handed out Stevie was making an appearance at the Nigerian song festival in Lagos. Still, host Andy Williams made an attempt at a live satellite feed from Nigeria, but sound and vision were rather poor. Andy Williams, who tried to talk to Steve via a telephone hook-up, had difficulties getting through to Steve, who was sitting near a television monitor tuned to Hollywood. Not being able to communicate with Stevie as he had hoped to, Andy Williams even made a faux-pas by asking him "If you can't hear me can you at least see me?" Andy Williams later apologized for that remark, but fortunately Stevie did not get cross about it. Instead, he said how happy he was to have won another four Grammies which shows that people obviously liked his latest album. *Songs In The Key Of Life* is an album about which Steve says: "I wanted it to be about a particular theme and I wanted it to go into a certain direction. We came up with the title *Songs In The Key Of Life* long before the album was released and you could take it as a kind of working title. I wanted the songs on the album to relate to as many things as possible dealing with the experiences that life has, my life and that of other people. And I wanted the album to hopefully express the kind of feelings that are shared by everyone."

Stevie's message has long been "survival through love" and most of the 21 tracks on this album deal with love in its various forms. Love: Man to Man Love, Man to God Love, Man to Child Love and Man to Woman Love. And they also deal with social-critical themes like *Black Man* or *Village Ghetto Land*, with which Stevie makes an even heavier social comment. Steve sings about fear, robbery, starvation, murder, disease, police corruption and politicians not caring:

> *Children play with rusted cars*
> *Sores cover their hands*
> *Politicians laugh and drink – drunk to all demands . . .*

Steve: "*Village Ghetto Land* doesn't only deal with one ghetto but with every ghetto throughout the world. People never realize how many ghettos there are." The song ends:

> *Now some folks say that we should be*
> *Glad for what we have*
> *Tell me would you be happy in Village Ghetto Land.*

As much as the lyrics of the song deal with ghetto life at its worst, the music to *Village Ghetto Land* is most pretty. It sounds like an eighteenth-century minuet, very classical and as if played by a whole orchestra of violins, cellos and basses. But in fact it is Steve on a Yamaha Electrone Polyphonic Synthesizer GX 10 which he lovingly calls his *dream machine*. Billy Griffin:

"This instrument is ridiculous. It cost Stevie 50,000 dollars but it's more than worth it. His dream machine is a keyboard instrument, a cross between an organ and a synthesizer, that simulates every instrument there is. And when I say simulate I mean it. It's like a twin to everything. I mean when you hear strings you can actually hear the bows coming down on the strings. Stevie is in love with this white instrument and he sits and plays it all the time."

The statement and the music of *Village Ghetto Land* are in extreme opposition to each other, and Stevie seems further to contradict this song's lyrics in *Have A Talk With God*. In this song that is the cut directly before *Village Ghetto Land* Steve finds life's solution in God. This track has been co-written by Steve's brother Calvin (while *Village Ghetto Land* was co-penned by the New York disc jockey Shatema Byrd) and again Steve plays all the music.

> *There are people who have let the problems of today*
> *Lead them to conclude that for them life is not the way*
> *But every problem has an answer and if your's you*
> *   cannot find*
> *You should talk it over to Him . . .*

Village Voice critic Robert Christgau commented on the contradictions on *Songs In The Key Of Life*: "Sometimes he almost seems to mean that bad thoughts are the source of all evil (*Love's In Need Of Love Today*), and I should point out to those sympathetic to his interpretation that its practicality is questionable, because it supplies no surefire method of eliminating the bad thoughts. I should also point out that Stevie acknowledges just this problem in *Village Ghetto Land*, which serves as an empiricist postscript to the idealist *Love's In Need Of Love Today* and *Have A Talk With God* by implying quite pointedly that poverty and happiness are often mutually exclusive.

"The man is obviously no giant ideologically, but he does have a reasonably accurate idea of what's going down. Ideology can hardly be his speciality in any case, because the locus of ideology is written language, whereas for Stevie books must talk. In fact, no verbal analysis can do him justice. What makes the contradictory platitudes of his lyrics worth following through is the rhetorical impetus of his music . . ."

Love's In Need Of Love Today is the opening cut of the album and it sums up its basic philosophy. Steve: "This song deals with all love for all people, with love itself, the meaning and feeling of love, the spirit of it. It is about sincerity of love, warmth, caring, concern of love. Not the physical expression of it." On this track Steve plays all instruments apart from collinga (Eddie "Bongo" Brown) and he starts the song and the album as the "friendly announcer" who leads the listener through this and all the other tracks:

> *Good morn or evening friends*
> *Here's your friendly announcer*
> *I have serious news to pass on to everybody* . . .

He talks about how hate breaks so many hearts and that

> *The force of evil plans*
> *To make you its possession* . . .

and that it is going to destroy everybody if we don't take "precautionary measures" for love to overcome all evil. But as Christgau says, Steve does not give a recipe for *how* we can overcome bad thoughts and begin to love one another . . .

This tune is followed by *Have A Talk With God* and *Village Ghetto Land* which goes straight into *Contusion*, a jazz orientated, electrifying instrumental with which Steve has been opening his live concerts since his accident. *Contusion* features Mike Sembello on lead guitar and Wonderlove with Raymond Pounds on drums, Nathan Watts on bass, Ben Bridges on rhythm guitar and Gregory Phillinganes on keyboards. All other instruments are played by Stevie, background vocal credits are given to Michael Gray, Josie James, Shirley Brewer and Artece May.

Side one of the album finishes with a happy dancing rhythm song about music. It is called *Sir Duke* in dedication to Duke Ellington, the king of jazz and it has the Big Band Sound. Steve used two trumpets (Raymond Maldonado and Steve Madaio), two saxophones (alto: Hank Redd, tenor: Trevor Lawrence) Raymond Pounds on drums, Nathan Watts on bass, Mike Sembello on lead- and Ben Bridges on rhythm guitar. Steve plays all other instruments. In *Sir Duke* – which was the second single to come off the album – Stevie praises the joy of music.

Apart from Duke Ellington, who Steve calls "the King Sir Duke", names other "music pioneers" like (Count) Basie, (Glen) Miller, Satchmo and Ella (Fitzgerald). Steve: "The song is a thankyou to people who have contributed so much to the world of music, although I've only mentioned a few by name."

The first cut on the second album side is the one that Stevie chose to be the first single taken off *Songs*. *I Wish* brings back childhood memories for Stevie, and certainly to most of the listeners: Steve recalls those childhood days where his only worry was what kind of toy he would get for Christmas, but even if he didn't get a thing he would be happy just with the joy that the next day would have in store for him. He remembers sneaking out backdoors, getting caught by his mother and trying his best to bring water to his eyes so that she would not whip his behind. He thinks back to when he played doctor with a girl. This time his brother is the one who caught him and he promised him everything and offered him anything not to tell mother. Steve talks about trading money for Sunday School for candy, "smokin' cigarettes and writing something nasty on the wall" for which he receives his sister's comment "nasty boy" and Renee is credited for "background". But despite all the hassles that he had doing "nasty" things, Stevie wishes those days when he was "a little nappy-headed boy" would come back once again.

> *You grow up and learn that kinda thing ain't right*
> *But while you were doin' it – it sure felt outta sight . . .*

The musicians are the same as on *Sir Duke* with the exception that Stevie does not use any guitars on *I Wish*. In the States this single went up to number 1 whereas in England it reached position 5.

Knocks Me Off My Feet is a love song that most critics could not see too much to. In most album reviews it has been dealt with in just one short sentence if it was mentioned at all and the *New Musical Express* wrote about this song as one "where Wonder's bubble-bath sentiment gets the better of him". Admittedly the verses are sweet as candy

> *. . . I reach out for the part*
> *Of me that lives in you that only two hearts can find . . .*

and carry clichés of what happy love is all about: pictures of lovers strolling through a park on summer days and laying beneath the stars are bound to bring scenes of the most touching love story movie to your mind. But as sentimental as the verses are, in the chorus Stevie catches exactly the feeling of what it is like to be in love. Madly, ridiculously, crazily, totally in love:

> *There's sumptin 'bout your love*
> *That makes me weak and*
> *Knocks me off*
>
> —
>
>   —
>
>   —
>
>   *my feet*
> *Knocks me off my feet . . .*

And being so helplessly, head over heels in love, all Stevie wants to do is tell his loved one that he loves her over and over again:

> *I don't want to bore you with it*
> *But I love you, I love you, I love you . . .*

For me, this is one of the most beautiful lines I have ever heard in a love song. Maybe this is *my* bubble-bath sentiment, but "I love you" are the most wonderful words that the one you love can say to you and you never get tired of hearing them. Or, like Stevie, saying them. But at the same time as Stevie keeps saying those three words he apologizes for maybe *boring* his lady with it. But like with probably most songs it depends on the kind of mood you are in when you listen to it whether you like it or not. As a critic and trying to be objective *Knocks Me Off My Feet* is most likely to be a song that you categorize as *Kitsch*. If you are madly in love yourself it will make you want to sing along with it as much as *I Wish* makes you want to get up and dance. And if you have just fallen out of love you probably hate it or call it the silliest song you have ever heard.

Pastime Paradise is another song where Stevie makes a social comment. He talks about people's habit of escaping into either a past time or future paradise instead of living today *for* a future paradise. But unlike to *Have A Talk With God* where He is near enough to talk to, in *Pastime Paradise* Steve wants us *not* to rely on God too much. Instead of waiting for anything to happen, Steve sings in the last verse:

> *Let's start living our lives*
> *Living for the future paradise* . . .

And while during the first half of the song Steve named exploitation, isolation, segregation and other evils of the world in the second half he does give us an idea of what can be done "to the peace of the world". He mentions integration, acclamation, world salvation to name but a few, only: how all these can be achieved he does not tell us. On *Pastime Paradise* Raymond Maldonado and Bobbey Hall play percussion while the seemingly big string orchestration is brought by Stevie and his dream machine. The West Angeles Church of God Choir and Hare Krishna sing the backing vocals. Steve: "I used the Hare Krishna people because they speak of looking toward the future and living for a future paradise. They speak of happiness and joy and the song does, too. That is why I wanted them for it."

In the booklet that goes with *Songs In The Key Of Life* Stevie says: ". . . I do believe it is that Stevie Wonder is the necessary vehicle on which Steveland Morris must be carried on his mission to spread love mentalism . . .

". . . *Songs In The Key Of Life* is only a conglomerate of thoughts in my subconscious that my Maker decided to give me strength, the love + love − hate = love energy making it possible for me to bring to my conscious an idea . . ."

Summer Soft is a song with which Stevie, as he says, musically revives his *Thank You Love* from the *Down To Earth* album.

"Musically it's the same punchline" he laughs, although the lyrics are quite different. "*Summer Soft* is about the relation between men and nature's seasons." And it also tells how fast time slips away:

> *And so you wait to see what she'll do*
> *It is sun or rain for you*
> *But it breaks your heart in two*
> *When you find it's October*

On this track Ben Bridges is on rhythm guitar, Ronnie Foster plays organ, Nastee Latimer percussion and Steve all other instruments.

The last tune on the second album side is *Ordinary Pain*. The musicians are Stevie Wonder, Mike Sembello on lead guitar and Hank Redd on alto saxophone. Steve wrote this song in Phoenix. "I had some problems at the time and all of a sudden, while I was trying to console myself, I thought: it's just an ordinary pain. I liked it as a line for a song, so I wrote some lyrics around it and when I went back to L.A. I cut it." *Ordinary Pain* is divided into two parts: the first with Steve singing the lead vocal (background vocals Minnie Riperton, Mary Lee Whitney, Deniece Williams and Syreeta Wright). He plays the part of a man who has been left by his woman. In this soft ballad he says that he does not mind her going away. He talks about holding back the tears when she says goodbye and telling yourself that you feel unnecessary pain in your heart. But at the same time he knows that he is badly hurt, only he does not want others – and least of all the girl – to know how wounded he is deep down inside:

> *Don't fool yourself*
> *But tell no one else*
> *That it's more than just*
> *An ordinary pain*
> *In your heart . . .*

In part two of the song the melody changes its tenderness into a harder, funkier rhythm. Shirley Brewer sings the reply (background vocals Linda Lawrence, Terry Hendricks,

Sandray Tucker, Charity and Linda McCrary and Madelaine "Gypsie" Jones). She tells him that

> *You're just a masochistic fool*
> *Because you knew my love was cruel . . .*

and that his friends had warned him not to let her go to his head. But it is only five lines that she half-sings, half-speaks, until the backing vocalists start singing "ordinary pain" between each of the thirteen lines in which she pretends to have fooled him right from the beginning. And you know that she is playing his game by not telling him that it also hurts her to leave him. She is also trying to fool herself by thinking of it as just an ordinary pain. But then she comes up with the truth:

> *You know I'd really like to stay*
> *But like you did I've got to play . . .*

As soon as she finds herself admitting that he broke her up she quickly changes her way again. Because all the time you hear the backing vocals "ordinary pain" – you know that she has not gotten over it and she knows, too. So now she tries if revenge makes her feel any better:

> *You're dumb to think I'd let you be*
> *Scot free without some pain from me . . .*

This time it seems to work. You still hear the backing vocalists with "ordinary pain" but now she has turned very bitter, remembering all the pain that he had brought to her when they were together. Compared to this, it is just an ordinary pain what she feels now. Her part ends with her telling him to see for himself how he is going to do while in the very end of the song you only hear the chorus "ordinary pain". She has found her way out, while he has only started to realize what he has lost and the pain he feels is getting stronger. How Stevie captured the mood of his and her situation is brilliant. Steve: "*Ordinary Pain* speaks of the many meanings of a broken heart. Love makes you happy one minute and it brings you down the next. But you need both. You have to know sadness to appreciate happiness."

Songs In The Key Of Life contains seven songs dealing with Man To Woman Love and it is amazing how much they differ from each other. *Ordinary Pain*, the story of a love that has ended and why and also a description of the feelings of the two people involved. *Knocks Me Off My Feet*, the song where Steve is so helplessly wrapped up in love that the only way for him to tell her how he feels is by repeating the three words "I love you" two dozen times altogether. He is unable to explain himself to her any otherwise, while in *As* Stevie, also head over heels in love, gives analogies of steadfastness:

> *As around the sun the earth knows she's revolving*
> *And the rosebuds know to bloom in early May* . . .
> *Just as time knew to move on since the beginning*
> *And the seasons know exactly when to change* . . .

Even death, he promises, could not take his love from her. Because deep in his mind he would still know about the love he had left behind and therefore be loving her always. Like *Ordinary Pain, As* also depends very much on backing vocals (Mary Lee Whitney). After two verses, a four-line-chorus and another three verses and a ten-line-chorus, whereby the chorus is built as an antiphony, Steve's soft vocal builds up to become intense. Now his lyrics are very much down to earth: saying that life certainly is not always what we would wish for but that just this should be reason enough for us to want to change it:

> *So make sure when you say you're in it but not of it*
> *You're not helping to make this earth a place*
> *sometimes called Hell* . . .

And if we cannot "change the words into truth and the truth into love", Stevie hopes that the next generation will. From then on *As* is a twelve-line-chorus, repeated three times, with affirmations of loving the loved one

> *Until the rainbow burns the stars out in the sky* . . .
> *Until the ocean covers every mountain high* . . .

In between each example of how endless his love is (sung by

the backing vocalist) Stevie either sings "I'll be loving you" or in the second repetition "always".

But while in *As* Stevie makes love everlasting in *Joy Inside My Tears*. Steve sings

> *I feel that lasting moments are coming far*
> > *and few between*
> *So I should tell you of the happiness that you bring*

Although the lyrics of this song are generally more joyful than its music might suggest, with the melody Steve underlines the melancholic touch matching his philosophy that you cannot value joy if you have not experienced what it is like to cry and be sad. *Joy Inside My Tears* is a slow ballad that if you did not understand English you would probably never connect the happy title with it. And still, despite the joy that Stevie sings about in this song it somehow seems to lack the usual positive and never-despairing Stevie Wonder attitude. It sounds rather like catching a glimpse of the sun but generally remaining darkness. Maybe apart from the music it is also the four lines with which Steve starts *Joy Inside My Tears* that give it a kind of heavy mood:

> *I've always come to the conclusion that "but" is the way*
> *Of asking for permission to lay something heavy on one's head*
> *So I have tried to not be the one who'll fall into that line*
> *But what I feel inside I think you should know . . .*

If It's Magic is a love song that has a few specialities: Stevie's singing is only accompanied by Dorothy Ashby's beautiful harp playing and at the very end by a few bars with Stevie on harmonica. But what makes *If It's Magic* unique is that although it is a love song throughout four verses and a chorus he never actually mentions the word "love". In the chorus Steve lyrically implies the all-curing power of love:

> *It holds the key to every heart*
> *Throughout the universe*

But in the verses as well as melodically Steve treats love as something very gentle, very fragile and airy. And while on one hand he presupposes love's infinity ("for there's enough for everyone") at the same time he asks:

> *If it's magic*
> *Then why can't it be everlasting*

And then Stevie chose to put the answer to this and even possible solution into the form of another question:

> *So . . . . . .*
> *If it's special*
> *Then with it why aren't we as careful . . .*

Another Star is like *Joy Inside My Tears*; and, as extreme as *Village Ghetto Land*, a song in which the music contradicts the lyrics. The melody is joyful, and has a lot of drive. The words of the song, directed to a lost love, put Stevie in a past time paradise:

> *For you*
> *Love might be for you to find*
> *But I will celebrate our love of yesterday . . .*
> *For you*
> *There might be another song*
> *But in my heart your melody will stay with me . . .*

This time Steve gives no explanation of why his love has left him. All he does is tell her that she will stay in his heart forever. Usually those kind of lyrics imply self-pity. But with the light and happy music that Steve put to these words they sound nothing like it. The melody brings the lyrics down to be just a statement – nothing else.

Man to Woman Love song number seven is *All Day Sucker* on the EP. Like *Ordinary Pain*, its theme is misused love. The song has a very melodic chorus with excellent backing vocals (Carolyn Dennis) although the general mood is pessimistic. And opposed to the girl in *Ordinary Pain* who finally draws the consequences and leaves the man who is mistreating her love, Steve this time plays the all-day sucker for love who cannot get himself to give up on the woman who just plays with him.

It has taken Stevie almost two tears to get it all together, but he has definitely achieved what he aimed for: to produce an album with one theme but nevertheless covering a variety of experiences that life and love holds. The first song on the third side of the album is one of Stevie's favourite tracks on *Songs*: *Isn't She Lovely*, the song about his daughter Aisha which is also a thank you to Yolanda, Steve's lover and mother of his children:

> *Londie, it could have not been done*
> *Without you who conceived the one*
> *That's so very lovely made from love . . .*

On this track Steve plays all instruments apart from keyboard (Gregory Phillinganes) and everybody who was in the studio when Stevie recorded it joined in clapping their hands – and Steve gave them a credit for it: Brenda Barrett, Shirley Brewer, Coleen Carleton, Carole Cole, Nelson Hayes, Dave Henson, Artece May, Edna Orso, (Ira) Tucker and Josette Valentino.

At first it looked as though this track would be the single. *Isn't She Lovely* got a lot of airplay in America as well as in England, but then all of a sudden Steve decided to take *I Wish* off the album and it took over. But sure enough as soon as *I Wish* came out as a single Pye was faster than lightning in releasing a cover version of *Isn't She Lovely* with their singer/songwriter David Parton. The backing track is a close copy of Stevie's arrangement and the record got into the British charts within a matter of weeks. It even beat Stevie's *I Wish*: the cover version of *Isn't She Lovely* reached position 4. David Parton: "To be quite honest about it, I suppose it is a bit of a cheek covering Stevie Wonder, but his is such a definitive version you can't really hope to improve on it, so you just get as close as you can. I was surprised that he didn't release it as a single himself, but then again he was bound to know that someone else would do it. I feel a little embarrassed about it because I'm a great fan of his and being a songwriter myself it's not the ideal way I'd have wanted a hit. But it's good to get one anyway."

Funnily enough it had not even been David Parton who was supposed to sing the cover version. Pye had dispatched him and Tony Hatch to produce a single with a "name" singer on it.

Parton does not say who the singer was but it looked like they had some problems with him singing Steve's tune. That is why Parton finally got down to sing it himself and this way make a name for himself. But as Lee Garrett once said in a radio interview where he was asked about Art Garfunkel covering *I Believe (When I Fall In Love It Will Be Forever)*: "It's bound to be a hit. Because what can you do wrong with a Stevie Wonder song unless you can't sing. And Art can." And so can David . . .

Isn't She Lovely is followed on the album by *Joy Inside My Tears*. The musicians are Stevie on his dream machine and all other instruments, Gregory Phillinganes on keyboard and backing vocals Susaye Green. Then comes *Black Man* with Hank Redd on alto and tenor saxophone, Steve Madaio on trumpet, George Bohanon and Glen Ferris play trombone and Stevie all other instruments.

Side four of *Songs In The Key Of Life* begins with *Ngiculela – Es Una Historia – I am Singing*. Steve plays all instruments but for the background percussion he credits Charles and Shirley Brewer, Renee Hardaway, Nelson Hayes, Marietta Waters, Nathan Watts, John Fischbach, Amale Mathews and Josette Valentino. *I Am Singing* combines the statement Stevie made in *Sir Duke* about music being an international language that everyone understands, with the outlook on a better tomorrow through love of *Pastime Paradise* and *Love's In Need Of Love Today*. Steve wants everybody to join into his song of love. To emphasize that people all over the world can do it he sings the same melody and words in Zulu (translation by Thoko Mdalose Hall), Spanish (translation by Raymond Maldonado) and English.

In the middle part of the song Stevie explains that this melody expresses exactly how he feels. That he has tried to put his feelings about all our tomorrows into words. And Stevie asks everyone again to join in the tune about love: The words to *I Am Singing* are not only among the printed lyrics to all the songs but also on the second page of the booklet underneath his foreword. The last sentence of his introduction to the album is at the same time the prelude to *I Am Singing*: ". . . So let it be that I shall live the idea of the song and use its words as my sight into the unknown, but believe positive tomorrow and I shall so when in evil darkness smile up at the sun and it shall to me as if I were a pyramid give me the key in which I am to sing, and if it is a key that you too feel, may you join and sing with me." It is not difficult to follow Steve's invitation and join into the happy samba.

This song is followed by *If It's Magic* and *As*. On this latter track Herbie Hancock is guest player on keyboards while Nathan Watts plays bass, Dean Parks guitar, Greg Brown drums and Steve plays all other instruments. Mary Lee Whitney sings the backing vocals and background handclap credits go to Herbie Hancock, Dave Henson, Yolanda Simmons, Josette Valentino, Nathan Watts and Stevie himself. The last LP track is *Another Star*. For this finale Steve got nine musicians together: Bobbi Humphrey (flute) and George Benson (guitar) as guest stars; Nathan Watts on bass, Hank Redd and Trevor Lawrence on alto- and tenor saxophone, Raymond Maldonado and Steve Madaio on trumpet, Nathan Alford jr. on percussion and Carmello Hungria Garcia on Timbales. The background vocals are sung by Steve, George Benson and Josie James.

Then follows the extended play, a 33 that looks like a 45 containing four tracks. And, as all the critics agreed, "it ain't no throw away", although it is a bonus EP. The first song is *Saturn*, co-written by Stevie and his lead guitarist Mike Sembello. (Musicians: Stevie Wonder, Mike Sembello on lead and Ben Bridges on rhythm guitar, Gregory Phillinganes on keyboards.) *Saturn* is a utopian story, where Stevie plays the part of a Saturnian coming down to Earth. He has been to this planet quite a number of times before "to find your strategy to peace is war" and as he realizes that nothing has changed since his last visit, he is

Going back to Saturn where the rings all glow . . .

Critic Bob Woffinden of the *New Musical Express* thinks of the song as extraordinary but at the same time as a kind of rip-off: ". . . sounding like bits of three Procul Harum songs Sellotaped together, even the use of the keyboards and brass are similar."

Ebony Eyes deals, as Steve says, "with all black women, not only one" although in the actual song he only talks about one lady:

> *... a girl that can't be beat*
> *born and raised on ghetto streets*
> *a devastating beauty*
> *a pretty girl with ebony eyes ...*

Ebony Eyes, a song of black beauty and black pride is played by Stevie, Nathan Watts on bass, Jim Horn on saxophone, Peter "Sneaky Pete" Kleingow on steel guitar and Steve gives special thanks to Tom Parma – "Z" articulation.

All Day Sucker is the first track on the second EP side and this one is played by Stevie, Ben Bridges and Mike Sembello on rhythm- and W. G. "Snuffy" Walden on lead guitar. The background vocals are sung by Carolyn Dennis and Steve gives special thanks to Steven St. Croix – Marshall Time Modulator.

The 21st and last song in the album package is *Easy Goin' Evening (My Mama's Call)*. It is a slow instrumental with a kind of lazy, relaxing mood to it and features Stevie on harmonical and Nathan Watts on bass.

Songs In The Key Of Life is an album that shows Stevie in love, full of love and he put it together with lots of love. The way Steve sums it up is: "The only way that you can challenge the things that are challenging you *is* with love. Love is the way and the answer to everything." He also says that "Love is eternal and infinite. It is only people who do not make it last for themselves and for others" but he very strongly believes that lasting love for each and every one of us does not have to remain a dream. In the foreword to *Songs In The Key Of Life* that Steve wrote in the booklet he states: ". . . An idea to me is a formed thought in the subconscious, the unknown and sometimes sought for impossibles, but when believed strong enough, can become reality . . ." (This sentence is indeed as ungrammatical as it reads.)

With *Songs In The Key Of Life* Stevie has confirmed the

"thousand images" that he was said to have since *Music Of My Mind*. As soon as the album came out it was talked about not only as the Album of the Year but as the Album of the Seventies. Like his last four albums Stevie produced and arranged this one, but for the first time since he started out on his own Robert Margouleff and Malcolm Cecil did not work with him on the recording. Stevie felt that he needed new inspirations, and a different working atmosphere for a change. After all, Steve, Bob and Malcom had been a creative team for a good four years. They had cut hundreds and hundreds of tracks together and come to know each other inside-out. The thrill of their working relationship had gone and it was time for all three of them to move on.

Songs In The Key Of Life was engineered by John Fischbach and Gary Olazabal with assistant engineering from Dave Henson (at Chrystal Industries Inc., Hollywood), Howie Lindeman (at Hit Factory, New York), Steve and Rick Smith (at Record Plant, Sausalito, California) and mastered by Andrew Berliner and Jeff Sanders (at Chrystal Industries). The programming was done by John Fischbach, Charles Brewer and Stevie Wonder. Bass EQ: Gary Olazabal.

In the booklet that goes with the album Steve dedicated two pages of thankyous to friends of his, people who have helped him along the way one time or another and people like Marvin, who have crossed Stevie's path only very briefly but gained a big place in his heart. He thanks his family: "To My Mama and Father – thank you for being my Mama and Father – thank you for letting me be your son. Renee, Milton, Calvin, Larry and Timothy – thank you for letting me be your brother!"

Stevie thanks relatives and the staff of various schools that he attended and to the staff and patients at hospitals that have either helped him or Yolanda when she had the baby. He says thank you to pressers, manufacturers, distributors and to everybody at the Apollo Theatre, New York. He thanks "All the Airlines, Stewards, Stewardesses, Checkers, Hotels, Friends, Enemies, Fans," and again he leaves some space for "................... YOU!". Stevie also says thank you to Motown and apart from this he lists a good 250 people by their names.

The back cover of the booklet is filled with phrases and inside jokes from the time that Stevie and his crew spent in the studio getting the album together. It is headlined "HOW WE GOT THERE" and when you read "Let's remix *Contusion* one more time" you can literally *hear* everybody in the studio go "*Oh no!*" Steve mentions peach cobblers and telephone calls (from and to Yolanda and Johanen Vigoda), cancelled studio sessions ("YOU'RE KIDDIN'!") and the delay of the album. In the first third of 56 lines:

"We're almost finished (smile)"

and the very bottom lines:

"WHEN IS THE ALBUM GONNA BE FINISHED?
We'll be finished next week.
YOU SAID THAT BEFORE!
Where's Mama Hardaway?
IS THIS THE FINAL CHA CHA ????"

Those personal pages make Stevie's friends smile. Gypsie: "Each line of the 'How we got there' reminds you of a certain situation and all the fun we had despite the hard work. It is good to know that later you can laugh at things that, at the time they happened, weren't necessarily funny. Like it was pretty hectic at times, and the studio was always crowded. But then – everyone who was involved in the album tried to be nice to all the other people around. Like when someone was in a bad mood before he got to the studio he wouldn't let it out on anybody. I think this is another great gift that Stevie has: he makes you feel at ease even though you're under stress."

John Fischbach: "Yeah, Stevie has a genius with people, too. He gets on to their wavelength. And although he is blind he can see a lot more than other people. Stevie has in-sight." And Deniece Williams says: "Just to be around Stevie and listen to the tunes he does makes you feel good. When you're in the studio with him you are the first to get the message of love that he conveys. I always listen to what he says – his understanding of love, people and life. It is good to know that there is a solution to everything."

301

The recording sessions that Stevie does can only be measured in extremes: they can be more fun and more inspiring than the work with other artists, but they are also the hardest. And the longest. Most of Steve's musicians – those he selects to be members of Wonderlove – do not get paid by the session but Steve keeps them on a regular salary. For Stevie this is killing two birds with one stone: for one, he has an exclusive on those musicians which saves him the hassle of co-ordinating their time schedule with his. He does not have to book them in advance but they are his employees and there whenever he needs them. On the other hand, paying his musicians a salary works out cheaper for Stevie in the long run. (In England, for instance, the approximate fee for an ordinary studio musician is £22.50 per three hours' recording. If a musician plays two instruments he get 25 per cent on top of the basic fee and if he plays three instruments he earns 50 per cent of the basic fee on top of it.) But at the same time a salary is an advantage for his musicians, too. This way they do not have to worry about insurances, and all the other things that the employer has to take care of. And they don't have to worry about the tax man coming around at the end of the year when they have spent all the money that they were supposed to hold back for him. Also, Stevie is very generous and he gives them a special treat every now and then. Jim Gilstrap: "When I was in Wonderlove and we were travelling with him, Stevie would give all of us excursion tickets that were valued longer than the actual tour was. That means we had a few days left to fly to wherever we wanted and have a good time."

Some of Stevie's session singers cannot live on the money that they make in the studio only. They have ordinary jobs during the day but they still do not mind sleeping only a few hours per night after a session to then get up and go into the office. Like Gypsie, who works as a secretary: "Well, working day and night gives you little red eyes and it makes you hate the alarm clock when it goes off only a couple of hours after you went to bed. But as soon as you're in the studio you know it's all worth it. Even though you sometimes don't sleep at all. Like I've come home at times and all the music was still going round in my head. It's really weird, like often I remembered the melody but not the lyrics. Although we'd done that particular tune over and over. And then you're trying to remember: what was I singing? and by the time you know you have to get up again.

"But it is all worth it. Even though some of us could hardly open our eyes we smiled. Somehow Stevie always managed to keep us on an energy level that you would think is impossible. He's got this enormous talent to motivate people. He fills you up with so much love that you want to go and pass it on to other people. And they give it to the next. Steve is a powerhouse of energy and love. It just pours out of him. It would be nice if everybody would open themselves up to take some of it. Steve's got enough for everybody! There is so much love in his music . . ."

But Stevie's mission to spread love does not end in his songs. In the foreword to his booklet with *Songs In The Key Of Life* Steve says: "I've never considered myself an orator nor a politician, only a person who is fortunate enough, thanks to all of you, to become an artist given a chance to express the way he feels and hopefully the feelings of many other people." But even so and although he does not join any political party to make his social-political statements, he still formulates his concerns other than in just his music. On the last page of the booklet he wrote:

"I am joining the fight, and I hope many will join us in the fight to help accused criminals that are denied a fair trial while sometimes others that have committed mass murders can be paroled in a matter of time, based on them knowing a friend who is a friend of a friend whose friend is a friend of that friend who has the magic power. There are so many 'Ike Whites' in this world – let's give these men a fare – making not the color of his skin his final fate for being behind bars."

When Stevie talks about human rights like this he knows what he is talking about. "Things have happened where a black man got shot for looking at a white chick. That's crazy stuff and completely off balance," he says. The information that Stevie has about prison situations does not only stem from what he has read or heard from people around him. Occasionally Stevie goes on a prison tour and talks to some convicts. And again, he does not want to get any publicity out of his concern and keeps quiet about those tours.

Stevie gets quite a lot of fan mail from prison, and some inmates even dedicate poems to him. This is one that Denise Hall from *Black Music* found in a poetry book that she discovered "in the wilds of Kentucky". It was written by a convict in a North Carolina prison and entitled *Music Makers In The Dark*:

> *Stevie*
> *I recall your sound*
> *As red roses petals*
> *Gave way to the summer*
> *Gave way to a woman's*
> *   soft kiss*
> *Gave way to a moment*
> *That invited me to enjoy*
> *The rise and fall of love's*
> *   surprise*
> *Stevie, could you sing a few*
> *   notes for me,*
> *So that I can learn my way*
> *   around this feeling?*

People's attempts to talk to Stevie in poems like he talks to them with his music is often touching. The helplessness with which the words are strung together for Stevie do not do justice to the loving thought that was there in the first place.

To put feelings into words and succeed in reflecting the feeling without any distortion, is a rare gift. Stevie has this gift. He considers it God-given for him to be a vehicle to spread love. And quoting Stevie from the booklet again he says: "It is to me a fact that Stevie Wonder is that temporary someone of myself even though we have come to know each other very well and realized because of who he is, the many doors that have been opened may have been closed to myself, Steveland Morris . . ."

Songs In The Key Of Life, so far Stevie's latest album, has been said to be the best thing that he has ever done. But again he himself says in the opening words in the booklet: ". . . In every album that I have and shall do, it is not my goal for that to be better than that and the next to succeed the others, but only that I do and give the best I can at the time of my doing and giving and that only happens because of the dis- or satisfaction that made me want to be a better someone . . ."

When this book went into print, Stevie was in the process of recording a new album of the working title *The Secret Life of Plants*. It looks like his fans are in for some more amazing surprises with the music that comes from his mind.

Stevie, so he says, has "only just started" to live. He is only 27 years of age today, and there will be a lot more from this man . . .

CHAPTER TWELVE

If Music Be The Food Of Love, Play On . . .

"In life you have to take a chance, you cannot live with the past. You have to move on." That is what Stevie said after *Where I'm Coming From* had come out but not been accepted by the public.

From there Stevie moved on to *Music Of My Mind*, which brought him worldwide recognition. The final breakthrough came with the next album, the *Talking Book* of Stevie's life. This record had turned platinum within six weeks of its release, and so did *Innervisions*, the album that proved that Stevie's high standard was to last.

Fulfillingness' First Finale and *Songs In The Key Of Life* went platinum on their day of release. You can't improve on that!

In two successive years Stevie won five Grammy Awards. The year after, in 1976, Paul Simon officially thanked Stevie Wonder for not having released an album in 1975. If Stevie had, Paul Simon said, he was not sure if he would have been Grammy awarded for *Still Crazy After All These Years*. Quite a compliment!

Musicians Stevie has supported in studio sessions like Eric Clapton, Jeff Beck, B. B. King, Stephen Stills and Graham Nash to name but a few, do not hide their admiration for Stevie.

The Rolling Stones, Taj Mahal, Elton John and other artists whom Stevie has joined on stage do not begrudge Stevie the storm that he creates in the audience when he guest-stars.

Paul McCartney dedicated his *Red Rose Speedway* album (1973) to Stevie, and a superstar like Paul Anka, one of the most secluded artists, is not too good to sing backing vocals on one track of Stevie's *Fulfillingness' First Finale* without getting any bigger credit for it than as a session singer.

To creative people, playing with Stevie means more than seeing their name on a million-selling album. They feel honoured to work with him and to contribute whatever they can to his music. Innumerable singers and musicians like to be part of what Stevie creates. Whatever studio he works in, there are queues of young artists hoping to get an audition with him. Sometimes people just come in the hope that Steve needs someone, at other times they know that he is looking for Wonderlove members. But Stevie's standards are incredibly high and very seldom do the kind of singers that he is looking for turn up to be auditioned. Mostly Steve bumps into them accidently. Like Gypsie:

"We met in San Francisco. Funny you should ask me that. Because not too long ago Steve asked me if I remember when we first met. I certainly do, just like yesterday. This is something you don't forget.

"I was at a theatre that belongs to friends of mine and where I had gone to see Gladys Knight perform. Afterwards there was a dinner party, and I was invited. That was at some private club and it was really strange. Because it didn't look like a restaurant at all and we sat there wondering if this was really the right place for us. We were starving. Anyway, about an hour later we get the menu, order some food and still could not smell or see any. So we took to the booze. By now we had almost gotten over our hunger and we were just laughing and drinking and joking and singing away, when all of a sudden Stevie walked in. Steve and his whole entourage.

"And Stevie walked right up to me and asked me if I was a singer. I laughed, 'Well, I've been trying.' He said 'You're pretty good. Are you from San Francisco?' I said no, from Los Angeles. So Stevie said 'Great. I'm looking for another singer and I'll be in Los Angeles in a few days from now. So why don't you give Calvin your telephone number and I'll ring you when I get there?'

"I never believed that Stevie would get in touch with me – but sure enough he did. Just like that. He asked me to come over to the studio and we started rehearsing at once. I feel honoured for him to ask me to sing on his album. It is like 'You're okay,' do you know what I mean? And I am grateful for being there to be part of him."

Quite a few people Steve has worked with over the last years have left Wonderlove to pursue a solo career. But most of them still sing sessions for him when he asks them to. Like Linda Lawrence and Susaye Green who joined the Supremes or Deniece Williams who is now recording for CBS. Deniece's single *Free* even beat Steve's single *Sir Duke* by topping the British charts while Steve came second. Stevie is not angry about it if his singers get a chance to get their own career started – he even offers his help. But there are two things that make it difficult for Stevie to give his ambitious session singers a push. Jim Gilstrap, who is with Roxbury Records: "Well, for one most of us want to make it on their own terms – not as Steve's protégés. And also the easiest way for him to get you into a recording company as a solo artist is if he'd put in a word for you at Motown. And that is not exactly the company you'd like to be with unless you're Stevie Wonder."

Motown, so the word goes, is one of the most authoritarian companies. The rules concerning artistic freedom are still very tight; and most other record companies offer better publishing deals. (The lastest group to have left the label were the Temptations.) Another thing at Motown is that their turnover in staff is extremely high. So whoever is responsible for promotion or other important departments may not get to know an artist well enough to work on him effectively. As soon as they know what it is all about most of Motown's employees turn around and leave.

Motown's front is all very nice and helpful – but when it gets down to doing something you are better off on your own.

Motown did *not* want a book to be written about Stevie. And the way I discovered this speaks volumes about the character of the company.

At first they refused to help. Then they changed their minds:

I was given Lee Armstrong's number (Motown International Department L.A.), and he promised to set up all the appointments I needed. Wonderful! I called his secretary, Rose Ann Nemes, the day I flew in to L.A.

She was very sorry, she had not been able to set up all the interviews yet, but I could talk to Ira Tucker the following day if I would see her in the morning to check the time. I went to see her, she called Ira's number, and he wasn't there. She was so sorry.

Fortunately I knew that Ira had flown to Detroit the night before. Motown knew too, of course. And I knew they knew. Their helpfulness was a smoke screen: they never intended to co-operate. *None of the people I had asked to see were ever approached by Motown*, as I discovered when I reached them on my own: Brian Holland, Clarence Paul, Syreeta, even Steve himself. When I met Steve on my third day in L.A. (Motown had told me he was in New York) I discovered he had not been told about the book.

Rose Ann later resigned from Motown and talked frankly to me. She admitted that Motown's tactics with "sneaky writers" were obstruction disguised as co-operation, and that her orders were to "make a few phone calls but don't take it seriously".

Thanks, guys.

Elaine Jesmer, who wrote *Number One With A Bullet*, had more or less told me what would happen. In trying to be objective about Elaine's experiences with Motown, let me quote the basic story from *Newsweek*'s pro-Motown article on Stevie:

"Motown, as it happens, has been upset by a recent novel *Number One With A Bullet*, about a black record company that keeps its artists on a tight rein. Written by Elaine Jesmer, a former girlfriend of Marvin Gaye, the book – which Motown has called 'pornographic trash' – details violence and corruption in a fictional family-owned black record firm that has been taken over by the syndicate. 'Godfather' producer Al Ruddy bought the screen rights to the book and received money from Paramount to develop the script. But Paramount which had a five-picture deal in works with Motown, suddenly cancelled the deal with Ruddy. Ruddy says he'll make the film with independent financing."

Number One With A Bullet is, in fact, pure fiction. That is what it says in the book and that is what Elaine says if you ask her.

Elaine: "They hired Louis Nizer who is the top criminal libel lawyer in this country. His name is famous. They hired him to see the galleys of the book prior to publication. And that just isn't done.

"So Nizer rang my publisher and told him that Motown had heard that there were certain things in the book that were detrimental to Motown. So they wanted to check up on it that nobody would have to be sued. But at the same time he very carefully mentioned that he was not hired but only making the phone call preliminary to legal action. My publisher told Nizer that he could buy *Number One With A Bullet* in the bookstores. It was too late.

"So Nizer disappeared again. He only takes winning cases and he couldn't have won this one. However, just to get Nizer to make this phone call must have cost a fortune. We kind of referred to it laughingly as the 50,000 dollar call."

Motown did not sue Elaine Jesmer, but one cannot help the feeling that they had something to do with stopping the movie. Elaine: "It is quite obvious why Paramount stopped the film. That is the kind of power that Motown obviously has – but they could not have gone through any legal action, because they would never have won the case. My book is pure fiction and this is what it says inside. And I have never said anything else about it, either."

Also, there is another equally good reason for a company not to sue anyone that quickly. Elaine: "At this time the justice department was conducting hearings investigating the record industry. Corruption in the record business. But the government cannot just walk into any company's door and start asking funny questions. However, once a company exposes itself in a court case, then the door is open in a legal situation immediately. Then any government agency or anybody who has anything to do with it can come in and start investigating.

"For example if Motown had sued me the government could have stepped right into my trial and start asking questions. Nobody goes through that kind of hassle unless they really have to." So Motown's doors stayed closed, and people still wonder what is locked into the heavy iron safes behind heavy iron bars on the seventh floor in the Motown offices on 6464 Sunset Boulevard, Los Angeles.

Steve tries not to get involved in any of the rumours that undoubtedly exist about Motown: "Motown's politics are not any different from those of any other record companies. Sure, there are faults at Motown but nothing which could not be corrected. And even so I don't want to talk about it. My thing is music."

Steve's thing has always been and will always be music. Doug Kee: "It is really hard to hold Stevie's attention. Because he's always going off into new directions with his music. He is creative all the time. Steve is just like a little kid with a new toy. Music *is* his toy. And for him it's the kind of toy that never gets old. There are so many ways that he can go with it and he never gets tired of his music."

Gypsie: "He even sings and composes new stuff when he sits on the toilet."

Lee Garrett: "Stevie is music. And he also finds security in his songs. He can just cut the rest of the world off by going into his music. That is where he feels most comfortable. Because this is the thing that he can do best. Best for himself and better than many others. With music Stevie doesn't have to rely on anybody telling him what it's all about."

Syreeta: "His creativity is something that is always there. I've often watched him get up with his music, create it all day long and go to bed with it. And I've often wondered just *how deep* does this man go. What will the next thing be like?"

In the early years of his writing career Steve has often said, that he relies with his writing on what other people tell him about things. Those days are gone. Steve today depends much more on his own feelings when he writes than on other people explaining this or that to him. Like when Stevie writes about *sunshine*, which he has never seen, for him it reflects a mood:

311

"Sunshine for me is a great inner warmth. Something that smiles all the time . . . "

When Steve talks about a *beautiful woman*, "then it is inner beauty I describe," he says. "Something that makes you feel good. That is the important thing. I suppose there are a lot of people with a beautiful outer face but inside they are empty or even ugly. And it can also be the other way around: someone very plain to look at can have the most sparkling inner beauty."

And when you hear a line like *Until the rainbow burns the stars out of the sky* you really begin to wonder how sensitive a man who has never visually seen the rainbow, the stars or the sky, can be . . .

Over the last few years Stevie has stated more and more often that he is in fact *glad* not to see with his eyes. "A handshake, a voice, they cannot lie. Because you cannot disguise them. Whereas everything you can visually look at can bear a mask. Make-up, luxury, a smile even. I think that when you have never learned what it is like *not* to see, it is much harder for you to strip off all other people's disguises. No, if that's what sight is all about, I'm glad I don't see."

According to Stevie, sight is also something that is responsible for materialism. "Everything has to be the most expensive looking stuff that people can get. That is why everybody is so fond of money. Materialism has become more important than the things that money can't buy."

Competition, which results from materialism, is another thing that Stevie can't stand: in Stevie's eyes competition does not breed champions but is one of the reasons for our Western civilization being so uncivilized: "Competition means fighting. Fighting is evil. How much better we could all live if we joined each other instead of trying to climb up just to be able to look down on others. Everyone wants to be better than their neighbour. This is what happens in everyday life as well as in politics. Be it man or country. And this is just ridiculous. Some countries have so much, that they throw their food away while in other parts of the world people are starving. But whoever is responsible for it only sees that it is cheaper to destroy the goods than to ship them to where they are needed."

The music business, Stevie thinks, has also reached a point where even to the audience money sounds better than music. "The music business is becoming a totally crazy scene. Like when I renegotiated with Motown and got the 13 million dollar deal the papers were full of it. I can see the point, because it is revolutionary and all that. Fine. But what annoyed me about it is that every article wrote the same shit. Like 'Steve's contract is bigger than that of Elton John and Neil Diamond combined.' Now can you tell me if the kind of deal that you have with a record company makes your music any better? The dollar sign doesn't say anything about how my music or Elton's music or anybody's music makes you *feel*. And also there are a lot of musicians out there who can probably hardly live on their music. And I am quite sure that some of them are making music that is better than any of the stuff that is in the charts. But it really looks like it that the sound that money makes seems to be the most beautiful music in people's ears. That is what I love about children, see: they can relate to things much better than most adults can. To them love and affection is the most important thing. It's like when you describe someone to a child you tell the kid what kind of voice he's got, if he likes animals, what he likes to do best and how he makes you feel. If you want to describe a certain person to an adult all you have to tell him is if he's rich or not. That's enough for them to make up their mind what he is like. It's crazy."

Another thing Stevie dislikes is appearing on television. (However in February 1977 he surprised with his guest appearance in a TV tribute to Dick Clark, who had then completed 25 years as the premier rock TV host in the States. Steve had even composed a "tribute" song especially for this event.). "Most TV producers want to produce commercial, slick and inoffensive shows. I don't go for that at all. I want to take a television recording as seriously as I take a recording in a sound studio when I produce my songs. I don't want to cheat my audience, and I don't want to settle for second best. I don't do it with my albums and I'm certainly not going to do it for television. Also being on certain shows puts you in a certain category. And it's really bad for an artist if he doesn't get the right kind of time spot or the right kind of show. Also there are shows with all different kind of acts on, and I get offered to do those rather frequently. But I don't dig it. They make me feel limited. I don't want to do that too much."

But there is one thing for which Steve does go in front of a camera: Ira Tucker is just producing a documentary on Stevie's life. He has taken bits and pieces from old movies Stevie made or from filmed events. And he also shoots Steve's life today. Like at the press review for *Songs In The Key Of Life* on the farm in Massachusetts, when Steve is in the studio, with his daughter, doing jam sessions or receives another one of the innumerable awards that he is presented with for various things. So far Ira has not decided how long it is going to take him to finish the documentary on Steve. But he hopes that it will be out before too long.

To Stevie, being the monstrous star that he is and getting one platinum album after the other, is not so much selling millions of records as millions of people wanting to hear his music. To show his fans his appreciation he sometimes does things that he would not have to do at all.

When *Songs In The Key Of Life* had just come out, Steve visited a few record shops around the country. This is actually called a promotion visit – but Steve did not do it for promotion. That he had had already. Stevie really wanted to thank people for making his album a number one – with a bullet – on the day of release.

Some of the record shops were crowded. At V.I.P. Records on Crenshaw Boulevard in Compton, California, more than a thousand people had turned up to see Steve. Other shops were empty. At Tower Records on Sunset Boulevard in Hollywood, California, only thirty fans had gathered, most of whom were there accidentally. Although Stevie's appearance had been announced on the radio and Tower Records had put a huge sign up, no one really believed that a superstar like Stevie Wonder would actually go there. He was one hour late, but at five o'clock in the afternoon he arrived.

Stevie and his entourage spent about 45 minutes at Tower Records. Steve talked to people, shook hands with some of them and finally got behind the counter to hold a mini-speech: "Thank you. You make me very happy. I'm sorry I kept you waiting with my new album. But I'm glad you like it. Thank you for listening to my music. Love to all of you." Then Steve's personal manager Chris Jones grabbed hold of Steve and took him back to the Mercedes. Guys from Motown's security department made way for Steve and watched out if anybody was getting any funny ideas like trying to hold Stevie back or something. But nothing happened. No fans were going crazy and Stevie could leave without any problems at all.

In the beginning of 1977 Stevie gave a special thankyou to all the people working at Motown's distributing office in Detroit. He flew into the city for one day to give all the people who had packed and stacked and distributed his albums a hand. Stevie did not just pose for photographs, he really stacked records for a little while . . .

Steve often acts spontaneously, and you are fortunate to be around when it happens. Lou Wilson, manager of the Continental Hyatt House Hotel on Sunset Boulevard, L.A. told me: "Johanen Vigoda, Stevie's lawyer, stays here when he is in L.A. That is rather frequent and often he meets Stevie here. And it has happened more than once that Stevie went in the hotel bar, sat at the piano and entertained our guests. How do you like that?"

The Continental Hyatt House Hotel is home for many musicians, when they are on the road and stop in Los Angeles. Gordon Lightfoot, the Doobie Brothers, the Who and Led Zeppelin to name but a few stay there. But Steve is the only one who gets up and plays music for free.

People also go out of their way for Stevie. In the beginning of 1976 Stevie had all of a sudden gotten the idea to celebrate his mother's 50th birthday at Nick's Fishmarket. So he sent his brother Calvin over to take care of the necessary arrangements. Only: Nick's Fishmarket *never* rent out their restaurant for private dinner parties. The restaurant and the discotheque are open seven nights a week and once they start making an exception for one star, every other showbiz personality who would want the same.

Nick's Fishmarket made one exception, though: for Stevie. Because he, they said, is something completely *different*! And that again, they think, should be clear to everybody else. And also: no one can deny Stevie anything, which means Nick and René could not either.

Lula Hardaway's birthday party turned out to be one of the biggest events in Hollywood. And that is something. Among the 250 guests was L.A.'s mayor. Minnie Riperton, everybody from Wonderlove, Lee Garrett, Syreeta, Steve's entire family and all their friends were there. And instead of 96 dinners, which is usually the most Nick's Fishmarket serves at one time, they brought out all the 250 dinners for the guests at one time. People and food were all over the place and everybody was glad that it was not he who had to do the tidying up the next morning. Lula's birthday guests did not mind that it was crowded and that some of them had to take the plates on their lap so that they could eat. There just weren't enough tables! But the mood and the food made up for it. Steve had ordered assorted cold appetizers like oysters, clams, shrimps, crabs and all the rest of it. Then they had a mixed salad with a cream of spinach dressing and shrimps on top. The main course was a veal and sole combination. The veal was sautéed in butter with asparagus and the lemon sole marnier sautéed in lemon butter. Garlic spaghetti and mushrooms were on the side. The dessert was strawberries romanoff.

The bar was open for everybody to drink whatever he liked – and the barkeepers just added the drinks up at the end of the party. They came to just over 600. How many bottles of wine and Dom Pérignon were emptied that night is something that no one remembers. It was lots and lots. The dinner party that had started at six o'clock in the late afternoon went on until four o'clock the following morning. For Lula Hardaway 50 is definitely no age to stop partying late nights. With Stevie, she has been used to odd hours for years now – visiting him at the studio or going to his concerts. The celebrity and her family were the last to go home. A few days later Stevie got the bill: the party had cost him 16 grand. That is undoubtedly a lot of money to spend on one party, but Steve does not make a habit of throwing feasts like this every night.

He spends very little money on himself, other than on instruments, women and wages. Some of his earnings go to charity, and the rest of it Stevie invests. His accountant John Ritter says: "Stevie has placed his capital in conservative straight-up ways to keep up with inflation. But any deals he makes are mostly not of financial but of ethical value to him. He uses a lot of money to help minority businesses to get started."

How much of his income Steve pays on salaries and other fixed costs every month Ritter will not say. He also does not give a figure on how much money Steve donates to organizations. Ira Tucker: "The trouble is that the more money you earn the more you have people knocking at your door to give you some of it. Now Steve donates an incredible amount of money to whoever he thinks needs it. But he does not like to talk about it. And the reason for me not to tell you is that the more people know you give money to others the more they feel inclined to have a part of it, too. And you just cannot give money to each and every organization. Even if you would like to."

Stevie is also a favourite with promoters who want to set up charity concerts. Ira gets a good dozen requests like this per week. And then he spends his time explaining to various people why Stevie does not want to do this or that or that he simply has not got the time to do all the concerts he is asked to do. Ira spends most of his life on the telephone anyway. When you meet him at his apartment at the Regency Hotel in L.A. you are lucky if you get to say three words to him before the telephone rings and interrupts you again. Actually, the best way to have a conversation with Tuck *is* to ring him up – then his phone can't disturb you.

However, Ira feels that quite a lot of people take Stevie's generosity for granted: "Sometimes you really get the feeling that Steve is obliged to do this and that for handicapped people because he is blind himself. But again, you just can't give free concerts all the time."

There is one concert though, that Stevie considers. Debbie

Torres, a young secretary told me: "I have a teenager sister who is multi-handicapped. Which in her case means that she is blind and mentally retarded. So far there are no facilities that deal with multi-handicapped people. There are only three ways: either you put people like this into a home for the blind, or you put them into a home for mentally retarded people, or you let them stay at home. None of the three possibilities take care enough of all aspects.

"Now some people in Los Angeles have decided to found a Therapeutic Living Center which is a project to give a human opportunity to multi-handicapped people. A guy called Bill Young is in charge of the programme – he has worked a lot with blind and/or handicapped people before. But one person can only deal with so many people that he takes care of. The idea is to set up a home for more than just a handful of multi-handicapped people, and to have trained staff to help those people to *live* and not just vegetate. But we need money to start the project off with.

"Strangely enough I had not even thought of approaching Stevie to do a benefit concert for us. But then I bumped into Herbie Hancock, who has now become a good friend of mine. And he suggested that he would play and that we should try and get Steve interested as well.

"So I had a tape made on which the whole project was explained to Stevie. It took me a while to get it to him but to cut a long story short, I finally gave it to Josette Valentino, his secretary who promised to pass it on to him."

Josette did. Only when Debbie finally met Steve herself on one of his promotion visits in a record shop, he had not listened to it. But Steve knew about the project and when Debbie talked to him he said that he was very interested to help the TLC. Debbie:

"Steve asked me to ring Chris Jones to tell him how and when we thought of setting this gig up and to co-ordinate Steve's time schedule with ours."

Debbie did. That was in October. By the time this book went to print she was still trying to get a definite idea about when Steve would be free to do the concert. Altogether Debbie has been trying for eighteen months to set this thing up. It took her one year to get through to Stevie and for the rest of the time she has been ringing Chris Jones as Stevie had told her to. Debbie:

"But every time I speak to him he says that he hasn't talked to Steve about it. That there were so many other things that he had to take care of first."

Debbie still believes that Steve wants to do this benefit concert. "It's not him, it's the people around Steve giving you a hard time," she says. "After all he told me to tell Chris to go ahead with it. And that he was *really* interested. If Steve wasn't he could have told me to jump into the lake."

I came across quite a few stories like this when I did the research on this book. Not regarding benefit concerts but all sorts of things where Steve makes promises and does not keep them in the end. And at times I really wondered if it really all goes down to the people surrounding Stevie.

After all, it is very easy to be nice and kind when you have people who do the "dirty" work for you by keeping everybody off your neck. Why should Stevie tell Debbie to go and get lost when Chris Jones can give her the message? This way Steve keeps his friendly image and his employees take the blame. But that's their job, that is what they get paid for.

When I mentioned thoughts like this everybody I spoke to got very cross and told me that I obviously did not realize how tough Steve's organization was. Lee Garrett: "How on earth can you dare think such a thing? I told you before that Steve keeps forgetting things but that he does not mean to. I'm sure that he doesn't think about the conversation that he had with Debbie any more and the tape that she forwarded to him probably ended up in some corner. *But* when Steve says that he wants to do something he really means it. Only he expects his employees to set it all up. If Chris came to him and gave him a date for the concert, Steve would be there and doing it."

Doug Kee: "Sorry – you're on the wrong track. If Steve had had no interest in Debbie's concert he would have told her. He's really straightforward, and after all, Debbie would have understood if Steve had explained to her that he gets hundreds of people asking him to do a benefit.

"Mind you, Steve can be a motherfucker. I'm not saying that he is all nice and that he is a saint. Steve certainly ain't no saint. He goes off like everybody else. I mean as much as he is a musical genius after all he's only *human*. It depends on the situation but when something or someone pisses him off he can get very snappy and bitchy. But isn't that what we all do? A lot of people just look at Steve as the star and they say 'Wow, listen to his music.' But they forget to look at him as a human being. He's got feelings and moods just like all the rest of us. He says it himself: Stevie Wonder and Steveland Morris are two separate people, although Stevie Wonder has taken over most of his personality. And when he promises something he really keeps it. Only how long it takes until he actually gets down to doing it doesn't often depend on him but on his organization. They really try to live his life for him and don't do the things that he wants done. And he really forgets things easily – apart from his music, of course."

Doug, for example, has no reason at all to tell me how sincere Steve is if he were not. Steve sacked him for more or less no reason at all. After Doug had been with Steve for a good three years he was told to leave because he "wasn't up to date with the equipment". Doug: "I know that wasn't the reason but what can you do? You know, just before I got sacked my father had left Steve in 1972. He had a lot of hassles with Motown and he left for personal reasons. There again, it didn't have anything to do with Steve but with the people around him. They were telling Steve a lot of shit about my father and it was all very unpleasant. So he decided to make a move. See, he's fifty now and he doesn't need all this aggravation. After all, he can work with other people. He's got a good name in the music business. He started out with Dizzy Gillespie in the old jazz days and he worked with the Four Tops, the Spinners and Gladys Knight and the Pips. Like the arrangement on Gladys' version of *The Way We Were*, that's his."

It seems a real pity that the people surrounding Stevie do obviously have enough power to break up old friendships, let alone that they prevent new ones. They keep strangers and friends away from him the same and strengthen their position by having a kind of exclusive on Steve. Joe Cocker told me:

"It's quite a few years back now, but some time in the early Seventies I had an experience with Steve's bodyguards. It was at some party that Stevie attended and I happened to be there, too. Anyway, Steve and I hadn't met before and his people obviously didn't know Cocker. Well, and as I walked past Steve and stopped to say hello, this huge bodyguard made a step toward me and said 'Cool it, man, *cool* it.' I really thought I was in a movie, the whole situation was so ridiculous. And I thought to myself well, maybe I happen to dig the wrong guy. But when I finally met Steve and got to talk to him I realized that all this wasn't his fault. He's innocent, you know. And he's such a great guy."

However, there is one thing that Steve's people cannot keep him from doing: when he feels like it he has them go out with him and watch other artists' gigs. And often he goes up on stage to join them in a jam session. Bob Fisher: "It's absolutely crazy. Now that the album is out every promoter is trying to get Steve for some concerts. Motown would like to see Steve on stage, too. They do – but only jamming with others. He did quite a few things in New York at the beginning of the year (1977) but only with Roy Ayres or other artists, and that wasn't planned so he didn't even get a billing."

Concert promoters have a hard time setting up gigs with Stevie. Like Danny O'Donovan who represents the Motown stable in Great Britain. The concerts he had promised the English audience in 1975 and 1976 had fallen through because of the delay of the album. Now that *Songs In The Key Of Life* has been released for half a year, O'Donovan still does not seem to get anywhere. Says an O'Donovan spokesman: "Can't you ask me an easier question? We've been mucking about for months now and we still don't know what's gonna happen. Danny is in the States now to set it all up but even then you can't rely on it. If Danny were given dates today it would take another four to six weeks until they are confirmed. Only God above and Steve know when he's coming to England.

It could take another few months or he could just turn up like that."

But even if Steve should "just turn up like that" everybody would be delighted. When Steve does a concert the news spreads in no time and the gig is sold out in a matter of hours. And every promoter would rather cancel other concerts than not to have the best concert hall for Steve the day he decides to do a show.

Danny O'Donovan's office did not make any statement about Steve's fee. British music magazines printed rumours saying that Stevie has a nightly rate of £20,000 or $35,000 in Europe. This sounds reasonable – after all Neil Diamond is supposed to have taken £50,000 per concert he did in England in June '77.

So far Stevie played the Nigerian Festival in Nigeria, Africa, at the beginning of 1977. And the same as with his album release dates Stevie is said to want to wait with his tours until his stars are in their luckiest zodiac position.

You could call Stevie an astrology freak. As soon as he meets new people his first question is "What sign are you?" and if you're lucky he will find yours compatible with his. Steve believes very strongly that the stars influence your life and he even makes them partly responsible for his marriage with Syreeta breaking up: "She's a Leo and I'm a Taurus. That means we both have very strong personalities and want to lead. But you can't have two leaders . . ." Steve also says that people might not expect any changes from him because he is a Taurus and supposed to be very steadfast. But then, he continues "Tauruses are also very stubborn. If they have an aim they want to reach they go towards it. And my aim is to make music but develop it . . ." According to the Chinese horoscope, Stevie, born in 1950, is a Tiger. And as well as Tauruses, Tigers are said to be always in the lead . . .

However, with a little luck Steve finds his stars to be in a zodiac position that allows him to come over to England between the time that this book gets printed and published. After all, it is more than three years now since we last saw Steve in the U.K. But with Stevie it is all worth the wait. He keeps getting better and better all the time, and his fans know it. After all, there are only few artists who can disappear from the public scene for a couple of years completely without having to try a comeback. But with Stevie it is as if he had never been away although there was no sign of him or his new album from the end of 1974 until late 1976. Apart from an occasional TV appearance or benefit concert that he did.

It is Stevie's high standard that allows him to do – or not to do – things that most other artists would not get away with. And up to today Steve's high standards have sold him almost twenty million records since 1971. Plus the thirty million records that Stevie had already sold from when he started off in the music business as a minor until he became of full age.

His talent is to combine meaningful lyrics and beautiful music in a unique way, but he also has a knack for putting commercial hook lines and funky dance rhythms together with intricate, thoughtful arrangements.

Singers who cover his tunes range from Peter Frampton (*I Believe When I Fall In Love It Will Be Forever*) to the Beach Boys (*I Was Made To Love Her*) to Sergio Mendes (*All In Love Is Fair*) to Liza Minelli and Frank Sinatra, who are only two of the innumerable artists to have recorded Stevie's *You Are The Sunshine Of My Life*.

Those times when Steve felt stigmatized by *Fingertips* or *Uptight* are long gone. He no longer has to fear that he could be categorized – unless it's under love, love, love.

Stevie, the black flower child knows where he is deep down inside himself. And he has taught people to accept his music for what it is: "I want people to know that I am sincere and that I do not mess about with them. I want it to be worthwhile for them to listen to my music as much as it is worthwhile for me to send out the message that has been given to me."

Hank Cosby, Steve's producer ten years ago, says: "Steve has always been a decade ahead of his time musically." Billy Eckstine once called Stevie "the Duke Ellington of our day". Then he added: "My God, what is this kid gonna be doing when he's 37 or 38 and has some idea about what's going on?"

It sounds like Stevie has already got a pretty good idea about what's going on. And about what he wants. Steve: "I want my music to last for a long time. Not just for a minute or two. Music can measure how broad our horizons are. My mind wants to see infinity."

The music of Stevie's mind is infinite.

So is the sunshine of his love. "Here is my music, it is all I have to give. Know that your love keeps me strong" was the message that Stevie gave on the American sleeve of *Talking Book*. He had written it in braille.

And those of us, who thought we knew what sight is all about, Steve teaches to begin to see with our hearts.

If music *is* the food of love –

play on!

Postscript

As this book went into print Stevie saved the life of his childhood friend Lee Garrett.

In the summer of 1977 Lee suddenly found himself under great emotional pressure which he did not think he could cope with. Lee: "Business and personal problems had built up over the last few months and in the beginning of July seemed so overwhelming that I didn't see any way out of them." Instead of turning to his friends and talking things over with them Lee panicked and wanted to shoot himself on Wednesday afternoon, 6 July. Fortunately one of Lee's sisters who had visited him realized the seriousness of the situation when she found that Lee had locked himself into the bathroom with a gun. Her first reaction was to ring Stevie who at this time was in the Chrystal Studios in L.A.

Lee: "Stevie turned up in no time. First of all that made me feel even worse, because until then it had always been me who had tried to teach *him* things about life – all the independence bit we've talked about before. Now Stevie caught me in a weak situation and that was exactly what he said. Although I can't recall all of what he said – my head was spinning like hell and I was really dizzy and desperate – I do remember one thing. 'Hey, man,' he said, 'what's all this bullshit? You're no nigger who gives up on life easily – think of all the stuff you've told me. About nothing should get you down – there's always a way out and that fighting makes you appreciate things more than if you'd got everything thrown at you. Come on, we'll find a way. Nothing is that bad that you cannot cope with it. You're *strong*, man, get yourself together.' "

Then, Lee says, Stevie reminded him of the re-incarnation Lee believes in so much. "You know that you've got to come back and take all the shit all over again if you commit suicide. That won't help you but only stop you from reaching your goal as soon as you would like to." Also Stevie told Lee about his own experiences with death. Lee: "Stevie talked about his accident and all the things that he felt then. And how much more he appreciated life since he's been so close to dying."

Four hours after Stevie had arrived Lee came out of the bathroom and dropped the gun. By now Lee's sister had reached a doctor who gave Lee some pills to calm him down and put him to sleep.

Unfortunately though the press had heard about the incident and the next day the papers were full of Stevie saving Lee's life. Even the American TV and radio-stations picked up the news.

A day later the British papers and radio-stations carried the news-item. When I read about it my first reaction was: this can't be true. Lee would *never* do a thing like this – it must be a stupid public relations gag and they are all sitting in L.A. and laughing their heads off. I did not even want to give Lee a call because I did not feel like making a fool out of myself. I could almost *hear* Lee say: "Don't be silly, Constanze, you know me better than that. I ain't no stupid nigger who wants to blow his brains out. So what's new in London . . .?"

Later on in the evening though I decided to ring Gypsie. She laughed into the telephone. "Hi, Constanze, I *knew* that you would call me."

"Did you?"

"Yeah. And I told Lee that I was expecting your call."

"Good public relations, hey?"

"No. True." All of a sudden Gypsie's voice had turned very serious. "No, it's true," she repeated. "And the wonder-boy talked him out of it."

"Why?" I asked. "Lee never gave me the slightest idea of being suicidal."

"I didn't believe it at first," Gypsie said. "But Stevie did. Isn't that amazing? Nobody else but Stevie believed it. How he *knew* God knows. And he really saved Lee by talking to him.

You know, there's a lot of shit gone down lately. Mainly businesswise. Lee's been messed about to an unbelievable extent. And even people like him can only take that much I think and then there's a breaking point. But don't worry, he's okay now. I'm gonna see him later on 'cause Stevie, he and I are gonna go to a movie tonight."

After I had spoken to Gypsie I still did not want to ring Lee. He would be getting so many phone calls now from "friends" who would all of a sudden remember him . . .

Hours later, at two o'clock in the morning (London) I turned on the radio. The first thing I heard was the first few bars of *Heart Be Still*, one of my favourite Lee Garrett songs. (This was covered by Frankie Valli on his album *Fallen Angels*.) Automatically I dialled his number.

"Hello?"

"Hello to you, listen to this!" I turned the volume up. *"Heart be still 'cause we can make it! Heart, please be still you and I can take it yes I know we can* . . .

"That's Capital Radio," I said. "They are playing you this very minute. And anyway, I don't quite know what to say – but don't do that again. That's bad public relations."

Lee laughed. "I won't. I ain't no stupid nigger who wants to blow his brains out. I just freaked for a minute, you know? I wasn't quite myself, understand? But now it's all over. I'm okay now. And anyway, what's new in lovely London . . .?"

Then he told me what had happened the night before and he added: "You know, the worst thing of all was that in that particular moment I thought that nobody loved me anymore. I felt so terribly lonely within my heart."

And I felt very guilty. What if Steve had been on tour or couldn't have been contacted? How do you know when you're in Europe that your friend in the States is going through a heavy patch in his life? *He* is not the kind of guy to ring you up and complain about life. And you don't ring L.A. every week . . .

But there is one thing, you should know, Lee Garrett: there are quite a number of people who love you. Even some of them who have only known you for a short time. Like Peter Sarstedt

327

and Joanna who you only met a few months before they moved back from L.A. to London. They rang me up the next day and both of them were as shocked as I was when I told them that the news-item was not a tasteless public relations gag. "*Why* didn't Lee let us know?" Joanna said. "There's always *something* that friends can do, no matter what. We're gonna get a cassette over to him right now. Jesus Christ, why is it always *good* people who get all the shit?"

Because good people are most likely to be the ones who are taken advantage of. Like Lee. But now Stevie is going to see to it that Lee is not messed about with any longer. And this time Stevie, who often comes along with his help just a little too late, made it just in time. And if he had not meant so much to my life already he would now – for saving the life of someone I care for a lot. And 'thankyou' sounds such a lousy little word for all what Steve has done for so many people and for me. But "thankyou Stevie!" is the only thing that I can say and deep down in my heart I hope that you know what I mean!

Discography

54157	I'm Wondering/Every Time I See You I Go Wild	14.9.67
54165	Shoo-Be-Doo-Be-Doo-Da-Day/Why Don't You Lead Me To Love	19.3.68
54168	You Met Your Match/My Girl	14.9.67

EIVETS REDNOW

| 7076 | Alfie/More Than A Dream | 25.6.68 |

STEVIE WONDER

54174	For Once In My Life/Angie Girl	15.10.68
54180	I Don't Know Why/My Cherie Amour	28.1.69
54188	Yester-Me, Yester-You, Yesterday/I'd Be A Fool Right Now	30.9.69
54191	Never Had A Dream Come True/Somebody Knows (Somebody Cares)	13.1.70
54196	Signed, Sealed, Delivered, I'm Yours/I'm More Than Happy (I'm Satisfied)	3.6.70
54200	Heaven Help Us All/I Gotta Have A Song	29.9.70
54202	We Can Work It Out/Never Dreamed You'd Leave In Summer	18.2.71
54208	If You Really Love Me/Think Of Me As Your Soldier	22.7.71
54214	What Christmas Means To Me/Bedtime For Toys	24.11.71
54216	Superwoman/I Love Every Little Thing About You	25.4.72
54223	Keep On Running/Evil	8.8.72
54226	Superstition/You've Got It Bad Girl	24.10.72
54232	You Are The Sunshine Of My Life/Tuesday Heartbreak	22.2.73
54235	Higher Ground/Too High	31.7.73
54242	Living For The City/Visions	18.10.73
54245	Don't You Worry 'Bout A Thing/Blame It On The Sun	14.3.74
54252	You Haven't Done Nothing/Big Brother	23.7.74
54254	Boogie On Reggae Woman/Seems So Long	23.10.74

54274 I Wish/You And I   18.11.76
58421 Sir Duke/Tuesday Heartbreak   3.77

U.S. Albums

Teach Me Tonight/Uptight (Everything's Alright)/Ain't That Asking For Trouble/I Want My Baby Back/Pretty Little Angel/Music Talk/Contract On Love/With A Child's Heart

272 *Down To Earth*   9.12.66
A Place In The Sun/Bang Bang/Down To Earth/Thank You Love/Be Cool Be Calm (And Keep Yourself Together)/Sylvia/My World Is Empty Without You/Lonesome Road/Angel Baby (Don't You Ever Leave Me)/Mr. Tambourine Man/16 Tons/Hey Love

279 *I Was Made To Love Her*   28.8.67
I Was Made To Love Her/Send Me Some Lovin'/I'd Cry/Everybody Needs Somebody (I Need You)/Respect/My Girl/Baby Don't You Do It/A Fool For You/Can I Get A Witness/I Pity The Fool/Please Please Please/Every Time I See You I Go Wild

281 *Someday At Christmas*   27.11.67
The Christmas Song (Merry Christmas To You) / Bedtime For Toys / Christmas Time/Twinkle Twinkle Little Me/A Warm Little Home On A Hill/What Christmas Means To Me/Someday At Christmas/Silver Bells/Ave Maria/Little Drummer Boy/One Little Christmas Tree/The Day That Love Began

282 *Greatest Hits*   25.3.68
Uptight (Everything's Alright)/I'm Wondering/I Was Made To Love Her/Hey Love/Blowing In The Wind/A Place In The Sun/Contract On Love/Workout Stevie Workout/Fingertips Pt. 2/Castles In The Sand/Hey Harmonica Man Nothing's Too Good For My Baby

291 *For Once In My Life*   11.68
For Once In My Life/Shoo-Be-Doo-Be-Doo-

Da-Day/You Met Your Match/I Wanna Make Her Love Me/I'm More Than Happy (I'm Satisfied)/I Don't Know Why/Sunny/I'd Be A Fool Right Now/Ain't No Lovin'/God Bless The Child/Do I Love Her/The House On The Hill

GORDY

932 *Alfie* (AS EIVETS REDNOW)   20.11.68
Alfie/More Than A Dream/A House Is Not A Home/How Can You Believe/Medley: Never My Love – Ask The Lonely/Ruby/Which Way The Wind/Bye Bye World/Grazing In The Grass

TAMLA

296 *My Cherie Amour*   29.8.69
My Cherie Amour/Hello Young Lovers/At Last/Light My Fire/The Shadow Of Your Smile/You And Me/Pearl/Somebody Knows Somebody Cares / Yester-Me, Yester-You, Yesterday/Angie Girl/Give Your Love/I've Got You

298 *Live*   6.3.70
Intro/Pretty World/Sunny/Love Theme from "Romeo And Juliet" (A Time For Us)/Shoo-Be-Doo-Be-Doo-Da-Day/Everybody's Talking/ My Cherie Amour/Yester-Me, Yester-You, Yesterday/I've Gotta Be Me/Once In A Livetime/A Place In The Sun/Down To Earth/ Blowing In The Wind/By The Time I Get To Phoenix/Ca 'Purange/Alfie/For Once In My Life

304 *Signed, Sealed, Delivered*   7.8.70
Never Had A Dream Come True/We Can Work It Out/Signed, Sealed, Delivered, I'm Yours/Heaven Help Us All/You Can't Judge

333

A Book By Its Cover/Sugar/Don't Wonder
Why/Anything You Want Me To Do/I Can't
Let Heaven Walk Away/Joy (Takes Over Me)/
I Gotta Have A Song/Something To Say

308   *Where I'm Coming From*   12.4.71
Look Around/Do Yourself A Favour/Think Of
Me As Your Soldier/Something Out Of The
Blue/If You Really Love Me/I Wanna Talk
To You/Take Up A Course In Happiness/
Never Dreamed You'd Leave In Summer/
Sunshine In Their Eyes

313   *Greatest Hits Vol. 2*   21.10.71
Shoo-Be-Doo-Be-Doo-Da-Day/Signed, Sealed,
Delivered, I'm Yours/If You Really Love Me/
For Once In My Life/We Can Work It Out/
You Met Your Match/Never Had A Dream
Come True/Yester-Me, Yester-You, Yester-
day/My Cherie Amour/Never Dreamed You'd
Leave In Summer/Travelin' Man/Heaven
Help Us All

314   *Music Of My Mind*   3.3.72
Love Having You Around/Superwoman/I
Love Every Little Thing About You/Sweet
Little Girl/Happier Than The Morning Sun/
Girl Blue/Seems So Long/Keep On Running/
Evil

319   *Talking Book*   1.11.72
You Are The Sunshine Of My Life/Maybe
Your Baby/You And I/Tuesday Heartbreak/
You've Got It Bad Girl/Superstition/Big
Brother/Blame It On The Sun/Lookin' For
Another Pure Love/I Believe (When I Fall In
Love It Will Be Forever)

326   *Innervisions*   3.8.73
Too High/Visions/Living For The City/Golden
Lady / Higher Ground / Jesus Children Of

334

America/All In Love Is Fair/Don't You Worry
About A Thing/He's Misstra Know-It-All

U.S. Compilation Albums

693   *Big Hits Vol. 11*   9.69
You Met Your Match

GORDY
946   *Motown Winners Circle Vol. 4*   10.69
Shoo-Be-Doo-Be-Doo-Da-Day

SOUL
720   *Switched-On Blues*   11.69
I Call It Pretty Music (But The Old People
Call It The Blues)/Some Day Pretty Baby –
Sammy Ward (Harmonic accomp.)

MOTOWN
703   *Motown At The Hollywood Palace*   3.70
I'm Gonna Make You Love Me (Duet with
Diana Ross)/Don't Know Why I Love You/
For Once In My Life

707   *Motown Chartbusters Vol. 1*   9.70
Blowing In The Wind

725   *Christmas Gift Rap*   10.70
Ave Maria/What Christmas Means To Me/
One Little Christmas Tree

727– *The Motown Story*   22.2.71
731   For Once In My Life/I Was Made To Love
Her/Uptight (Everything's Alright)/Fingertips

732   *Motown Chartbusters Vol. 3*   5.71
For Once In My Life

734   *Motown Chartbusters Vol. 4*   5.71
Signed, Sealed, Delivered, I'm Yours

744   *Motown Chartbusters Vol. 5*   12.71
I Was Made To Love Her

795   *A Motown Christmas*   29.5.73
What Christmas Means To Me/Ave Maria

M*   337

731	Never Had A Dream Come True/Somebody Knows (Somebody Cares)	3.70
744	Signed, Sealed, Delivered, I'm Yours/I'm More Than Happy (I'm Satisfied)	6.70
757	Heaven Help Us All/I Gotta Have A Song	10.70
772	We Can Work It Out/Don't Know Why	5.71
779	Never Dreamed You'd Leave In Summer/If You Really Love Me	7.71
798	If You Really Love Me/Think Of Me As Your Soldier	1.72
827	Superwoman/Seems So Long	9.72
841	Superstition/You've Got It Bad Girl	1.73
852	You Are The Sunshine Of My Life/Look Around	5.73
869	Higher Ground/Too High	9.73
881	Living For The City/Visions	11.73
892	He's Misstra Know-It-All/You Can't Judge A Book By It's Cover	4.74
908	Don't You Worry 'Bout A Thing/Do Yourself A Favour	7.74
921	You Haven't Done Nothing/Happier Than The Morning Sun	10.74 10.74
928	Boogie On Reggae Woman/Evil	12.74
1054	I Wish/You And I	3.12.76
1068	Sir Duke/Tuesday Heartbreak	4.77
1083	Another Star/Creepin'	7.77

U.K. E.P.'s

STATESIDE (SE)

1014   *I Call It Pretty Music*
I Call It Pretty Music/Workout Stevie
Workout/Monkey Talk

TAMLA MOTOWN (TME)

2006   *Stevie Wonder*
Fingertips/Hey Harmonica Man/Happy
Street/Square

U.K. Albums

ORIOLE (P.S.)

40049	*Tribute To Uncle Ray* As America	8.63
40053	*12-Year-Old Genius – Live* As America	8.63

STATESIDE (SS)

10078	*Jazz Soul Of Little Stevie* As America	11.63
10108	*Hey Harmonica Man* as "Stevie At The Beach"	1.65

TAMLA MOTOWN (STML)

11036	*Uptight* As America	9.65
11045	*Down To Earth* As America	4.67
11059	*I Was Made To Love Her* As America	12.67
11075	*Greatest Hits* Shoo-Be-Doo-Be-Doo-Da-Day/A Place In The Sun/Uptight (Everything's Alright)/Travelin' Man/High Heel Sneakers/Sad Boy/Kiss Me Baby/Workout Stevie Workout/Fingertips Pt. 2/Hey Harmonica Man/Contract On Love/Castle In The Sand/Nothing's Too Good For My Baby/I Was Made To Love Her/Blowing In The Wind/I'm Wondering	8.68
11085	*Someday At Christmas* As America	9.68
11098	*For Once In My Life* As America	2.69

11128   *My Cherie Amour*   1.70
       As America

11150   *Live*   6.70
       As America

11164   *Live At The Talk Of The Town*   10.70
       Pretty World/Never Had A Dream Come
       True / Shoo-Be-Doo-Be-Doo-Da-Day / My
       Cherie Amour/Alfie – Drum Solo/Bridge
       Over Troubled Water/I Was Made To Love
       Her/Yester-Me, Yester-You, Yesterday/For
       Once In My Life/Signed, Sealed, Delivered,
       I'm Yours

11169   *Signed, Sealed, Delivered*   12.70
       As America

11183   *Where I'm Coming From*   6.71
       As America

11196   *Greatest Hits Vol. 2*   12.71
       Signed, Sealed, Delivered, I'm Yours/We
       Can Work It Out/For Once In My Life/If
       You Really Love Me/Shoo-Be-Doo-Be-Doo-
       Da-Day/You Met Your Match/My Cherie
       Amour/Yester-Me, Yester-You ,Yesterday/
       Never Had A Dream Come True/Heaven
       Help Us All/Don't Know Why/Never
       Dreamed You'd Leave In Summer

TAMLA MOTOWN (STMA)
 8002   *Music Of My Mind*   5.72
       As America

 8007   *Talking Book*   1.73
       As America

 8011   *Innervisions*   8.73
       As America

M.F.P. SOUNDS SUPERB (SPR)

90003 *Uptight* 9.73
Uptight/Ain't That Asking For Trouble/
Love A Go-Go/Hold Me/Pretty Little Angel/
Music Talk/I Want My Baby Back/Thank
You Love/Be Cool, Be Calm (And Keep
Yourself Together)/Angel Baby (Don't Ever
Leave Me)/Hey Love/More Than A Dream

8019 *Fulfillingness' First Finale* 7.74
As America

TAMLA MOTOWN (TMSP)

6002 *Songs In The Key Of Life* 30.9.76
As America

U.K. Compilation Albums

TAMLA MOTOWN

11001 *A Collection Of 16 Big Hits* 3.65
Hey Harmonica Man

11007 *Motortown Revue Live* 4.65
I Call It Pretty Music (But The Old People
Call It The Blues)/Moon River

11019 *Hitsville U.S.A.* 12.65
Kiss Me Baby

11027 *Motortown Revue Live! In Paris* 2.66
High Heel Sneakers/Funny How Time Slips
Away/Fingertips

11030 *Motown Magic* 6.66
Uptight (Everything's Alright)

11043 *A Collection Of Big Hits Vol. 4* 3.67
High Heel Sneakers

11055 *British Motown Chartbusters* 10.67
I Was Made To Love Her/Blowing In The
Wind

343

11237   *The Motown Sound Vol. 2*   8.73
         Keep Running/I Love Every Little Thing
         About You

11301–   *The Motown Story*   9.73
11305   Fingertips/Uptight (Everything's Alright)/
         I Was Made To Love Her/For Once In My
         Life

SOUNDS SUPERB
90010   *It's Christmas At Motown*   9.73
         Someday At Christmas/One Little Christmas
         Tree/Christmas Song

TAMLA MOTOWN
11246   *Motown Chartbusters Vol. 8*   10.73
         Superstition/You Are The Sunshine Of My
         Life

11244   *Disco Classics Vol. 4*   4.74
         We Can Work It Out

11278   *Disco Classics Vol. 5*   12.74
         Uptight (Everything's Alright)

12003   *Motown Gold*   11.75
         Yester-Me, Yester-You, Yesterday

U.K. Chart Placings

RECORD RETAINER/MUSIC WEEK CHART

Date of Entry		Highest position
26.2.66	Uptight (Everything's Alright)	14
20.7.66	Blowing In The Wind	29
21.1.67	A Place In The Sun	20
29.4.67	Travelin' Man	50
5.8.67	I Was Made To Love Her	5
21.10.67	I'm Wondering	22
11.5.68	Shoo-Be-Doo-Be-Doo-Da-Day	46

4.1.69	For Once In My Life	3
19.4.69	I Don't Know Why	14
2.8.69	My Cherie Amour	4
22.11.69	Yester-Me, Yester-You, Yesterday	2
11.4.70	Never Had A Dream Come True	6
1.8.70	Signed, Sealed, Delivered, I'm Yours	15
21.11.70	Heaven Help Us All	29
15.5.71	We Can Work It Out	27
19.2.72	If You Really Love Me	20
10.2.73	Superstition	11
26.5.73	You Are The Sunshine Of My Life	7
13.10.73	Higher Ground	29
2.2.74	Living For The City	15
13.4.74	He's Misstra Know-It-All	10
19.10.74	You Haven't Done Nothing	30
11.1.75	Boogie On Reggae Woman	12
14.12.76	I Wish	5
5.4.77	Sir Duke	2

U.S. Chart Placings

BILLBOARD POP 100

Date of Entry		Highest position
6.7.63	Fingertips Pt. 2	1
5.10.63	Workout Stevie Workout	33
29.2.64	Castles In The Sand	52
13.6.64	Hey Harmonica Man	29
28.8.65	High Heel Sneakers	59
5.2.66	Uptight (Everything's Alright)	3
14.5.66	Nothing's Too Good For My Baby	20
13.8.66	Blowing In The Wind	9
10.12.66	A Place In The Sun	9
4.3.67	Travelin' Man	32
22.4.67	Hey Love	90
8.7.67	I Was Made To Love Her	2
28.10.67	I'm Wondering	12
4.5.68	Shoo-Be-Doo-Be-Doo-Da-Day	9
20.7.68	You Met Your Match	35

Date of Entry		Highest position
3.8.68	You Met Your Match	2
16.11.68	For Once In My Life	2
8.3.69	I Don't Know Why	16
14.6.69	My Cherie Amour	4
1.11.69	Yester-Me, Yester-You, Yesterday	5
14.2.70	Never Had A Dream Come True	11
4.7.70	Signed, Sealed, Delivered, I'm Yours	1
24.10.70	Heaven Help Us All	2
20.3.71	We Can Work It Out	3
21.8.71	If You Really Love Me	4
27.5.72	Superwoman (Where Were You When I Needed You)	13
30.9.72	Keep On Running	36
25.11.72	Superstition	1
24.3.72	You Are The Sunshine Of My Life	3
18.8.73	Higher Ground	1
10.11.73	Living For The City	1
6.4.74	Don't You Worry 'Bout A Thing	2
10.8.74	You Haven't Done Nothing	1
16.11.74	Boogie On Reggae Woman	1
11.12.76	I Wish	1
16.4.77	Sir Duke	1

From 23.11.1963 until 30.1.1965 Billboard did not publish R & B charts.

ALBUMS

13.7.63	The 12-Year-Old-Genius Recorded Live	1
18.6.66	Uptight	33
28.1.67	Down To Earth	92
30.9.67	I Was Made To Love Her	45
27.4.68	Stevie Wonder's Greatest Hits	37
11.1.69	For Once In My Life	50
11.10.69	My Cherie Amour	34
11.4.70	Stevie Wonder Live	81
29.8.70	Signed, Sealed, Delivered	25

Gold Singles

Fingertips
Uptight
I Was Made To Love Her
For Once In My Life
My Cherie Amour
Yester-Me, Yester-You, Yesterday
Signed, Sealed, Delivered, I'm Yours
Heaven Help Us All
If You Really Love Me
Superwoman
Superstition
You Are The Sunshine Of My Life
Higher Ground
Living For The City
You Haven't Done Nothing
Boogie On Reggae Woman
Don't You Worry 'Bout A Thing

Gold Albums

Music Of My Mind
Talking Book
Innervisions
Fulfillingness' First Finale

Songs In The Key Of Life
Stevie Wonder Greatest Hits
Stevie Wonder Greatest Hits Vol. 2

Platinum Records

Signed, Sealed, Delivered I'm Yours
Superstition
Talking Book
Innvervisions
Fulfillingness' First Finale
Songs In The Key Of Life

Stevie Wonder as a Session Guest and/or Producer

The Detroit Spinners	It's A Shame/We'll Have It Made	Singles
B. B. King	To Know You Is To Love You	LP
Rufus	Rags To Rufus	LP
Minnie Ripperton	Perfect Angel	LP
Dixie Hummingbirds	We Love You Like A Rock	LP
The Supremes	Bad Weather	Single
Buddy Miles	More Miles Per Gallon	LP
Pointer Sisters	Steppin'	LP
Roberta Flack	See The Sun In Late December	
Syreeta	Stevie Wonder Presents Syreeta	LP
	Syreeta	LP
	Harmour Love	Single
"Junior Walker And The All Stars"		LP
Originals	Game Called Love	LP
Main Ingrediant	Afrodisiac	LP

This list is not comprehensive!

Cover-versions on Stevie Wonder Compositions
(non-comprehensive list)

You Are The Sunshine Of My Life
Engelbert Humperdinck/Buddy Greco/Andy Williams/Rod

McKuen/Grover Washington jr./Sacha Distel/Brenda Lee/
Liza Minelli/James Last/Blue Mink/Perry Como/Bobby
Humphrey/Ray Coniff/Percy Faith/Johnny Mathis/Hugo
Montenegro/Frank Sinatra/Junior Walker/Petula Clark

Superstition
Mel Tormé/The Osmonds/Sergio Mendes/Beck, Bogart &
Appice

I Believe (When I Fall In Love It Will Be Forever)
Cleo Laine/Peter Frampton/Art Garfunkel

Living For The City
Ray Charles/Ultrafunk/Maynard Ferguson/Ike & Tina Turner/
Ramsey Lewis

To Know You Is To Love You
B. B. King/String Driven Thing/Margie Joseph/Syreeta

All In Love Is Fair
Shirley Bassey/Jimmy Helms/Hank Crawford/Billy Eckstine/
Barbra Streisand/Jimmy Castor Bunch/Junior Walker/Nancy
Wilson/Sergio Mendes

Uptight (Everything's Alright)
Nancy Wilson/Geno Washington/Diana Ross & the Supremes
and the Temptations/Ramsey Lewis/Brenda Lee/Bill Cosby/
Jackie Wilson/The Osmonds

Never Dreamed You'd Leave In Summer
Joan Baez/Three Dog Night

Tell Me Something Good
Rufus/Ivonne Fair/Phil Upchurch & Tennyson Stephens

I Was Made To Love Her
The Beach Boys/King Curtis/Tom Jones/Barkays/Junior
Walker/Jackie Wilson/Ramsey Lewis/Sil Austin

My Cherie Amour
Stanley Turrentine/Al Martino/Tony Bennett/O. W. Smith/
Andy Williams/Engelbert Humperdinck/George Benson/
Ramsey Lewis/Rhythm Heritage

Isn't She Lovely
David Parton
Happier Than The Morning Sun
Captain and Tennille

Stevie Wonder and Stevie Wonder/Syreeta Wright Compositions for Syreeta's Albums

Black Maybe/How Many Days/Come And Get This Stuff/
'Cause We've Ended As Lovers/Waitin' For The Postman/
When Your Daddy's Not Around/I Wanna Be By Your Side/
Keep Him Like He Is/Baby Don't You Let Me Lose This/To
Know You Is To Love You/I'm Goin' Left/Spinnin' And
Spinnin'/Your Kiss Is Sweet/Heavy Day/Just A Little Piece
Of You/Universal Sound Of The World/Harmour Love

Index

353

355